Compassionate Listening

and Other Writings

by Gene Knudsen Hoffman

Quaker Peace Activist & Mystic

Edited by Anthony Manousos

Western Friend is the official publication of Pacific, North
Pacific and Intermountain Yearly Meetings of the Religious
Society of Friends.
Opinions expressed in this book are those of the authors, not
necessarily of the Yearly Meetings.
For more information, please contact
Western Friend editor at editor@westernfriend.org

Cover by Meredith Jacobson
Layout by Susanna Combs
ISBN 0-9700410-6-7

First printing 2003 in the United States of America
Revised, second printing 2013 in the United States of
America

Table of Contents

Foreword

GENE KNUDSEN HOFFMAN was a mother and grandmother, international peacemaker, counselor, Quaker, poet, actress, writer, teacher, and so much more. She was a remarkable individual who influenced many during her lifetime.

The founder of Compassionate Listening, Gene was my treasured mentor from 1996 - 2004, until her mind rejected coherent patterns of recognition and communication. She died peacefully on July 19th, 2010. Even though I had lost her years before, her death affected me deeply.

I keep a three inch thick "Gene file", full of her letters, transmissions, and articles. I am still amazed at her voluminous outpouring and sharing. Some people never find or recognize their mentors. I am grateful that I found Gene, and that we both recognized the nature of our relationship.

In the early 1990s, I was leading citizen delegations to Israel and Palestine for the Earthstewards Network. I felt frustrated that my work seemed to be adding to the polarization of the conflict in a part of the world where I had lived, and had grown to love so dearly. I brought participants from the United States and most were either pro-Palestinian or pro-Israeli. Almost all of us fell into taking sides, and I knew that I needed a stronger reconciliation framework for my efforts. I had witnessed the transformative power of listening in 1982 during several months of training at Neve Shalom / Wahat al Salam's now-famous School for Peace in Israel, so I was naturally drawn to Gene's articles on listening.

Gene had begun her international listening work in the 1980s in the former Soviet Union. After Glasnost, like many working in the citizen diplomacy arena, she turned her reconciliation efforts to Israel and Palestine. As a young peace activist, I regularly came across Gene's articles and pamphlets. We were both members of the Fellowship of Reconciliation (FOR) and clearly shared many overlapping interests.

I finally called Gene in the spring of 1996, and invited her to join my next delegation and teach us how to practice Compassionate Listening with Israelis and Palestinians. Gene and I met the following week in Oregon. Despite our forty-year age difference, we discovered an instant "soul sister" connection that bridged the generation gap. It seemed that with every subject we discussed, we found another network of connections. We knew and loved the same people, the same projects, authors, and ideas. We shared similar experiences and feelings about our activist histories, and the "enemy making" we experienced in the peace movement. We acknowledged the challenges of working with conflict and our own self-righteousness.

Gene immediately agreed to come with me to the Middle East that November. She also felt that Richard Deats, former director of FOR and then-editor of *Fellowship* magazine, would be ideal for the delegation. Richard was an expert in nonviolence whom Gene had wanted to introduce to Yasser Arafat, founder of the Palestine Liberation Organization.

From the day we met, Gene had a mission to educate me about her reconciliation efforts, and most specifically, her Compassionate Listening work, and I had an equal hunger to absorb her transmissions. After our first delegation together, it was clear that she recognized me as one who would carry her work forward.

Gene wrote of our partnership and our mutual commitment to reconciliation, "Sixteen years of one-on-one listening passed. My journeys resulted in more articles, more explanations, but no converts, as far as I knew. Before Leah, no one else had wanted to work with me because they said I didn't advocate for anything. When you advocate, you pick a side and you have enemies. I didn't take a side. When people asked me who I was advocating for, I told them, 'I'm advocating for reconciliation.'"

I was the eager recipient of Gene's typed notes, letters and articles on Compassionate Listening, love, forgiveness, anger, and post traumatic stress syndrome (PTSD). She sent hand-written letters outlining details of our shared projects and practical applications. She sent notes and cards about her favorite books, photocopies of letters, and quotes and teachings from various teachers she admired. Two of the people she considered her closest mentors were Adam Curle, senior Quaker mediator, and Thich Nhat Hanh, Buddhist monk, peacemaker, and poet.

It was FOR who sponsored Thich Nhat Hanh's first U.S. and international speaking tour in 1966. Gene wrote, "I was so interested in this young Buddhist who had so much to contribute to peace. In 1985 I went for a month to Plum Village, his center in France. While there, he asked me to organize his first retreat with Vietnam Veterans, which I did. Thay, as we learned to call him, is particularly strong and powerful in his teachings on reconciliation. The international program I founded, Compassionate Listening, is based on his teachings."

Gene helped me secure funding to produce a film of our second Compassionate Listening delegation in Israel and Palestine – a delegation for Jewish participants that included religious leaders. We dedicated the film, *Children of Abraham*, to "Gene Knudsen Hoffman, Compassionate Listening Pioneer." In early 1999, shortly after the release of the film, Gene began to receive so many invitations to screen the film that she thought she would have to hire someone to help her. She wrote that she was "overwhelmed, but of course thrilled" to watch the active spread of Compassionate Listening. In the same letter, she encouraged me to lead delegations to listen to Slobodan Milosevic and Saddam Hussein.

Gene developed a Compassionate Listening curriculum in 1998 and began offering inquiry-based classes in Santa Barbara. Her curriculum is included in her *Sourcebook on Compassionate Listening*. The following year, I began to offer Compassionate Listening trainings in the U.S. with a different model. Several times, Gene, our Training Director Carol Hwoschinsky and I gathered with our growing community of Compassionate Listening practitioners from North America to deepen our collective understanding and practices.

Despite Gene's intention of being a full partner in the non-profit organization (we had changed the name from "Mid-East Citizen Diplomacy" to the "Compassionate Listening Project"), she eventually came to terms with her limitations and wrote to me that her traveling days were over. She asked to remain on the Board of Directors as "Co-Founder and originator of Compassionate Listening."

In 2002, I founded the Jewish-German Compassionate Listening track with my German friend and trainer, Beate Ronnefeldt. In the last letter I received from Gene, dated April 10, 2004, she thanked and honored me for pioneering the Jewish-German work, which she called "thrilling" and "an ambitious undertaking."

Gene had thanked me profusely those last two years for this project, a testimony to her passion for Jewish-German reconciliation. In her work in Israel in the early 1990s, Gene had researched and written extensively about PTSD among Jewish Holocaust survivors in Israel, and its role in the Israeli-Palestinian conflict. She had interviewed Israeli psychologists who were considered experts in the field, and published articles and a Pendle Hill pamphlet on the subject called *No Royal Road to Reconciliation*.

Those of us who study, practice, and teach Compassionate Listening can continue to learn much from Gene's articles and essays. We practitioners have a powerful lineage, and our work is infused with Gene's research, study, and practice in the art of reconciliation. She was a pioneer in a new field, always seeking to clarify and challenge her fellow peacemakers.

In a letter from Gene to a fellow colleague, dated June 3, 2000, Gene wrote:

"About nonviolence: I question whether a gospel of nonviolence will save us. I think we have the doctrine, but not the necessary respect and concern for the unhealed suffering of oppressors and other violent people. It seems we rarely consider listening to them as a possibility for wider understanding. Instead, we have Nuremberg laws, and kill or otherwise destroy perpetrators through vengeance. We forget that Gandhi spent much of his time with his 'enemies,' listening to them and learning how to love them. I think it was his loving truth which was grounded in his respect for them as human beings that enabled them to set India free."

In August 2001, Gene wrote to me, "I think I've found a motto we can all use as the subtitle of 'Compassionate Listening' on publications, stationary, and brochures. I think it expresses in a 'nutshell' what we are doing. It's the title of one of my essays – An Enemy is One Whose Story We Have Not Heard. What do you think of that?"

I love to think about Gene's delight, knowing how far her work has traveled, and how many have benefited from her understanding that "an enemy is one whose story we have not heard."

In 2003 we created an Advanced Training and Facilitator Certification track. Our facilitator community has spent years developing curricula and honing practices that we have shared all over the world at conferences, universities, religious and spiritual centers, mediation programs, schools, communities, and in public workshops. Compassionate Listening has been integrated into many programs worldwide. Our annual delegations to Israel and Palestine continue—we've led 28 to date—and we've held many trainings for Israeli and Palestinian peace leaders. Our community has taken the work in recent years to Liberia, Rwanda, Burundi, Jordan, Syria, Lebanon, and Guatemala.

Gene, I honor you for your remarkable lifetime quest in service to personal and collective healing. Thank you for your love, belief and investment in me personally, and in our wider community of compassionate listeners. You are and will remain the founder of Compassionate Listening, and the birth mother of a movement.

With great love for you,

Leah Green
Founder & Executive Director of
the Compassionate Listening Project
http://www.compassionatelistening.org/

Editor's Preface

I planned to write a short biography of Gene Hoffman as part of a study of peace activists who also consider themselves mystics.[1] I had spent all summer gathering material about Gene's life and work, and was looking forward to spending a nice, quiet day at my word processor writing up my observations.

But God or the Universe had other plans. When I called up Richard Deats, editor of *Fellowship* magazine, to ask him some questions about Gene, he said that "things were kind of hectic" and asked if I had seen the news on television yet. I told him that I was too busy writing, but since he insisted, I turned on the TV. What I saw filled me with horror and dread. The images of planes crashing into the Twin Towers, the fiery explosions, the clear blue skies suddenly darkened with smoke, repeated over and over again, obsessively, like a nightmare, didn't seem real, yet I knew that it wasn't a movie. I knew that the world, and my life, would never be the same.

I also knew that Gene Hoffman's insights were more crucial than ever before. After spending much of her life trying to understand the root causes of violence, she had concluded:

> Some time ago, I recognized that terrorists were people who had grievances, who thought their grievances would never be heard and certainly never be addressed. Later, I saw that all parties to every conflict were wounded, and that at the heart of every act of violence was an unhealed wound. I began to search for ways we peace people might help to heal these violence-causing wounds.[2]

During the two years that I have spent collecting and editing this remarkable anthology of Gene's writings, our country has tried to fight terrorism through preemptive violence. Our leaders have authorized the invasion and occupations of two countries, killed thousands of people, curtailed civil rights, escalated the military budget beyond all reason, and alienated most of the world. Terrorist acts have increased worldwide, and US citizens feel less secure than ever before. It will undoubtedly take a generation, perhaps longer, to undo the damage caused by our misguided response to the terrorism.

Deeply versed in psychology and spirituality as well as social activism, Gene provides an alternative to our nation's compulsive cult of violence. She insists that the key to overcoming terrorism is through deep listening to another's pain and inner conflict. "An enemy is one whose story we have not yet heard," is one of her favorite sayings. But Gene is not naively optimistic about this approach. She knows how hard it is to listen deeply and to transform an enemy into a friend. She recognizes that to become peacemakers, we must face up to our inner conflicts and be willing to be transformed by the Spirit.

Gene has been active in the struggle for peace and social justice for over fifty years—since the days of Senator Joe McCarthy and loyalty oaths. At age eighty she continued to give workshops and write articles for the alternative press. Her writings are filled not only with spiritual and psychological insights, but also with vivid portraits of people that bring to life the peace and justice movement during the past half century. As we prepare ourselves for the long struggle ahead to restore sanity to our nation and the world, Gene's example can help us remember that peacemaking is a lifelong commitment—one that is full of joy and adventure as well as hard work.

This book could not have been completed without considerable help from Friends. First, I want to thank the Bogert Fund for Christian Mysticism, which provided seed money to conduct research on "activist mystics." Publication of this book was made possible through generous donations from Frances McAllister and Helen Bross (in memory of her beloved husband John) as well as other donors who contributed. Finally, I am grateful to all who have read the manuscript, shared stories about Gene, and provided encouragement and constructive criticism.

Anthony Manousos, Editor

1. See p. 253 for a discussion of "Activist Mysticism."
2. *Pieces of the Mideast Puzzle*, p. 9.

Introduction and Biography

As the shadow of terrorism and war looms large in the consciousness of America and the world, Gene Hoffman's message of healing and hope seems more relevant than ever before:

> Some time ago, I recognized that terrorists were people who had grievances, who thought their grievances would never be heard and certainly never addressed. Later, I saw that all parties to every conflict were wounded, and that at the heart of every act of violence was an unhealed wound. I began to search for ways we peace people might help to heal these violence-causing wounds. [4]

For the past twenty years, Gene Hoffman has been engaged in efforts to seek out the deep, psychological causes of violence and to help bring about healing and reconciliation through a process she calls "Compassionate Listening."

An active Quaker and member of the Fellowship of Reconciliation (FOR) for over fifty years, she traveled dozens of times to the Middle East and the former Soviet Union during the 1980s and 1990s to do reconciliation work. In 1989, after American planes downed two Libyan planes, she went to Libya with an FOR delegation to meet with Libyan leaders. She has met with and listened to Palestinians and Israelis, and published articles, books, and pamphlets about her experiences, including *Pieces of the Mideast Puzzle* (1991) and *No Royal Road to Reconciliation* (1995). When Alaskan hunters and fishers and indigenous people came into conflict over hunting and fishing rights, Gene helped to arrange Compassionate Listening sessions through the American Friends Service Committee (AFSC). She has published over one hundred articles as well as books, poems and pamphlets and given innumerable workshops and talks about peacemaking. Her work has inspired numerous others, including Cynthia Monroe, AFSC staff person in Alaska, and Leah Green, founder of Mideast Citizen Diplomacy's Compassionate Listening Project. Gene has been rightly called a "pioneer" in the Compassionate Listening movement, and has worked with such other notables as Adam Curle, Herb Walters, Virginia Baron, and Richard Deats.

"Gene is a real prophet," said Judith Kolokoff, former AFSC regional director in the Pacific Northwest. "And she's a remarkable facilitator. She has the capacity to bring out the very best of the truth in each individual."

Gene's approach to compassionate listening is rooted in both psychological and mystical perspectives. A founder of the Santa Barbara Night Counseling Center in the 1960s, she earned her Masters in pastoral counseling from Goddard College and worked with Ben Weininger, a "Zen-Hasidic" psychiatrist. With her background in counseling, Gene came to see all parties in a conflict as "wounded," as having suffered psychological traumas that need healing.

But Gene's work also has a spiritual dimension, as Dennis Rivers, a communication skills instructor from Santa Barbara, observes: "Gene is a Quaker mystic. Her calling was to carry pastoral counseling out of the pastor's study into public life. What has energized her work over the years is the Quaker teaching that 'there is that of God in every person.'"

As Gene herself puts it: "The call, as I see it, is for us to see that within all life is the mystery: God. It is within the Contra [opponent of the Sandinista government in Nicaragua], the Nazi, the Africaaner, the Israeli, [the Palestinian], and the American. By compassionate listening we may awaken it and thus learn the *partial* truth the other is carrying, for another aspect of being human is that we each carry some portion of the truth. To reconcile, we must listen for, discern, and acknowledge this partial truth in *everyone*." [5]

To appreciate fully Gene's approach to peacemaking and conflict resolution, we need to understand something about her intense inner struggles. To do so, we need to follow her along a spiritual journey that she aptly calls "a peace pilgrim's progress to inner healing." [6]

From Fairytale Childhood to Stormy Adolescence

Probably no peace activist has been more honest in sharing her life story, even the painful and problematic parts, than Gene Hoffman.

Gene's life was not supposed to be painful; it was supposed to be a fairytale or the American Dream come true. That's how Gene's parents saw their own lives and that's what they sought for their daughter. But Gene has had the courage and faith to explore the dark as well the enlightened parts of herself in her two autobiographical works—her unpublished Masters thesis called *Toward Turning* (1976) and an account of her stay in a mental institution, *From Inside the Glass Doors* (1977).

According to Gene, her father's story was a "typical Horatio Alger one." Thorkild ("Tom") Knudsen, emigrated from Denmark in 1909. He arrived penniless and slept on a park bench his first night in New York. He then went west, founded the Knudsen Creamery in Pasadena, and became rich and powerful. According to Gene, "this one-time impoverished farm boy rose to such distinction that he was knighted by the King of Denmark and became a confidant of royalty and presidents," including the Quaker-turned-Cold-Warrior, Richard Nixon, who was treated like a member of the family. [7]

Gene's mother, Valley Mary Filtzer, was (in her daughter's words) a "beautiful, vital, vivid, and ambitious woman" who dreamed of becoming an actress. When Valley's father died, the family's fortunes declined and Valley had to quit school to work in her mother's small restaurant. Valley attended night school and became secretary to the president of the Arden Diary, where she met and fell in love with Gene's father. Their parents at first did not approve of the marriage. Valley's parents disapproved because Thorkild was a foreigner. Thorkild's family disapproved because Valley's family background was reputedly Jewish. Gene has always been proud of her Jewish connection, even though it was denied by her parents:

> I was twenty two when my grandmother [Anna Stalp Filtzer] told me my grandfather [Samuel] was a Bohemian Jew. That knowledge had been hidden from me by my parents. Perhaps she thought it was time [that I knew]. I was thrilled and returned home in great excitement to tell my parents how glad I was to be a Jew. They denied it. But I continued to cherish this awareness of the Hebrew seed in me, the seed of prophets and seers.[8]

On January 3, 1919, Elinor Gene Knudsen was born in Los Angeles, California, to a family whose fortunes were on the rise. From an early age Gene was encouraged to believe that she had been singled out for an extraordinary destiny, that she would become a great stage actress, and that she would marry a Prince Charming and have a perfect life. Her childhood was in many ways idyllic—full of "camping, traveling, holidaying, huge family gatherings, many Danish traditions, and celebrations of every kind."[9]

Gene's religious education was shaped by the contradictory attitudes of her parents. Skeptical of organized religion, her father idolized free thinkers such as Thomas Paine, Thomas Jefferson, and Robert Ingersoll. He encouraged Gene to be a freethinker and question everything intellectually. Gene's mother, on the other hand, had what Gene called "a simple faith in God" based on feeling, not intellect. Valley conveyed to her daughter the consoling sense of a personal and loving God. She exposed Gene to a smorgasbord of religious practices—from Unitarianism to the Foursquare Gospel Church of the flamboyant evangelist Aimee Semple McPherson. To ground her daughter in a particular faith, Valley had Gene baptized in a Presbyterian church at age four, apparently against the wishes of her husband, who didn't attend the ceremony. As a child, Gene loved the church and all its rituals, particularly the hymn singing, but she found some teachings of the Bible hard to accept. In this respect she may have been influenced by her father, who didn't want his wife to give Gene a Bible, saying, "Don't give her one; she might believe it." [10]

Gene had a rich imaginative life nourished by the idealism of poetry and religion. As a child, she prayed to Jesus from time to time and experienced a quasi-mystical experience when she attended a mass at St. Peter's Cathedral in Rome at age nine.

According to Gene, one of the most memorable religious moments of her childhood was reciting Edgar Guest's "Let Me Live in a House by the Side of the Road" during a family gathering at age twelve. When Gene finished her recitation, she noticed her father in tears. She says that this poem was to become a moral "compass" that influenced her to make her various homes into gathering places for those in need, and for peace activists.[11]

Another religious attitude that her parents endorsed can be summed up in the biblical phrase: "From those to whom much has been given, much will be required" (Luke 12: 48). The Knudsens expected a great deal from their children. Gene was not their only daughter; the Knudsens adopted a Danish girl, Marie Christiansen, to be Gene's companion. When Marie became pregnant out of wedlock as a teen, Gene's father disowned her and threw her out of the house. Despite paternal disapproval, Gene and her mother continued to have a close relationship with Marie over the years. As a child, Gene was frequently disciplined with "spankings" and other punishments when her behavior was not up to the family standard.[12] As a result, Gene suffered from bouts of depression, insomnia, and various physical ailments that persisted throughout much of her life.

Valley, Gene's mother, was a woman who demanded much from herself, as well as from her daughter. A tireless organizer, she was involved in numerous charitable and humanitarian efforts, including a tree-planting beautification program called Los Angeles Beautiful. Gene calls her "a liberated woman," whose influence on many people (including her daughter) was compelling.

Gene was born to be an artist, as far as her parents were concerned. As soon as Gene was old enough to talk, her mother took her to acting lessons. The acting coach told them to come back when Gene could read. Gene's parents encouraged her artistic talents in every way possible, and she did the same for her children (she often says, "I raised my children to be artists: writers, painters, musicians," and their art works line the walls of her home)[14]. In junior high and high school, Gene was constantly involved in plays and recitations. Instead of college, she went to the Pasadena Playhouse where she spent four years studying drama (she later received a B.A. in acting when the Playhouse became a degree-granting institution). In 1939, she traveled to Stratford, England, to study Shakespeare and was

14

the first American invited to study at the Royal Theater School in Copenhagen. Arriving in Denmark just as Hitler attacked Scandinavia, she abruptly returned home.

During her teenage years Gene fell in love with a brilliant and talented young musician named David Nater, who was seven years her senior. After a passionate affair that lasted several years but was not "consummated," Gene broke off their relationship. David committed suicide soon afterwards, and the story became front-page news. His parents blamed Gene, who was devastated. As she explained in her spiritual autobiography, *Toward Turning*, "I wondered where God was—if God was—how could He let this happen? I prayed for understanding. None came."[15]

After a time of soul-searching Gene decided to go back to the theater and study acting seriously. She played her first starring role under the direction of a famous and extremely demanding Hungarian director named Barbara Vajda. Gene's performance was stellar, and she felt overjoyed.[16]

In the flush of success, feeling that she was "in love with the world" and "the whole world was in love with" her, Gene found a new lover named Werner Klemperer (1920-2000), who was the son of the famous conductor/composer Otto Klemperer. (Werner later became a well-known actor—his most famous role being that of Colonel Klink in the TV comedy *Hogan's Heroes*.) Of Catholic-Jewish background (his father fled Germany to escape the Nazis), Werner opened Gene up to new religious as well as artistic vistas. Through Werner and his family connections Gene met some of the world's great musicians: Bruno Walter, Igor Stravinsky, Ernst Toch, and Arnold Schoenberg. [17]

In 1940, she also met a New York playwright and director named Noel Langley who aroused in her the same passionate feelings as her former lover David. Noel wanted her to move to New York, star in his play, and help him to usher in a "new age of theater." Werner also wanted to move to New York, so they went together and rented apartments in the same building. Even though Gene continued to be involved with Werner, she longed for Noel. The only problem was that he was married and had five children.

After four months in New York, Gene's relationship with Werner fell apart, and Noel wanted Gene to become his mistress. Her Puritan conscience rebelled, so she begged her mother to come to New York.

Her mother reacted with shock and despair when Gene called and explained her predicament. But she also helped her daughter by buying her new clothes and setting her up in a safe haven for well-to-do young women, the Barbizon Hotel for Women.[18] Gene's emotional turmoil reached the point where she sought psychiatric help for the first time. Her psychiatrist was a woman, a student of Freud's, who told Gene that she cried too much, and that men don't like women who cry too much, and dismissed her. Gene did not return.[19]

Gene continued to see Noel from time to time on a friendly basis, but these encounters were fraught with anxiety. Torn between her powerful desire and equally powerful conscience, Gene was at a loss about what to do with her life.

Seeking Normalcy: Her First Marriage

In 1941, she met Raymond Chamberlin Boshco, whom she describes as "ambitious and fun-loving, well-to-do, and the ideal hunting and fishing companion for my father." He soon fell in love with her and asked her to marry him. Seeking "normalcy," she accepted and they were married on Valentine's Day, 1942. Gene regretted the decision almost immediately, but decided to be a dutiful wife as well as she could. The couple moved to Boston where Gene "lived in a doll's house," like the repressed heroine of Ibsen's play. While her husband worked for his father's woodworking company, Gene juggled the duties of housewife and career woman. Gene's father arranged for her to write a newspaper column which was published in all the Los Angeles papers and was seen as good PR for the family business. She also produced and performed in a children's radio program, "Stories Children Love." She even sold war bonds.[20]

At the same time, she was haunted by memories of her former lovers and turned for consolation and inspiration to literature—particularly the writings of English novelist D.H. Lawrence, Irish poet W.B. Yeats, American science fiction writer Philip Wylie, and fantasy/science fiction writer Joan Grant, whose book, *Winged Pharoah*, opened up for the first time "the possibility of a non-violent life." She dreamed that she was destined for some Great Mission, though she wasn't sure what it would be.[21]

Then, she became pregnant. After an extremely hard labor lasting 37 hours, she gave birth to her first child, a boy called Nikolas, on May 30, 1944, in Springfield, Massachusetts. She was overjoyed. Soon afterwards, the family moved to the West Coast, her husband was drafted into the navy, and Gene became pregnant again. When her husband was sent overseas, Gene returned to live with her parents in Glendale and felt peaceful and safe for the first time in many years. On August 12, 1945, her daughter Valley was born, much to Gene's delight.

But she soon became restless once again and returned to her creative endeavors. Her mother hired someone to care for the children while Gene plunged into a frenzy of work writing columns, producing radio programs, and acting in plays. Her absent husband was not missed.

When he returned in 1947, they set up housekeeping in Pasadena. A Danish au pair girl who was hired to take care of the children and domestic chores became Gene's best friend. As Gene pursued her demanding career as a writer and performer, her life seemed successful and happy. But inwardly she felt "lost, isolated, detached." She called her life a "prison of perfection."[22]

Divorce, Re-marriage and Discovery of Quakerism

In 1947, her life took another abrupt turn. When she began reading children's stories on the radio, she sought the services of a recording studio run by a man named Hallock Hoffman. Their business relationship blossomed into a friendship, and he invited Gene and her husband to dinner. As the guests socialized, Gene and Hallock found themselves alone in the library where they spoke of "God and the Spirit and Ultimate Reality and Emerson and Gibran and the many worlds of the Spirit and making peace in the world."[23]

Gene immediately felt that she had found her soul mate and that her marriage to Ray had ended. She told her husband of her feelings, and he suggested that she have an affair (as long as it didn't disrupt their family life). But Gene's conscience wouldn't allow for a marriage of convenience.

Gene's parents were dismayed by and strongly opposed her decision to file for divorce. But Gene was adamant: "I knew I had found true love, because I could write poems again—poems of ecstasy and joy and pain and anguish, and of seeking and finding God again. And I searched the Scriptures and the poets I loved. They all seemed to affirm my direction."[24]

With this inner confirmation, Gene left her husband and her home, went to Nevada with her two children, filed for a divorce, and married Hallock on July 20, 1948—all within the space of four months. Their son Paul Craig was born on June 8, 1949.

In 1950, Hallock gave up a lucrative business career to serve as associate regional director of the AFSC in Pasadena. He also resigned his commission as a captain in the air force and became a conscientious objector. This was a major step since Hallock's father, Paul Hoffman (1891-1974), was a major political figure in Washington, DC circles, as well as president of the Studebaker Automobile Corporation. Paul Hoffman headed the Marshall Plan, was president of the Ford Foundation, and nominated Dwight Eisenhower for President during the 1952 Republican Convention. Hoffman used to say to his liberal son and daughter-in-law that if Eisenhower lost by two votes, he'd know whom to blame.

Soon after the birth of their son Erik Thorkild on September 10, 1950, Gene and Hallock discovered Orange Grove Quaker Meeting in Pasadena. Gene immediately felt she was among kindred spirits. When she and her husband were accepted into membership the following year, she remembers "dancing down the street, feeling exultant that I had joined so great a company of seekers, people of God. I felt that together Hallock and I would perform miracles."[25]

Hallock and Gene set out to become "perfect Quakers." Gene and Hallock bought a modest home in Pasadena and happily settled into a life of Quaker simplicity. Gene's creative energies were at their peak. Over the next decade, she was involved in numerous projects and wrote many articles. Besides hosting a children's radio program called "Stories Children Love," she acted in many plays (her acting career continued until the late 1960s.)

She also bore three more children: Kristian Robert, Nina Kiriki and Kaj Lathrop. Gene feels that bearing children was "one of the most creative experiences of my life."

A major change in Gene's life began in 1957 when Hallock was invited by Robert Maynard Hutchins to join the Fund for the Republic. Hutchins, a former Chancellor of the University of Chicago, started this Fund in order to "restore democracy to America" during the McCarthy era. This bold project was originally funded, and then disowned, by the Ford Foundation because of its controversial nature.[26]

During the years in which Hallock worked for the Fund (and later for its West Coast branch), Gene's lifestyle underwent a dramatic change. In 1957, five months after their son Kaj was born, the Hoffmans moved to New York, bought a 20-room house, mingled with the rich and famous, and were even invited to a state dinner at the White House. Along with her radio and writing work, Gene became involved in teaching Great Books courses (a project initiated by Hutchins and Mortimer Adler to make the seminal ideas of western civilization more widely available). [27]

Espousing her own brand of feminism, Gene advocated letting women develop and express their full potential as human beings. When she noticed that no women were given leadership roles at the Center for the Study of Democratic Institutions (the West Coast branch of the Fund for the Republic), Gene asked Hutchins when women would be included. He replied, "When they are able to think."[28]

Gene demonstrated in many ways her ability to think independently. When she wrote a column favoring the United Nations, she was "fired" from the columnist job that her father had secured for her. Gene also took a controversial stand against the loyalty oath. In 1954, she became involved with a lawsuit against the city of Pasadena because it used a form requiring property owners to swear a "non-disloyalty oath."[29] Partly because of her family connections, her case attracted media attention, and Gene received hate mail from anti-communists.

"I responded politely to every single letter," Gene recalls. "And sometimes people were so surprised that they wrote letters apologizing for their rudeness."

Taking a strong stand on civil rights, Gene insisted that her children attend an integrated school in Pasadena—something that was not common for families of her background in the 1950s.[30] When she published an article on her family's experiences with integration, she was invited to become the first white columnist for the African-American newspaper, the *Amsterdam News*. During this period she wrote articles on racial topics with such topics as "Black *Is* Beautiful" (in which she talks about the importance of acknowledging and celebrating one's ethnic/cultural identity).[31] Gene also wrote many articles for publications such as *Fellowship Magazine* and *Friends Journal* and became widely known in peace and justice circles.

The Sixties: Breakdown and Breakthrough

In 1959, having reached the age of forty (what Dante called "*nel mezzo del cammin di nostra vita*")[32], Gene left New York and moved with her family to Montecito, a community near Santa Barbara, California. Hallock had been assigned to help develop a West Coast branch of the Fund for the Republic, which was called the Center for the Study of Democratic Institutions. The move to New York with seven children and the intense pace of East Coast life had been quite stressful, so Gene looked forward to the idyllic charms of the California coast. When Hallock invited Gene for a walk along the beach, Gene anticipated a romantic moment. Instead, her husband announced that he was having an affair with his secretary; he even wanted his mistress to move in with the family! Although Gene knew that their marriage was having problems, the news came as a severe shock. Suffering a nervous collapse, she was hospitalized with a diagnosis of "suicidal schizophrenic episode."

Despite, or perhaps because of, this setback, she was determined to overcome her emotional distress, win back her husband, and save her marriage.[33] She sought out the best therapist she could find. Gene was fortunate in finding an extraordinary therapist who also became her guru: Dr. Benjamin Weininger. Gene describes him a "beloved mentor, friend,

Zaddick,[34] and psychiatrist" who played a crucial role in her spiritual as well as psychological development. She writes:

> Day after day he sat with me, listening to me as I poured out my anguish and pain and self-hatred. Day after day he would seek to help me loosen the bonds of my absolutist view of life and the universe. Day after day—year after year he was there, encouraging me, reminding me that there was a whole life before me, filled with riches, that this was but a moment in time, a learning-how-to-live moment.[35]

Weininger had had a profound mystical experience in his early twenties, and in later life was influenced by the teachings of Zen Buddhism, Hasidism, and Carl Rogers' interpersonal psychology.[36] One of Weininger's goals as a therapist was to help his clients overcome "dis-equilibrium" and become "unified instead of divided" persons.

Thanks to Weininger's ministrations, Gene managed to weather her crisis and keep her marriage together, albeit precariously, for another twelve years.

During the tumultuous 1960s, Gene's children became adolescents and her home in Montecito became a hangout for young people rebelling against social conventions. With her flair for the theatrical and colorful, Gene loved—and was loved by—the "flower power" generation.

After several years in Montecito, Gene decided to build her "dream house" in the mountains above Santa Barbara (Gene loved designing homes, though she has had no architectural training). When the family moved to their mountain retreat in 1963, Gene felt extremely isolated and missed their big, friendly old home near the beach.

On September 9, 1964, a tremendous fire started in Coyote Canyon and raged through the Santa Barbara mountains. Gene's "dream house" burned to ashes, along with most of her papers.

The family moved back to Montecito where they stayed for the rest of the decade.

In 1965 Gene's father Thorkild ("Tom") Knudsen died of a heart attack while hunting—one of his favorite activities. Thorkild was a member of the Order of the Elephant and killed tigers, elephants and other wild animals that he stuffed and proudly displayed on the walls of his den. Gene facetiously called it the "room of dead heads."

Thorkild Knudsen's funeral took place at Forest Lawn in Glendale, California. So many people attended that they couldn't fit in the service area; a massive public address system was set up so that everyone outside could hear. Gene's daughter Valley recalls that there was "a HUGE wreath ... maybe 20 feet in diameter ... with the word 'DAD' emblazoned in the center. He was a father figure to many."

The '60s were an incredibly busy time for Gene. She and her husband were both active in the anti-war as well as civil rights movements. Returning to the theater, she acted in and directed plays. Under Weininger's guidance, she became a counselor and helped start the Night Counseling Center in Santa Barbara. As its director, she at one point supervised 35 lay counselors. [37]

Then, in 1969, another crash came. By now Gene had five teenage children, all in various stages of adolescent rebellion. When one of her sons was arrested on a drug charge, Gene flew to Denver to bail him out. That same week Hallock lost his job at the Center for the Study of Democratic Institutions, and Gene's mother was taken seriously ill with Parkinson's disease.

It all proved too much for Gene. During lunch with a friend, she broke down and wept uncontrollably. When she was taken home, she began screaming, and it became clear to her friend that more than just a vacation was needed. She advised Gene to check into a small private psychiatric hospital in Los

Angeles as a voluntary patient. Feeling overwhelmed and out of control, Gene made the fateful decision to commit herself.[38]

This experience proved to be another turning point in her life—one that she equated with Dante's *Divine Comedy*. Describing her experiences in a mental asylum, Gene refers to her doctor as "my Virgil"—an explicit allusion to Dante. Virgil was Dante's wise and compassionate guide through hell and Purgatory; he also helped Dante to see his mid-life crisis from a literary perspective. In a perhaps unconscious reference to Dante's "*selva oscura*" or dark forest, Gene gives her therapist the pseudonym Dr. Forester. It is Dr. Forester ("the one who takes care of the forest") who allows Gene to enter the *selva oscura* of her past and re-live old childhood hurts:

> In Dr. Forester's office I had hallucinatory visions of myself as a small golden-haired child in a circle of golden light, at the bottom of a black well....Suddenly the vision blacked out, and I heard my voice, small and piteous, telling him, 'They've taken away the trust...' Then began my journey through a Dante-esque hell which I continued to describe to him while tears flooded the words. Old angers and fears I thought were long since exorcised by my 'reason' rushed out through the feelings into words."[39]

It is significant that Gene's teacher, Ben Weininger, interpreted Dante in psychological terms: "The *Inferno* is a poetic account of the sensations of a schizophrenic episode."[40] According to Weininger, Dante's feelings of isolation and exile allowed him to identify with the torments of the damned.

In a similar way, Gene's keen sense of her psychological disturbance allowed her to empathize with the suffering of her fellow patients. She writes with shrewd and compassionate insight about patients and staff, describing each one vividly in a manner reminiscent of Ken Kesey's *One Flew Over the Cuckoo's*

Nest. Many of her fellow patients were young people around the same age as her children. Most had drug-related problems and difficult family situations.

The walls of the institution were covered with psychedelic posters on which patients had scrawled quotations from Bob Dylan ("I shall be released" being the most popular) and peace signs. Gene wondered if the problems of these young people were related to our society's obsession with violence and war:

> Most, if not all, the teen-agers were peaceniks. I have since wondered about the relationship between their political radicalism and the fact they were there. As I reflect, mine made [my ideas] unacceptable to my parents, [particularly my father] and [his] deep disapproval was certainly a factor in my uncertain self-esteem.[41]

During her month at the hospital, Gene came to appreciate keenly the importance of listening to patients—listening beyond words to the deeper truths that patients were trying to express with their art work and their sometimes bizarre behavior. She recognized that listening is one of the most important elements of therapy.

"Whenever I was listened to respectfully," she wrote, "I came to my own understanding and could often communicate more fully to my therapist." She also came to realize that each person has a unique perspective, a unique "truth," that must be respected. "Another need that became obvious to me is that the therapist must recognize the validity of the patient's truth, of his/her knowledge about him/herself." This is often difficult for a professional therapist to do. As she herself acknowledges, "As a counselor, I was often quick to diagnose for my client and then try to fit his/her unique situation into my diagnosis. I now know I was wrong."[42]

Sometimes patients could listen better, and therefore be more helpful, than trained therapists. This insight drew her into a practice called Re-evaluation Counseling, which was very popular with Quakers at the time.[43]

As so often has been the case in Gene's life, she turned a personal crisis into an opportunity for psychological growth and spiritual renewal. After her stay in the hospital, Gene enrolled in Goddard College's extension program and earned her Masters in pastoral counseling. She converted her autobiographical writing into a Masters thesis (*Towards Turning*) as well as fascinating book called *From Inside the Glass Doors*. Of this book psychologist Carl Rogers wrote: "I found... I couldn't put it down. It is a deeply moving document." Her teacher/therapist Ben Weininger gave it his highest praise: "Gene Hoffman makes a significant contribution towards understanding of human needs—a remarkable transformation of a disturbed and confused soul to an actively involved healing presence."

What makes *From Inside The Glass Doors* both moving and significant is its frank depiction of the journey from borderline insanity to psychological health—or as Dante would say, from the depths of the Inferno to the ineffable heights of the Paradiso. Gene does not conclude with a beatific vision, however, but with a simple and down-to-earth truth:

> I needed to place my trust—not in a particular person, a particular relationship, a particular situation—but in life (which is synonymous for me with God). I needed to trust the process—to welcome whatever happened to me as though I'd prayed for it.[44]

This powerful aphorism—"Accepting whatever happened as though I'd prayed for it"—is one that Gene continues to use. It may be rooted in an Hasidic story.[45] Among other things, it means accepting and embracing the totality of life—the pain and joy, the inner demons and the beatific visions—both in oneself, and in others. Gene's book ends with a poem expressive of her hard-won wisdom:

"In the midst of darkness
Light persists."—
Mr. Gandhi said—
I'm beginning to
See the pinpoint
Of light after
Sometime in darkness—
And it all comes clear—
I don't have to be a
sun
   or a moon
      or a planet
Not even a star—
Not even a flashlight!

Just can be—
That's enough
And being—perhaps
I can shine enough
To light my own way
And perhaps—
For a moment—
Yours

The phrase—"To light my own way, and perhaps—for a moment—yours"—suggests another important influences in Gene's work, namely, the Jewish philosopher/theologian Martin Buber. The title of Gene's Masters thesis is taken from a passage in Martin Buber's *The Way of Man* (1958), as she explains in the following passage:

"Turning," according to Martin Buber, means man's turning from his aberrations to the 'way of God.' "This is the fundamental act by which man contributes to his redemption." By taking the turning, the human being unifies the soul. "Soul," in Martin Buber's terms means: "The whole (person), body and spirit together."

"Only with a united soul" will our work and our life be "all of a piece."[46]

This process of unification is "never final," according to Buber. It is an ongoing work that grows more "relaxed" and "steady" as the soul becomes more unified.

For Gene, as for Martin Buber, the divine reality is revealed not in a sudden enlightenment experience or a final beatific vision, but in ongoing relationships that gradually bring the soul into balance. Gene is fond of telling the story of the time when Martin Buber was meditating in his office, and a young man knocked on the door. Deep in meditation, Buber replied, "Come back later." Buber was horrified to learn that the young man had come to his office in desperate need, and had committed suicide. From that point, Buber decided that God can best be experienced not as an "it"—an object of contemplation or cognition—but as an I-thou—an ongoing relationship. Perhaps because Gene had a similar experience with a suicidal young man when she was a young woman, this story moved her deeply and spoke to her condition.

In 1971, Gene suffered another emotional shock, though it was by now far from unexpected. Her husband Hallock finally left her for good. Soon afterwards, he married a woman who was younger than his daughters.

Gene went through the usual anguish of divorce, but managed to cope with remarkable success thanks to her spiritual support network. Returning to Quaker meeting, she found a community as well as a spiritual practice that enabled her to express her feelings and visions in a creative and healing manner. Fundamental to her recovery was the practice of daily prayer:

My emergence [from the "dark wood" of despair] began about five years ago when I consciously began to worship each morning. It was so restless and tentative at first! I could hardly sit the five minutes I had allotted myself: was always secretly peering at my watch to see if it was up....

These days I find my worship periods vary....Sometimes I linger over something that is troubling me. Sometimes I am in pain and I watch myself quietly being in my pain. Sometimes I feel only the presence of timeless love, timeless peace.[47]

In the summer of 1973 she attended the annual gathering of Pacific Yearly Meeting, shared with Friends some of her personal struggles, and was asked to write a paper on divorce for the following year. She "blithely" agreed.[48]

In the fall of 1973, she went to Pendle Hill, the Quaker retreat center near Philadelphia, which was founded in 1929 to foster "study and contemplation." Adults going through crises in their lives often find in Pendle Hill a safe haven in which to heal as well as to explore spiritual frontiers.

In the midst of a blustery Pennsylvania winter, Gene sat down and wrote about what led to her divorce. What emerged was an autobiography very much in the spirit of George Fox, the founder of Quakerism, who described with powerful emotions the "ocean of darkness" he had to pass through before he could see "the ocean of light."[49] In a similar vein, Gene writes:

I do not know why I had to go through so much anguish and pain. I don't know how much I have yet to experience. But I no longer care why. I know now, somewhat [as] James Nayler[50] did "fellowship with them who live in dens and desolate places in the earth." And I would not trade this fellowship for anything else. I am blessed.[51]

During her stay at Pendle Hill Gene increasingly felt a deep and joyous connection to a "blessed community" of "wounded healers" and fellow seekers, many of whom were not much older than her children. In the Pendle Hill world of freedom and openness Gene's creativity returned with an intensity that she had not experienced for many years, if ever. She had mystical visions and psychedelic experiences of unusual intensity (although she refrained from the use of drugs—she clearly didn't need them). For her final paper, Gene wrote a "Vision of Pendle Hill" in language reminiscent of Walt Whitman and D.H. Lawrance:

> Pendle Hill is a seed bed—germinating giants
> And the plants (we people here) are cracking through our shells. And we are trembling before our songs. And we dare to speak of the Spirit. And we dare to brood darkly. And we dare to shine, sometime.
> And we joy (sometime) in our existence; and we joy in the existence of one another. And that we are various. And that we are come together at this moment.
> And we are come together to liberate one another, to redeem for one another our divinities. I have come to redeem the divinity in you; you have come to redeem the divinity in me. And we are all redeeming that golden-dark-and-purple-flaming-out-divinity-in-each-other.
> (And I don't want to go home; I just want to stay here and expand and be intoxicated by the Spirit and I don't want to go home and I don't want to go back to dryness—and I don't want to go out in the world and I don't ever want to be in an unhallowed place again and I don't want to be told I'm too much and
> I WILL FLAME OUT.... And you WILL NOT COME BEHIND ME WITH A FIRE EXTINGUISHER.[52]

With passion and joy and wry humor, Gene goes on for a dozen more pages describing the "divine sparks" she senses in her fellow Pendle Hillers ("here is Pat, the coming crescendo, who will pour forth in torrent of song...and here is Bethy—shy spirit, wood nymph. And here is Dan of the red patriarchal beard and the shy child in his green eyes...") Then, in a remarkable display of verbal pyrotechnics, she depicts her final encounters and her final meeting for worship on her last day at Pendle Hill:

> Like a Bach Fugue—swelling and welling to its glorious crescendo. Through me, through Scott, through Bob, through others...the Meeting where I learned so great a learning—how various we are and how right it is that we are various....

She concludes with her homecoming to Santa Barbara. Basking in the afterglow of the Pendle Hill experience, in a room full of light and rainbow colors and peace, she feels the presence of her children and friends, transfigured and transformed by the mystery of love.

If Gene's story were to end here, it would be remarkable enough. She has plunged into the Inferno of her childhood traumas and mental illness, trekked through the Purgatory of an unhappy marriage, and at last tasted Paradise ("the garden of love and delight") among sympathetic Friends.

Her new sense of life's possibilities—and the possibilities of Quakerism—are enthusiastically expressed in an article she wrote for *Friends Journal* in 1975:

> I believe we Friends have the possibility of being among the most creative people on earth—for we know and have proven that all things are possible through the Spirit. And we know and we have proven that the

Spirit is within us. By attending to it faithfully and following its leadings, miracles can and have happened.

And I believe they will happen as we move more into worship together and apart. We will have available to us any talent we need. We will once again walk and talk with princes and with kings, or with wayfarers and with strangers. We will understand everything and speak in love to everything—to flowers and animals and plants and stones.[53]

Compassionate Listening:
A New Approach to Peacemaking

But where Dante's story ends, Gene's is just beginning. Not content with ecstatic visions and a renewed commitment to Quakerism, she began to seek a new approach to peacemaking. In 1971, she quit the Night Counseling Center. As she explained in an interview, "I want to devote the last quarter of my life doing everything I can to educate people for peace."[54] During this period she completed her Masters degree in pastoral counseling and wrote articles on the subjects ranging from interpersonal psychology to logotherapy.[55] But peace activism was definitely her primary concern. With Richard Nixon in the Presidency and the Vietnam War still raging, Gene attended disarmament conferences and participated in rallies. In 1981, she turned her Santa Barbara home on Sola Street into "The Gathering Place," where activists of all ages hung out.

Allan Solomonow, Middle East program coordinator for the American Friends Service Committee, recalls this period: "Gene had an open house where everyone could come, and she made very good cookies... She was quite different from most older persons and was considered a little unconventional. She was passionately interested in the Cold War. And she also meditated and was intrigued with all the healing and listening movements that were considered cutting edge or 'weird' back then...."

As Gene sought to integrate her spiritual and psychological practices with her peace activism, she came to believe that the traditional methods of peacemakers were not working. Rallies, conferences, and confrontation ("speaking truth to power") did not address the underlying causes of violence. Nor did peace activists confront the subtle (and sometimes not so subtle) internalized violence caused by unresolved psychological issues.

> During my lifetime I have worked with many peace people and peace groups. Rarely were the people I worked with peaceful. Perhaps I was the least.
>
> In the peace movement I found wondrous people, people who sacrificed themselves, who often turned the other cheek, who could write eloquently of compassion, forgiveness, love of the enemy...
>
> I found, too, that the seeds of all society's ills were also in us, often hidden or disguised. Few of us recognized or admitted this to ourselves. We felt exempt. But the anger, the anxieties, the jealousies were still in place, camouflaged. Peace people, I found, weren't all that different from non-peace people except that we had found a humane goal to work toward.[56]

Because many peace activists suffered from unresolved inner conflicts, Gene felt that they often failed to reach out to those most in need of their message. She diagnosed the problem by saying "we were trying to heal ourselves from the outside.... We didn't understand that inner healing had to take place first."[57]

In articles and workshops she shared techniques for inner healing that she found effective, ranging from Al-Anon to Zen meditation. She enthusiastically embraced the practice of "engaged Buddhism" taught by a kindred spirit, the Vietnamese monk/peace activist/poet Thich Nhat Hanh. From Hanh she learned the important lesson that we must "be peace" by practicing and exemplifying peacefulness/mindfulness in our daily lives. She was so impressed by Hanh's approach that she helped to fund the publication of his first book, *Being Peace*.

During the 1970s the Parkinson's disease of Gene's mother Valley progressively worsened. For many years Valley lived more or less in a coma and was on life support. She finally died in 1976. Her funeral was attended by many who remembered this remarkable woman's many public philanthropies. What her granddaughter Valley recalled was her grandparents' kindness: "When I was very young, before we went to New York, my grandparents were basically my 'salvation.' I visited them maybe once or twice a year and I remember they let me come into their bed and they would hug me... something my parents NEVER allowed."

By the end of the 1970s, all of Gene's children had left home and were on their own. In 1980, at age sixty-one, Gene went on a pilgrimage around the world, visiting peace centers and peace activists in distressed areas. It was a personal journey, unaffiliated with any peace organization, that led to another turning point in Gene's life:

> I was walking in London when I saw a huge sign which read: "Meeting for Worship for the Tortured and the Torturers." It was sponsored by the London Quakers. I was astonished. As a Quaker Pacifist, I believed that I should have no enemy and should care for the wounded on all sides of every battle—but— put the torturers on the same level as the tortured? I'd never thought of that.
>
> A whole new chapter of my life opened. I wondered why people tortured others, and thought that if I could know that answer, there might be new possibilities for peacemaking and reconciliation.[58]

Soon after this breakthrough moment, Gene revisited the Middle East, interviewing Palestinians and Israelis, hoping to find ways to bring about reconciliation.

Gene's first visit to Israel took place in 1960, when she went with her husband Hallock and Robert Hutchins on an official tour sponsored by the Center for the Study of Democratic Institutions. During that visit she met Israeli Prime Minister Golda Meir and was deeply impressed by the idealism of the Israelis. But by 1980, the scene in Israel had changed dramatically. "Israel was heavily armed, frightened, defensive, and persecuting the Palestinians," wrote Gene. "What had happened to this promising nation and its people to cause it to become so bellicose?"[59]

Gene came to believe that many Israeli leaders were suffering from post-traumatic stress syndrome (PTSS), caused by their experience with the Nazis. Gene consulted with numerous psychologists specializing in this problem and wrote articles and papers showing how PTSS was influencing the behavior of both Jews and Palestinians. This was a very controversial idea at the time.

"Gene was doing pioneering work," recalls Solomonow. "The AFSC published a couple of her papers on post-traumatic stress."

Using techniques she had learned in counseling, Gene listened deeply to the Israeli and Palestinian point of view. She found that the practice of listening non-judgmentally helped to create a climate of understanding (if not agreement). Her interviews and reflections appeared in articles and in pamphlets called *Pieces of the Mideast Puzzle* (1991) and *No Royal Road to Reconciliation* (1995). In Gene's view, traditional advocacy work tended to focus on one side of the conflict and led to polarization. What was needed, Gene felt, was a new approach. She called it "compassionate listening."

Gene became a very skillful and sensitive interviewer. One of her most unlikely subjects was former President Richard

Nixon, whom she contacted in 1983 when she was working for FOR in Nyack, New York. "I just called Nixon up and told him that I was Valley Knudsen's daughter," recalls Gene. "He sent a driver to pick me up." (Nixon was willing to meet with her because of family associations: she had attended Pat Nixon's 47th birthday party at the White House in 1959 and had been present when her father had given the Nixon Chair of Political Science to Whittier College in Whittier, California.)

To interview Nixon and to hear the truth that he had to express, Gene had to struggle against her own mixed feelings and those of the peace community.

"Nixon was the son my father never had, and his name was a holy word in the house where I grew up," recalls Gene.

During the Cold War and Vietnam War Gene's views were diametrically opposed to those of Nixon, much to the chagrin of her parents. Furthermore, despite his Quaker background, Nixon had refused to meet with Quakers during his presidency. Gene's interview with Nixon was therefore an historic occasion.

During the first interview, which took place in Nixon's New York office in December 1985, Gene asked: "What can be done about terrorists? It is they who might easily spark World War III."

"We must be more honest about it," Nixon replied. "We are against terrorists only when terrorists are against the things we like."

"I feel people become terrorists when they feel they aren't heard, will never be heard, and their grievances will not be addressed," was Gene's response.

"I agree," replied Nixon. "But the real problem is there must be a whole change....War is evil. The idea of unconditional surrender, which we insisted on in 1945, was totally wrong, catastrophic."

During her second meeting with Nixon in San Clemente, California, he surprised Gene by coming out strongly in favor of the nuclear test ban treaty and affirmed that "the military option is out...we must seek peace without victory."

After these surprising encounters, Gene concluded: "It is more important than ever to listen to those we consider to be our adversaries.... I found wisdom in much of what Richard Nixon said. There was much I disagreed with—and more I did not understand—but there were areas to build upon, corners where small trusts might be established. This, I believe, is the attitude we should carry to all people."[60]

"Many people were outraged that I could condone him," added Gene. "But I didn't condone him, I interviewed him. If I'd stuck with only the part of me that opposed him, I never would have found out the truths that he held."

According to Gregg Levoy, Gene demonstrates that "it takes tremendous energy and hard work not to take sides when we experience conflict, but to stretch the soul wide enough to encompass *both* sides, stretch the imagination almost to the bursting point and understand that two utterly contrary stories can coexist even within the same person." [61] This was certainly true of Nixon, as well as of many others whom Gene painstakingly interviewed. She was able to embrace the paradoxical in others because she had learned to accept the paradoxes within herself.

In the early 1980s Gene met Richard Deats, who was director of the Fellowship of Reconciliation (FOR). "There was a chemistry between us as soon as we met," recalls Deats. In 1983, Gene moved to Nyack, New York, to work as a volunteer at the FOR office.

There she helped create the US/USSR Reconciliation Program. She organized delegations and peace tours to the Soviet Union during a period when President Ronald Reagan was stirring up fears by calling the USSR an "Evil Empire," and nuclear war seemed imminent. In 1983 she went to the Soviet Union for the first time and met with the Soviet Peace

Committee for a discussion of "human rights, threats to global ecology, terrorism, and an exploration of various freedoms from religious to ethnic self-expression." Gene chose to participate in the task force on terrorism "because that seemed… the one most closely related to nonviolent alternatives." Discussions were frank and lively, and Gene came to believe that *glasnost* and *perestroika* (Gorbachev's policy of openness and democratization) were real, though at a still fragile stage. She hoped that out of gatherings such as these would come "the new consciousness we need to create a society that is worthy of human beings, one that will include peace and good will to all."[62]

One of the important steps that ordinary Americans took to demonstrate "peace and good will to all" was to become "citizen diplomats." Gene organized several peace tours that helped Americans and Russians to appreciate one another as people after decades of separation and suspicion. Gene paints a vivid picture of how citizen diplomats were greeted by the Russians:

> Some 60,000 Americans went to the Soviet Union in 1983. Many of us brought home stories of our warm welcome by people who had been strangers to us, stories that were never published in the newspaper or shown on TV. Many of the stories were like mine: of visiting the early morning open market in Yerevan, Armenia, and leaving laden with gifts of fruit and vegetables in exchange for Fellowship buttons that said *peace* in English and Russian. Stories of meeting strangers who, with few words between us, led me where I wanted to go; of a fifteen-year-old girl who guided us through the city of Tbilisi, Georgia, and would not let us pay on the cable car up the mountain or for rides on the Ferris wheel at the top; of taxi drivers who refused fares, strangers who invited us home for dinner and would not let us leave without gifts of remembrance; of the gold shower of creativity in the Children's Art Museum in Yerevan and the

generosity of the director and his wife, who took us through museums and described their delight at discovering talent among youngsters in remote villages.[63]

Gene's group met with Soviet peace committee people and had interesting exchanges of views. Although the atmosphere of these meetings was cordial, challenging questions were also posed, like: "Why are Soviets afraid to be seen with Americans? Why don't they correspond with American friends?"

Gene also connected with non-governmental peace groups like the Independent Group to Establish Trust between the US and USSR. Given the complexities of Cold War politics, she wondered: Were these dissident groups truly sincere? Or were they pawns of the Pentagon?

In her encounters with Russians, she sensed dread of nuclear holocaust and the same ambivalence about peace that Americans felt. She perceived that Russians had much in common with their American counterparts:

> They are not a 'peace nation,' any more than we are. They are an anti-war nation, and there is a difference. They have a huge nuclear arsenal, just like ours. They play power politics, practice espionage, seek to keep countries on their borders "friendly" through military occupation, and are terrified of strange planes flying over their territory, and function from fear, just like us.[64]

After a year working at the FOR office in New York, Gene returned to Santa Barbara to continue her work there. She wrote two booklets for FOR's peace program. Her first project involved researching all the Soviet-American peace and reconciliation projects in the USA. She discovered so many that she produced a booklet called *Directory of Initiatives*. In its introduction she wrote: "American initiatives for the US and USSR are springing up like wildflowers all over our nation. Everywhere, it seems, individuals, congregations, classes, and organizations are reaching out, seeking to build trust and understanding between our two countries.

"We need to know the Soviet people," she continued, "to understand their history, to begin to care about them—to begin to think about saving their lives."

The idea of saving Soviet (and American) lives was new and exciting to her. It inspired her second booklet called *Loving the Stranger* (New York: Fellowship of Reconciliation, 1983). This was a discussion guide to help readers increase their understanding of Russians, explore their feelings toward them, and examine the possibilities for change. Gene focused on nonviolent ways to alleviate the fear and hatred of the Russians that many felt at this time.

To counter the culture of fear, Gene worked on projects to develop and increase trust and understanding. She went to the Soviet Union many times during her six years of involvement with the US/USSR Reconciliation Project. One of them was called "Seeds of Hope." Americans were encouraged to send seed packets of marigolds to the Soviet Embassy and the White House as well as to Soviet and American people. The packet bore this legend in Russian and English: "To our friends, the Soviet People, let us plant a garden together; flowers, not fear. Marigolds, not missiles. Together let us choose life so that we and our children can live."

Senator Mark Hatfield's office agreed to tabulate the number of seed packets sent to the White House. The idea became so popular that when Gene went to the Soviet Union, she was surprised to see numerous marigold gardens in the Soviet Union.

In 1984, she initiated an art project called "The World At Peace." Children were encouraged to paint pictures of peace in their countries. Different schools in the United States exchanged paintings with Russian children. "We had some remarkable exhibits of the Russian children's paintings in Santa Barbara and other places," recalls Gene.

One of Gene's most successful projects was called "Forbidden Faces" (a title derived from a poem by Catholic priest/poet/ activist Daniel Berrigan). These were slides of Russian people of all ages, which Gene presented on speaking tours throughout the United States from 1983-86.

Another event was called "Window on the USSR," which took place in 1985. The Santa Barbara chapter of FOR created a week of music, dance, songs, films, exhibits of Russian crafts, and public occasions where Russian culture and people were celebrated. John Iwerks created a huge street drawing of Santa Barbara's sister city, Yalta, and people were invited to paint portions of it. Later Iwerks was sent to Yalta where he helped create a similar painting of Santa Barbara for the Russian people to paint. Events like these took place throughout the United States.

For Gene, the highlight of this project was bringing four Russian women for a retreat at the Casa de Maria, an Immaculate Heart retreat center in the hills near Santa Barbara. The leader of the Soviet group was a woman whom Gene had met in the Soviet Union. Gene invited fifteen interfaith religious peacemakers from the USA to attend, and the Casa de Maria offered their beautiful House of Prayer and full hospitality for the entire group.

"It was an astonishing experience," recalls Gene, who led the retreat. "It turned out to be a time of discovery for both sides. The Soviet women could speak very little English and the Americans were unable to speak Russian, but we had superb volunteer translators and were able to understand one another fully."

Gene asked all the participants to share the story of their lives, beginning in childhood through adulthood. "The common humanity became obvious, as did the differences in political lives," recalls Gene. "The Russian women spoke approval for everything in their society. Some of the American women became upset about this because there was absolutely no criticism of anything in the Soviet Union. Fortunately, the problems were worked through and the retreat ended on notes of caring, understanding, and wishing each other well.... Many of the Americans had never seen a Russian person before...."

This exchange was not without its difficult moments. The Soviet plane was not allowed to land in the USA, so it had to land instead in Canada. FOR members had to cross the border in the dead of winter, pick up the Russian women, and take them to an airport in the USA. There were also protests at the airport when they left.

Modest though these trust-building efforts may have seemed at the time, they played an important role in creating the atmosphere that ended the Cold War, as John Tierman has pointed out in *The Nation*, Nov. 1, 1999. The combined efforts of citizen diplomats and antiwar protesters sent politicians an "unmistakable message" that the Cold War no longer enjoyed popular support.[65]

The Cold War ended, but serious world conflicts still remained, particularly in the Middle East, where Gene decided to focus her energies and talents as a peacemaker. "Gene is so creative with her ideas and so daring," remarked Deats in a recent interview. "She is always willing to do the unexpected."

One of the unexpected things that Gene did was to write to alleged "terrorists" such as Muammar Qaddafi and Yasser Arafat. In 1986, when American planes bombed Libyan civilians and Qaddafi's home and family in Tripoli, Gene wrote a letter telling him that she "grieved for the suffering that we caused him and his people, urged him to explore a nonviolent response, and said I hoped one day to listen to his grievances." He thanked her for her concern.[66]

Three years later, when American planes downed two Libyan planes, Gene went to Libya with Virginia Baron, editor of *Fellowship Magazine*, and an FOR delegation. They spent a week meeting with various officials and members of the "Libyan Arab Solidarity and Peace Committee." Most were highly educated professionals who had studied in the West. All but one spoke warmly of the United States (the exception was the former ambassador, who had been deported in 1980). All the Libyans expressed dismay with Reagan policies. Gene and the group listened to and took note of the Libyans' grievances:

> The Libyans' main concern was our attempted assassination of Qaddafi and the killing and wounding of his family, as well as many other civilians, in 1986. Next on the list were the economic sanctions against Libya, the embargo on all trade, the freezing of Libyan assets in the US, the banning of all Libyans from the United States, the ban on the travel of US citizens to Libya, our efforts to dismantle Qaddafi's regime, and the campaign of disinformation about Libya in the US.[67]

Along with serious discussions, there were opportunities for fellowship and entertainment. Gene paints vivid portraits of various Libyans she met and befriended. She and her delegation gathered a wealth of information about the Libyan people and their views, but when they returned to the United States, they discovered that the government was not interested in hearing about their experiences:

> We were not permitted to speak to any member of our government in Washington, for we had gone to Libya illegally, and it was against the law for anyone to listen to us. So we wrote our articles and spoke on radio and TV, but could not follow up on our Libyan visit because there was a ban on Libyans coming to

the United States and we were considered—and
were—law breakers.[68]

Because of her interest in the Middle East, and particularly
the question of terrorism, Gene was invited to join a delegation
from the American Friends Service Committee to meet Yasser
Arafat in 1992. Gene proved that she was not only a good
listener, she was also willing to speak out. According to Richard
Deats, when Arafat was lecturing the delegation on the
grievances of the Palestinians, Gene suddenly interrupted and
said, "You ought to learn about non-violence, and you ought to
meet with Richard Deats."

Much to everyone's amazement, Arafat expressed interest
and agreed. Gene followed up with a letter, and was invited to
return for a second meeting and to bring along Richard Deats.
In October 1992, Gene, Richard Deats, Scott Kennedy, and
Karim Alkahdi (FOR's first Muslim national chairman) went
to Tunisia to meet Arafat. They were met by Zudhi Terzi, former
PLO representative to the United Nations. He uttered prophetic
words:

> The more nonviolence is unfruitfully pursued, the
> more room there is for fanatics who will oppose the
> peace process out of desperation. There is the danger
> of the rise of Islamic fundamentalism. Fundamentalists
> reject any political settlement and consider the peace
> negotiations treason. The hope Hamas (the Islamic
> fundamentalists) offer are arms, money, and the belief
> that the Palestinian-Israeli deadlock will be broken
> with 'the help of God.'[69]

During their meeting, Arafat greeted the delegation warmly
and described the Palestinians' grievances at length. Deats spoke
of his experiences teaching nonviolence in the former Soviet
Union, particularly Lithuania. This country, Deats felt, could
be a model for the Palestinians in their struggles to become a

state independent of Israel since Lithuana was a small, poor country with no allies, yet it mounted effective resistance to Soviet rule and won its independence. Arafat was so impressed that he suggested that FOR form a nonviolent center in Jerusalem because, he said, "You cannot be arrested, tortured, or shot—you can only be deported."[70]

FOR was unable to fund this project, but did lend its support to peace groups in Israel and progress was made. Soon after the Oslo Accords, Gene wrote optimistically, "Since then, both [Arafat] and Prime Minister Yitzak Rabin made nonviolent initiatives to each other that were beyond my wildest dreams." The course of Palestinian-Israeli relations have undergone continual "mood swings," reaching a nadir during the latest bloody Intifada [Palestinian uprising]. As current events demonstrate all too clearly, the key to world peace may lie in resolving the conflicts between Israelis, Palestinians, and the various Islamic states in the region. These conflicts will never be solved, Gene insists, until we learn to listen to all parties, including terrorists, with compassion.

Passing on the Legacy of Compassionate Listening

During the past decade, Gene's expertise as a teacher of compassionate listening has been increasingly in demand. In 1996, Gene received a phone call from young woman named Leah Green who was Director of the Middle East Program for Earthstewards Network.[71] Leah explained that she was becoming frustrated because the encounters she was setting up between Jews and Palestinians were leading to polarization, not understanding. "Participants came with their minds made up," explained Leah. "I felt we weren't making a contribution."

When Gene agreed to help teach compassionate listening skills, Leah was delighted. "We did a pilot project together in November1996, and it made a phenomenal difference," recalls

Leah. "We trained our participants in compassionate listening and it really pushed the project forward. We've brought hundreds of Americans over and we listen to everybody, on the right and the left. We've listened to thousands of Israelis and Palestinians with the intention of discovering the human being behind the stereotype. No one has declined a listening session with us. We've sat with people in homes, offices, streets, refugee camps, the Israeli prime minister's office, the Palestinian president's office, and on military bases. We've listened to settlers, sheikhs, mayors, rabbis, students, Bedouins, peace activists, and terrorists. We've learned that it is easy to listen to people with whom we agree. It's when we listen to those with whom we disagree, those we hold as our 'enemies,' that listening becomes a challenge. We listen with the intention of putting ourselves in their shoes, and it's made a huge difference. Gene was the inspiration for this model."

Two of Gene's most important works during this period were *Pieces of the Mideast Puzzle* (1991) and *No Royal Road to Reconciliation* (1995). The first consists mainly of interviews with Palestinians and Israelis. Some of them are troubling, others heartening—all reveal deep pain and a deep desire for peace and reconciliation.

Gene led creative writing as well as compassionate listening workshops, and published a book of poems called *All Possible Surprises (1995)*. In her introduction to this book, she says that ever since she was a young girl, phrases would flash into her mind, and she would write them down, and they would become the seeds of poems. "It was years later I learned I was writing instructions to myself on how to live my life," Gene notes. After becoming a Quaker, Gene realized that these phrases came from her "inner voice" and were directing her to areas where she needed growth. For Gene, the act of creation is also an act of listening, and responding, to one's inner voice.

One of her poems is a response to a phrase by British peace activist Muriel Lester, one of Gene's role models:

"The job of the peacemaker is"
> to know there is no enemy
> what we fear are fear-masks
> worn by ourselves
> and the 'other side.'
> And behind each mask
> —the hooded Klansman
> —the complacent housewife
> —the rich who seek more riches
Is something trembling
to be born:
something pure in eclipse
some love waiting to be released
a person deserving
> reverence and faith.

Helping people to remove their "fear masks" and discover the "inner person deserving of reverence and faith" is the primary goal of compassionate listening.

Gene was one of several pioneers in this technique. As Gene recalls, "Adam Curle supported the Compassionate Listening Project when I presented it to the International Fellowship of Reconciliation. So did Herb Walters. Both came to Holland to be with me."

Compassionate listening techniques have been applied in a variety of situations and settings. Curle is the senior Quaker mediator from England. Walters developed his unique Listening Program in North Carolina. "He did great work in the South," notes Gene. "He now listens to people all over the world."

In 1999 Gene led compassionate listening training sessions in Alaska and the state of Washington, where conflicts over hunting and fishing rights have arisen between indigenous people and professional and recreational hunters and fishers. Gene went to Alaska at the request of Cynthia Monroe, an AFSC staff person, to train people in compassionate listening. Jeff Smith, an AFSC staff person in Washington, used Gene's approach when the resumption of whaling by the Makah tribe caused some non-native people to respond with racism and anger. In both instanceseveryone had strong opinions, and no one was listening to the other side. "This issue is tearing the town apart," said a frustrated activist in Port Angeles, Washington. Compassionate listening sessions helped to defuse some of the tensions and enabled people to have a better understanding of each other's viewpoints.[72]

During the past decade, Gene has found numerous ways to teach the techniques and principles of compassionate listening. She has led workshops, given talks, written articles, and even become an "Internet Presence" (although she doesn't herself own a computer, preferring instead the telephone and typewriter). Thanks to Dennis Rivers, two of her booklets—a collection of essays entitled *An Enemy is One Whose Story We Haven't Yet Heard* and *A Compassionate Listening Handbook: An Evolutionary Sourcebook*—are available for free in PDF format at www.coopcomm.org. Leah Green has produced a compelling 34-minute video based on Compassionate Listening called *Children of Abraham* which is available at http://www.mideastdiplomacy.org/video.html. Another video called *Alaskans Listening to Alaskans* is in the works.

Although compassionate listening skills can to some extent be conveyed through books and exercises, the *presence* of a sensitive and experienced teacher is extremely important in the learning process. A teacher must model compassionate listening in his/her own life and encourage his/her students to do so likewise.

"We say very clearly in our guidebook that compassionate listening is a spiritual practice," says Leah Green. "I couldn't adopt compassionate listening in any aspect of my life until I realized that it's a way of life, a religion. Before I rush to dehumanize anyone, I use a mirror. When we have a strong reaction to people, it's because we have traits in common."

Gene's capacity to listen deeply has enabled her to become an extraordinary teacher whose influence continues to grow. As Leah Green observed, "I consider Gene one of my most treasured mentors. In fact, I consider her one of our national treasures." This sentiment is widely shared by Gene's friends, colleagues, and students.

Did I Love Enough?

Given her dynamic personality and turbulent emotional life, it is not surprising that Gene's relationships with her children have not always been easy or peaceful. During much of their marriage Gene and Hallock were so caught up in their careers and personal issues that their children often had to fend for themselves. In her essay "Children Are Guests in Our Lives," Gene talks about her struggles to "give [her children] the careful attention they deserve, recognize their gifts, and let them go."

The family placed a great deal of emphasis on learning, but not upon formal education or degrees. All of the children attended college, but only three have degrees. It took her children many years—and (in some cases) lots of therapy—to find their own way in life.

Artistic self-expression played an important role in the lives of her children and helped them to bond as a family. Nikolas works as a musician and owns a recording studio; he has five children. Valley was a dancer and became a line-producer/production manager for film companies such as ABC and Disney. Paul was an artist, animator, home re-modeler, gardener, and composer. Kristian works as a musician and composer. Erik is an internationally known contradance caller as well as a music and dance teacher who has been hired as far away as Denmark and England. He is married and has a son. Nina Kiriki has a vibrant contralto voice, plays various instruments, and became an award-winning novelist and short story writer (one of her recent fantasy novels, *A Fistful of Sky*, describes a large family of magical people that has an uncanny resemblance to the Hoffman clan). Kaj is an artist, designer, musician, and yoga teacher.

When the family gathers periodically for reunions, they tend to be musical occasions. During the most recent reunion, which took place at the end of September 2003, the family went to Paradise Valley, in the mountains overlooking Santa Barbara, to listen to Nick play rock and roll oldies with his band FOG. Family members danced, sang, and cracked jokes and Gene was in seventh heaven (although she chose to wear earplugs because of the amplified music).

In January 1994, when the family met in Santa Barbara to celebrate Gene's 75th birthday, the family had some very disturbing news. Paul told his mother in private that she should say good-bye to him. He had been HIV-positive for about thirteen years, and the AIDS was finally progressing. He made a first suicide attempt in February, but his partner, Kenneth Coleman, found him and called the hospital. Paul's second attempt succeeded. He died on March 9, 1994. Paul was very close to his siblings and to his mother; and his death deeply affected the whole family. "Even though his body has gone," writes Erik, "there is still a large part of him present. We miss him!"

Gene and her husband Hallock continue to see each other from time and have an amicable relationship. "I don't believe in holding grudges," says Gene. (Hallock, married for the fourth time, lives near Palm Desert, California; Raymond Boshco also re-married and lives on the East Coast.)

Now that Gene is 84 years old and in declining health, she can no longer can travel on peace missions, but she still sees life as full of "possibilities" (the title of a column she writes for the alternative magazine *HopeDance*). Reflecting on the meaning of old age and being an elder, Gene writes:

> [According to Jack Kornfield, a Buddhist teacher] at the end of your life the only question worth asking is, "Did I love enough?" My internal answer was, "Of course I haven't, and perhaps never will. But I can begin trying—whatever happens, it will keep me well-occupied for the rest of my life."

It is typical of Gene that even though she is an octogenarian, she still sees herself as a beginner, with new and exciting possibilities for self-discovery ahead. She concludes:

> Life is full of not-knowing-how-to-love and finding new ways to act, to be, to respond, to live. Since I think this may take several lifetimes, I can't waste any more time. The assignment is before me. I'm here to focus on being a warm, loving human being, just like my sons and daughters are already. Maybe I'll be able to listen more compassionately to them and to my grandchildren—and I'm sure never to be bored. [73]

In the summer of 2003, Nina Kiriki wrote the following poem that sums up how many of her children feel about their mother:

Dear Mom,

You are a peace pioneer, a passionate listener,
The one who says yes to life
with colors, flowers, open arms.
You find friends everywhere.

Thank you for your fiery spirit,
Your ardent desire to help, to heal,
To find ways to connect.

Thank you for acknowledging mistakes and making amends.
Thank you for listening to the Spirit, for finding wisdom
in the words of sages now and before.

Thank you for your bright and seeking spirit,
Your love, your kindness and hospitality.
Thanks for sharing your gifts.
Thank you for always, always,
Being willing to shine.

FOOTNOTES

---

[4] *Pieces of the Mideast Puzzle*, p. 9.
[5] *Pieces of the Mideast Puzzle*, p. 10. The addition in square brackets is by Gene.
[6] "A Peace Pilgrim's Progress to Inner Healing," *Awakening*, Februrary 1990.
[7] *From Inside the Glass Doors*, The Turning Press, NY: 1977, p. 4.
[8] "Crevices in the Rock," *Fellowship Magazine*, 1981.
[9] *"Toward Turning,"* p. 12. (Unpublished Masters thesis from Goddard College.)
[10] *Toward Turning* pp. 13-19.

[11] *Toward Turning* p. 19.

[12] *Toward Turning*, p. 11.

[13] *Toward Turning*, pp. 11-12.

[14] See "Gene Hoffman," an article in *Santa Barbara Magazine*, 1971.

[15] *Toward Turning*, p. 33.

[16] *Toward Turning*, p. 34.

[17] *Toward Turning*, p. 36.

[18] The National Park Service's website notes that "Barbizon Hotel represents one of the earliest residential alternatives for women moving to New York City to take advantage of the new professional opportunities of the 1920s. Young women began leaving the traditional family home in search of career opportunities brought on by the era's economic expansion. The Barbizon provided a refuge for many of these women, and its owners sought to create an environment that reinforced the values of the families from which the women had come. Codes of Conduct and Dress were enforced, no men were allowed above the lobby floor, and prospective tenants needed three letters of recommendation to be considered. Despite these apparent constraints, the Barbizon later hosted many social, intellectual and athletic activities and, and in recent years attracted a variety of famous tenants, including entertainers Grace Kelly, Candice Bergen and Liza Minnelli." (See http://www.cr.nps.gov/nr/travel/pwwmh/ny25.htm).

[19] *Toward Turning*, p. 33-36.

[20] *From Inside the Glass Doors*, p. 7.

[21] *Toward Turning*, p. 45.

[22] *Toward Turning*, pp. 48-49.

[23] *Toward Turning*, p. 51.

[24] *Toward Turning*, p. 51.

[25] Toward Turning, p. 52.

[26] The Center for the Study of Democratic Institutions was established at Santa Barbara, California, in 1959 and based in Los Angeles from 1988. Hutchins organized the center and headed it and its parent corporation, the Fund for the Republic (chartered in New York in 1952), for 25 years.

[27] *Toward Turning*, p. 54.

[28] In *Dimensions of the Future* (Maxwell H. Norman, 1974, p. 65), Gene wrote an essay called "Sexual Equality is Not the Issue": "I don't want equality with men, or anybody else. I want something much more. I want recognition of my value and uniqueness as a person—not as a woman. I want opportunity to perform creative work. I want to be listened to in any council for which I have prepared myself. I want full freedom, and cooperation to evolve as a human being, to gain wisdom and knowledge. To be sure, I want certain rights guaranteed to me, not because I am a woman, but because I am a human being," p. 3.

[29] *Fellowship Magazine*, December 1955, p. 5.

[30] "Trapped by Thomas Jefferson," *Liberation*, February 1959.

[31] *Liberation*, November 1968, p. 34. Other articles for *Liberation* include "Let the Rage Uncoil" (March 1967) and "Is The Problem Really Sex?" (Summer 1963).

[32] "In the midpoint of our life's road." *Inferno*: 1.

[33] *Toward Turning*, p. 55.

[34] In Hasidic Judaism, one of the "righteous ones" upon whom the fate of the world depends.

[35] *Toward Turning*, p.55.

[36] In an unpublished paper entitled "A Psychiatrist's Experiential View of Hasidism and Zen," Weininger wrote: "I see mystical experience as an intuitive happening from our genetic inheritance to help us continue our development, especially when there has been too much of a block in a given area of our personality. In the Western culture, these peaks appear to take the form of a breakout in the areas of the social sense, a necessity for survival in persons who are too much self-centered and lack a social sense. Hasidism emphasizes the aspects of the communal nature of man. In the Orient the opposite is true. In everyday life, the importance of the family rather than the individual self has priority. So, in Zen Buddhism, the mystical serves as a breakthrough in the need for privacy, a perception of the uniqueness of the person in his sense of unity and the community is felt within one. In this way, a person who is over-balanced in one area moves towards more of a balance, becoming a unified rather than a divided person."

[37] *From Inside the Glass Doors*, p. 23.

[38] *From Inside the Glass Doors*, pp. 25-26.

[39] *From Inside the Glass Doors*, p. 61.

[40] From a paper called "Asceticism and Religious Experience" given at the American Psychiatric Association Convention in St. Louis in 1963. Weininger wrote: "The preparation for religious opening or enlightenment may be a sense of isolation. One famous literary illustration is Dante's poem, 'The Inferno.' The Inferno is a poetic account of the sensations of a schizophrenic episode. (Before he wrote the poem, Dante had actually been exiled from his home city in Italy.) His vivid pictures of the torments of the damned ring true to people who have lived through the acute isolation of schizophrenia, and any practicing psychiatrist who has heard the same stories—in less elegant language—time and time again." Weininger goes on to say: "The role of the healer is to bring the sufferer back from exile so that he can again feel a part of his human community."

[41] *From Inside the Glass Doors*, p. 31. Bracketed comments are by Gene.

[42] *From Inside the Glass Doors*, p. 71.

[43] Gene later dissociated herself from Re-evaluation Counseling because she felt that its founder was too controlling and tried to impose his own interpretations of reality on those seeking help. In her unpublished paper, "Re-evaluation Counseling and the New Pietism," she concludes: "Listening *is* powerful and it can be used for evil as well as good ends. I am not sure RC [Re-evaluation Counseling] ends are those I approve, and even if they were—I would want people to come to them in their own way and in their own time." With typical generosity of spirit, Gene adds: "In closing I want to remind myself and my reader that there is the seed of truth in RC. Love *is* listening, and each of us bursting with the message of ourselves. I learned how to listen, and

was generously and caringly listened to because of Re-evaluation Counseling" (p. 19).

[44] *From Inside the Glass Doors*, p. 84.

[45] In *Tales of the Hasidim* (1972), Buber tell a story about a rabbi who was always happy and smiling. When asked why, he replied: "I never know what I want until God gives it to me." Weininger frequently used stories like these with his patients.

[46] *Toward Turning*, p. 3. *The Way of Man, According to the Teaching of Hasidism* was published in 1958 and later reprinted as a Pendle Hill pamphlet in 1960. It is available electronically at www.pendlehill.org. Buber's work was widely read and appreciated by Quakers.

[47] "Quakerism and Creativity," *Friends Journal*, March 15, 1979, p. 25.

[48] "Redeeming Some Sparks Through Divorce," unpublished paper, 1974.

[49] Elsewhere, Gene makes clear that she identified with Fox's internal struggles. "[Quakerism's founder] George Fox described how he had to know all conditions so he could speak to all conditions. I feel that something like that happened to me during my years being lost 'in the dark wood.'" "Quakerism and Creativity," *Friends Journal*, March 15, 1979, p. 25.

[50] James Nayler was a charismatic early Quaker who was felt by many of his followers to be another Messiah. After entering Bristol, England, surrounded by women shouting "Hosannah," he was tried for blasphemy, tortured, and imprisoned. He emerged from prison broken in body, but not in spirit. His final words before dying are much quoted among Friends: "There is a Spirit that I feel that delights to do no evil, nor to revenge any wrong, but delights to endure all things, in hope to enjoy its own in the end. Its hope is to outlive all wrath and contentions, and to weary out all exaltation and cruelty..."

[51] "Redeeming Some Sparks," p. 22.

[52] From Gene Hoffman's unpublished writings.

[53] "Jesus the Christ, Quakers and I," *Friends Bulletin*, January 1975, p 71.

[54] *Santa Barbara Magazine*, 1971.

[55] The "Third School" of Viennese psychology, started by Victor Frankl, who believed that human beings are motivated by an existential and spiritual need to find meaning and direction in their lives.

[56] "A Pilgrim's Progress to Inner Healing," *Awakenings*, February 1990, p.8.

[57] "A Pilgrim's Progress to Inner Healing," *Awakenings*, February 1990, p.8.

[58] "Trauma: Tragedy or New Creation," *Harmony: Voices for a Just Future*, p. 7.

[59] "Trauma: Tragedy or New Creation," *Harmony: Voices for a Just Future*, p. 7.

[60] "Reflections on Meeting with Richard Nixon," *Friends Journal*, November 1, 1986.

[61] *Callings: Findings and Following an Authentic Life*, Gregg Levoy. New York, Harmony Books: 1997, p.58.

[62] "Creation Continues," *Fellowship*, March 1989, p. 4.

[63] "Sowing," *Fellowship*, 1984.

[64] "Sowing," *Fellowship*, 1984.

[65] For an account of how peace activists helped to end the Cold War, see p. 216 and footnote.

[66] "Listening to the Libyans," *Pax Christi*, Fall, 1989.

[67] "Listening to the Libyans," *Pax Christi*, Fall, 1989.

[68] *Friends Bulletin*, November 2001, p. 4.

[69] "After the Peace Accords—What?" *Harmony* 1994, p. 18.

[70] "After the Peace Accords—What?" *Harmony* 1994, p. 18.

[71] "An Enemy Is One Whose Story We Have Not Heard," Gene Hoffman, *Fellowship*, May, 1996. Some of the comments came from an interview with Leah Green conducted in October, 2001.

[72] "Compassionate Listening in Alaska" and "Compassionate Listening about Makah Whaling," *Friends Bulletin*, September 2001, p. 8.

[73] "Aging: A Time of New Possibilities," *Fellowship*, Oct. 2001, p. 17.

Part I:
Witnessing Against McCarthyism

Soon after joining Orange Grove Friends Meeting in Pasadena, California, in 1951, Gene took a principled stand against the loyalty oath—an issue that was especially important to Quakers during the McCarthy era.

Quaker opposition to swearing oaths dates back to the time of George Fox, the 17ᵗʰ century English founder of Quakerism.[74] During this time many Quakers suffered persecution and imprisonment because of their decision to follow Jesus' injunction not to swear oaths (Matthew 5:34-36 and James 5:12). For this reason, the loyalty oath became a pressing religious as well as political concern of Friends during the 1950s. As Susan Auerbach notes in her history of the American Friends Service Committee (AFSC) in the Pacific Southwest: "Just as Friends were urgently concerned about the draft in the '40s, they were outraged by the loyalty oath in the '50s." Friends Committee on Legislation, the first religious lobby in California, was founded in 1954 to respond to McCarthyism and the loyalty oath. A Pasadena Friend named Robert Vogel became involved in a lawsuit that questioned the constitutionality of a California law requiring all state employees to sign an oath.

Sad to say, this law is still in effect in California. All state employees, including teachers, are required to sign an "affirmation" oath. In 1997, Friends Bulletin *published an article about H.A. Tillinghast, pastor of the First United Methodist Church of Eureka,*

California, who was hired to teach a religion class at Humboldt State University in September 1995. When he refused to sign an "affirmation" oath, he was denied a job, even though the entire Religion Department signed a letter on his behalf. [75]

Gene's opposition to the loyalty oath attracted considerable attention because she and her husband came from prominent families. As Gene points out in one of her first essays published in Fellowship *magazine, her opposition to the loyalty oath was rooted in a deep religious concern for integrity as well as a political concern for protecting freedom of conscience.*

FOOTNOTES

---

[74] See p. 245 for Gene's explanation of Quakerism.

[75] See *Friends Bulletin*, May 1997, in which various recent cases are discussed. Teachers and other employees must sign an oath agreeing to "defend the state of California against all enemies foreign and domestic." Exceptions can be made in the case of those whose religion forbids them to sign oaths. Quakers presumably fit into this category.

The Oath and I

Fellowship Magazine, February 1, 1955

I am opposed to violence of any kind on religious grounds. I believe oaths are a form of violence, an attempt to coerce the individual. As a Quaker I accept the Christian charges to "love my enemies," and to "swear not at all . . . to let my answers be simply yea or nay, for anything more comes of evil." I believe in the single standard of truth, that a man's word should be accepted as good, and that requiring any further gesture, like swearing, breeds suspicion and doubt of one another which lead to violence.

As an American citizen, I feel it is my duty to preserve our freedoms. One of them is to be believed harmless until proven guilty of illegal acts. Society has the right to govern our acts— not our words, thoughts, or opinions. When the state, or another person, prescribes what one must or must not say to prove one's loyalty, it can prove nothing except that it is a force powerful enough to make one say certain words. Loyalty cannot be demonstrated by words or thoughts; loyalty is a matter of freely given love and respect. When the state attempts to direct thoughts and words, it is invading an area which belongs solely to the individual and his conscience or his God. When it forces an individual to make his private political opinions a matter of public record, it is violating the Federal Constitution.

Fortified with these beliefs—I met The Oath

On March 23, 1954, the Deputy for the County Tax Assessor's office of Los Angeles came to our home. I had been prepared for her visit, for I was aware that a "non-disloyalty" declaration, intended by law only for veterans and tax-exempt organizations, had been so placed on the tax statement that the property owner would either have to sign it or strike it out. I felt that being forced to do either was a violation of my rights as a free citizen.

Therefore, I asked the lady Deputy why the oath was included on my tax statement. At first she appeared not to understand what I was talking about. I drew her attention to the part that disturbed me—the non-subversive declaration—and said I didn't think it should be included in the statement for private citizens. She told me coolly that I could strike it out. I said I didn't think it proper to have to strike it out to avoid signing it. That would force me to make a matter of governmental record what I believe should be my private political opinion— my opinion on loyalty oaths. The lady became very disturbed. "It is a law that was passed by the legislature," she told me. I explained that I knew of the law, and that only churches, tax-exempt organizations, and veterans seeking tax exemption were required—by law—to make such a declaration.

An Unsecured Statement

She was extremely upset and handed me the tax statement saying she would leave it with me to do as I pleased. She further explained that if I did not sign it, it would be an "unsecured statement" and I would be billed earlier than usual.

Before she left, I asked her if she was careful to point out the oath clause to other householders. She said, "No, they all know about it," and went quickly out the door, closing it on me as I was speaking. I was indeed suspect.

I then decided to pursue my investigation further. I called the office of the County Tax Assessor and asked for a separate property statement form for citizens not claiming veterans' exemption, one without the non-disloyalty oath, and was referred to the Chief Clerk, a Mr. Livingstone. He was very patient. When he heard my objections, he explained that this particular form had been used because at the time the California Constitutional Amendment, requiring loyalty oaths of some citizens, was passed, the wording seemed to apply to house-owners. "There was even a question," he continued, "whether the State Legislature could exempt householders."

Since they had to make up these forms far in advance, and order them from eastern printing houses, the County Tax Office had thought it safer to print them this way. "After all," he told me, "if people don't like it, they can strike it out." He then assured me there were very few people who objected, and concluded by saying the county was saving the taxpayers thousands of dollars by printing only one form.

If we taxpayers understood the implications of having to state our private political opinions publicly (by striking out the offending clause), I was sure we would be pleased to pay for two forms, I explained. I then suggested that an irresponsible state government could certainly use such information against its citizens. He hastened to assure me that all property statements were secret documents, not open to public inspection, nor could they be disclosed in response to a subpoena. To my objection that I had understood FBI reports were secret and they were then being made available to McCarthy's committee, he read the Code of California on Revenue and Taxation. All information required by the Assessor is not a public document. He also quoted some legal judgments to me over the telephone.

Since it was obvious he could not change his opinion, I asked him if the deputies should not explain that the non-disloyalty oath was on the form and give householders their choice about signing it. The deputies, he replied, were "supposed to draw attention to the clause." I told him the deputy who had visited me had not done so and requested she be instructed to do so in the future.

Yet he was grateful I had called, explaining he could not know whether the deputies understood and carried out instructions unless citizens did call. He agreed to enter my protest against the inclusion of the non-disloyalty oath in the form given private citizens.

I did not sign the property statement. I never heard from anyone about my complaint again—and I was duly billed.

However, there is always another year, another tax statement, and—in California—another non-disloyalty oath. In 1955, when the deputy appeared again, so did The Oath. This time, my husband and I decided to "do something about it." We decided to sue the county Tax Assessor to restrain him from including the oath on statements not intended for veterans, et cetera. Since our home was in my name, I had to be the plaintiff.

The suit was entered on March 26, 1955, six days after our sixth child was born—a lovely new daughter. My delight in her arrival was not lessened, but certainly colored by this event. Because of my relationship to a rather well-known Hoffman, the papers and news commentators gave the story important billing and the letters and cards began to flood in. Those in favor outnumbered those opposed about 4-1. The letters of understanding and support cheered and encouraged me. The letters of condemnation shocked and chilled me. It easily took four letters in favor to overcome the effect of one anonymous threat to "send me back to Russia" or the anonymous phone call from a man who said he was recording every word I said and wanted to know "if I was now or ever had been a Communist."

I suggested to him that his question was improper and I did not think I could answer it. "Oh," he said, "so you're one of *those*." This ended our conversation.

Refused to Answer

I was surprised to discover the effect this attempt at coercion had upon me. I could easily have "cleared" myself by saying I was not, indeed had never even been approached by anyone who wanted to convert me to Communism, but I could not. The coercive nature of his question seemed to be a deep violation of my personality and integrity. At the moment the only thing I could possibly do was refuse to answer.

On April 15th, the case was heard by Judge Kurtz Kauffman in the Superior Court of Pasadena. My attorney was A. L. Wirin of the ACLU. One interesting sidelight on the proceedings was the collection of tax forms from nearly every other county in California which we presented as evidence. In no other tax form was the non-disloyalty declaration placed on the form as in the county of Los Angeles. There were either two forms, one for veterans and one for householders not claiming exemption; or there was a special "box" on the forms for veterans to sign. This box refuted the County Counsel's position that it was necessary to increase tax expenditures by the printing of two forms. Then Judge Kauffman issued a temporary injunction requiring the county tax assessor to strike out the non-subversive declaration on the forms where exemption was not claimed, and advised him to obtain new tax forms without the oath for 1956, pending court settlement of the suit. Since the tax assessor did not take any action to answer this ruling, it was won by default. We will take further court action to test the constitutionality of any non-disloyalty oath on tax forms in the county of Los Angeles if funds for it can be raised.

It was the county tax assessor and not I who was found guilty of subverting our democratic processes, yet this did not seem to impress those people in our society who fervently believe in loyalty oaths. No amount of "washing" can eliminate the stain of "disloyalty" associated with any person who questions the security area of government encroachment upon private citizens. The bureaucracy which deals with private thought and speech is large, unwieldy, and well entrenched. Lack of education for freedom makes most citizens either apathetic or hostile. The conformity sickness is acute. This is understandable because economic sanctions are quickly put into effect against one who refuses either to conform or be silent.

I am sympathetic with the problems of employers, for small groups institute effective economic boycotts against companies who employ "controversial" people, sponsor controversial radio or television talent, or take any public position on issues of importance. There are few companies who feel they can withstand such pressure—and perhaps they should not. Perhaps the proper end of a business is to sell its products, not to become involved with moral or political issues.

The individual is faced with the same dilemma as the business. Even though he would turn against the tide of the majority, if he feels the majority is wrong, he cannot do so without reprisal. Business—in these days—must face the prospect of losing some customers; the individual of losing his livelihood, a degree of social acceptance, and some "respectability." The decision is far from unclouded.

What the answer is, I do not know—it may be different in each individual case. But nothing is won without some sacrifice. If the business sacrifices principle for immediate gain, it loses the long-term gain of operating in a free society. If the individual sacrifices principle for immediate security, he loses the security of a free society. I believe that if more of us understood and took public stands against these encroachments on freedom, the tide might be turned. Every time we keep silent, we strengthen the power of conformity—and ultimately slavery.

The choice in the short term appears to be freedom or economic security. Economic security without freedom is no security. The question is: will we voluntarily choose to be insecure in the cause of freedom—or shall we let the inevitable insecurity of totalitarianism sneak up and overtake us?

Fortunately we were in a position to sustain the blows that followed our stand on the loyalty oath. Perhaps we have to learn that we are always strong enough to sustain blows in a good cause.

Part II:
Building Bridges
Between Races

Quakers speak not of beliefs, but of testimonies—a public witness that gives evidence of one's inward faith. As a Friend, Gene not only believed in Equality and Civil Rights, she was also willing to put her beliefs on the line and take risks that many middle class white liberals shunned. Much to the chagrin of her white neighbors in Pasadena, California, Gene insisted that her children attend an integrated school—something that was not common even for liberal families to do in the 1950s. When she published an article on her family's experiences with integration, she was considered so radical that she was invited to become the first white columnist for the African-American newspaper, the Amsterdam News.

Sending her children to a mostly black school had a profound impact at a personal level. Leonor Boulin, the girl mentioned in "Trapped by Thomas Jefferson," became a life-long friend of Gene's daughter Valley, who was a bridesmaid at her wedding. "Valley has been one of my best friends," said Leonor, "Someone who validates who I am..."

This friendship also meant a lot to Valley. "Leonor was my hero in 6ᵗʰ grade," recalled Valley. "I was the only white person in the class and it was a scary time. There were fights on the playground and it could get very violent. Leonor would come around and the kids would leave me alone. She was my protector.... She is a gorgeous person."

Leonor became a professor of sociology and founding chairperson of the African-American studies department at the Arizona State University. In 2001, she organized a gathering to honor a black philanthropist named Leon Sullivan and invited Gene to participate for personal as well as professional reasons. "Gene and her family have been so important to me psychologically," observed Leonor, "that I don't know how to talk about it."

During the racially turbulent 1960s Gene wrote articles on such topics as "Black Is Beautiful" (in which she talks about the importance of acknowledging and celebrating one's ethnic/cultural identity). She also ventured into Watts and met with black militants whose "Black Rage" helped her to deepen her understanding of what it means to be black and oppressed in American society.

During one confrontation, Gene discovered that she actually savored the vociferous arguing back and forth between black militants and white liberals.

"I was enjoying the fight," she exclaimed to herself, in amazement. Then she realized how different this exchange was from the usual polite exchanges that took place between cautious middle class whites and blacks:

> Here I was, treating black people like white people. Shouting out my resentment at their injustice against me just like I would have shouted at white people.
>
> "My God!" The thought flashed, "We're locked in a real human encounter. This is great!"

Her willingness to confront her own and other's feelings about race enabled her to understand some of the failures of the Civil Rights movement:

> I think I understand better now why nonviolent movements have lost ground. In the interest of a superficial love and unity, we clamp down the lid on a lot of reality. A big chunk of reality in all human

relations, particularly between the different racial groups, is suspicion, hate, fear, and pain. If we can bring this up to the surface and admit it to ourselves and to each other without guilt feelings—maybe the real caring might come.

It was through such encounters that the seeds of "compassionate listening" were first sown. What Gene learned, and what many contemporary psychologists and activists now acknowledge, is that it is very difficult for whites and blacks to listen to each other at this deep level. This is an ongoing problem with race relations in the United States that can be remedied to some extent through compassionate listening.[76]

FOOTNOTES

---

[76] To help whites to listen to the concerns of people of color, the American Friends Service Committee set up a "Listening Project" which gathered together thousands of testimonies by people of color and presented them at the UN Conference on Racism that took place in Durban, South Africa, just prior to the September 11th terrorist attacks. The US pulled out of this gathering because it didn't want to listen to what Palestinians and Africans were saying about racism and oppression.

Trapped by Thomas Jefferson:
How Our Family
Declared Independence in Pasadena

Liberation, February 1959

For six years my husband [Hallock] and I led a Great Books discussion group. For six years we discussed everything from the God of St. Augustine to...*The Motion of the Heart* [by William Harvey, 16th century British physician]. (I didn't get much out of that.) For six years we figuratively broke old ideas into little bits and put new ones together—ones we hoped would make for better living.

Right on the first page of the first document we dissected, Thomas Jefferson said: "All men are created equal." He also said this was a self-evident truth. It wasn't self-evident to a lot of us. A variety of opinions were expressed that evening and many evenings since. Opinions ranging from "Equal before God—equal before the law" to the opinions that all Jefferson did when he wrote the Declaration of Independence was to window-dress us for the world to present half-truths, no truths, and B.W.—or bellywash, as one member put it.

I was one of the minority who took Mr. Jefferson's words seriously. I thought then, and still do, that there was something to them. I had the notion that there was a kind of equality about people which, though it wasn't completely clear to me, was real enough. Anyway, I decided it was important to live as if Jefferson's opinion were true. My husband felt the same way.

Not long after this revelation, we had the opportunity to try to practice what we had begun preaching. I still don't know quite where we came out. The only thing I can be sure of is that my findings have turned me topsy-turvy: it appears that it's all right, even desirable, to talk about equality and "the way things should be" but it's positively frightening when you seem ready to act. We discovered we belonged to a "class"—white, privileged, well-to-do, socially prominent, thoughtful about social issues. This was fine so long as we didn't step into action—for when we did, we were, in effect, traitors.

This is how our de-classification came about:

Right after the birth of our sixth child we needed a bigger house. We asked our agent to find us one. Now our "agent" is also our friend. He is an upstanding young man who sells houses within whatever limitations his clients want. However, he believes the best of his clients unless they tell him otherwise. He operates his real estate business on the theory that houses should be sold to people who want houses and can pay for them, not to people of certain colors. He is a staunch advocate of Jefferson and the American Dream. This makes him a fly in the hypocrisy of the real estate trade which has to pretend not to discriminate, although it does. This is said to be why the Pasadena Realty Board denied him membership.

Well, John found us a house. His description sounded ideal. Nine bedrooms—or rooms which could be converted to sleeping—living room, dining room, pantry, playroom—and everything else—including a guest house which could be rented to pay our taxes, a three-car garage with a full room and bath, two and three-fourths acres of land, and a public park at the bottom of the canyon.

The price for this establishment astonished us. We discovered we could afford it—if we subdivided and sold off an acre. We had known that big old houses were going for songs but we hadn't realized they'd reached so low a pitch. We soon learned why "ours" had.

Only people with lots of children want big houses. People with lots of children are concerned about schools, and our house was in an "undesirable" school district. A few years ago Pasadena school zoning laws were so relaxed that parents were permitted to send their children to the schools they wished. Those who lived on the "East Arroyo"—where our new house was located— used to send their children to a lovely school in one of Pasadena's finest (this means whitest) residential districts on the "West Arroyo." Thus the East Arroyo remained fashionable—though old—and its residents could remain unaware that a few blocks away was Pasadena's Negro district.

How Equal Should We Get?

By 1955 all this had changed. One of the reasons for Pasadena's Great School Crisis was that the then Superintendent of Schools, Willard Goslin, announced that he intended to stop parents from transferring their children outside their own school district. This meant that all children living on the East Arroyo had to attend Abraham Lincoln Public School if they went to public school.

Lincoln School is unique in Pasadena. Its student population is roughly fifty percent Negro, thirty-five percent Oriental and Mexican-American, and fifteen percent white. The parents on the East Arroyo didn't want to send their children to Lincoln. They couldn't send them across the Arroyo any more, so they sent them to Catholic and private schools.

We understood our neighbors' reluctance to send their children to Lincoln School. We accepted the fact that not everyone had the zeal for integration we had. We were partly reluctant to send our children to any public school, because we would have liked higher academic standards than public schools provided. However, Lincoln sounded like an ideal setup for us. We had begun to preach understanding and equality—now we could start practicing it. Like most adults in America, we had few nonwhite friends. Like most children in America, ours lived almost entirely in a white world. Quite properly, our protestations were open to question. Here was the opportunity to test their validity. We welcomed it.

Before we bought the house, I interviewed the principal of Lincoln School and spoke with some of the teachers. I asked the principal the usual questions. Would our children be discriminated against? Would they be favored? Were Lincoln's academic standards lower than the standards in other Pasadena schools? How was integration working?

To each of my questions he gave a reassuring answer. With pride he told me of his school's record, of the fine relationships among the children. He told me our children would love it; if we gave Lincoln two weeks of their time, they wouldn't want to go anywhere else. He cited the case of one boy who had been taken out of Lincoln and sent to a fashionable private school where he was so unhappy that his parents had to send him back. He assured me that our children could proceed as rapidly as their intellects would permit them.

My conversation with the teachers was equally reassuring. I discovered that they were serious people with a fine understanding of children, that their emphasis was on the unique contributions of all peoples, and that their attitude toward teaching was one of concern for each child's growth and development.

Encouraged by this information and with the hope of subdividing the property, we took on a substantial mortgage and bought the house. Then the fun began.

The lovely people who were selling us the house gave a cocktail party to introduce us to our soon-to-be neighbors. The owner had for years been the head of the Bill of Rights Day celebration in Los Angeles. His wife had remarked that they sent their children to a private school, but that she wished they'd had the courage to do what we were doing. Armed with this approbation, we arrived at their party with enthusiasm.

Everyone converged upon us. They were most friendly. There was much talk of their delight at having a new batch of children in the neighborhood. I was busy discovering the names and ages of nearby children when someone asked me what school our children would attend. I responded with "Why, Lincoln, of course. I think it'll be exciting for them and us."

There was a sudden silence. I felt a strange prickle along my spine. The lady with whom I had been chatting said, "Well, I hope you like it," and left me to talk with someone else. From then on old neighbors talked with old neighbors. As soon as it was proper we left.

My husband and I looked at each other. Why the sudden silence? What had I done?

We were soon divested of our innocence. The principal of Lincoln had given me the names of other white families dotted along the East Arroyo whose children went there to school. There were three in all. As soon as we were decently settled, I invited the mothers and their children to visit us. Enlightenment came quickly. These older hands felt that East Arroyoites not only did not want to send their children to Lincoln, they didn't want anyone else on their tight little island to do so either, because they were still agitating for the resurrection of the old zoning conditions. We speculated about their reasons. Perhaps they thought that people who sent their children to Lincoln might ultimately sell their house to Negroes. Maybe they thought that children who associated with Negroes might bring them home. Maybe they took this as an indication that the white children might be of "lower" caliber. One family told us that they had been visited by a delegation as soon as they moved into the East Arroyo district and had been firmly advised not to send their children to Lincoln——advised so firmly the family took it as a threat.

However, neither threats nor ostracism nor the displeasure of their neighbors intimidated them. Their reasons were various, and ranged from a profound conviction in the dignity of each individual to a hearty, inarticulate belief in democracy. We were pleased to join their ranks.

Next we had to sell the lot. Our friend the agent advised us—though he said it wasn't absolutely necessary—to secure the signatures of our new neighbors on a petition for permission to subdivide our property. We drew up the petition and he began making the rounds to get the signatures. Not one neighbor would sign our petition. At first they resisted on technical grounds, but when we met all their conditions, they still refused to sign. We finally learned why.

Our preaching had got around. They thought that people who kept saying they believed in integration and then moved into a house so that their children could go to school with Negroes would hold an open sale of the property. They were right. We intended to sell our lot to people we thought would make good neighbors. This had nothing to do with the color of their skin. This seemed to us to follow from Mr. Jefferson's principle. Our intention was not met with enthusiasm by our neighbors. After placing every legal roadblock he could think of in our way, the lawyer of one of our neighbors confided to a talkative person that he'd heard we might sell to a Negro and that he intended to stop us at any cost. We heard through someone else that another neighbor, who is Pasadena's biggest real estate agent, had declared that if we sold our lot to a nonwhite family, he would fight us through every court in the State. We were not making ourselves popular.

At this point I telephoned a member of the zoning commission and described our situation. She said that if our papers were in order, the zoning commission would put them through. She also said that this kind of pressure was precisely what the zoning commission hoped to eradicate. So without a single signature on our petition, we went before the zoning commission and won the right to subdivide.

I wish we could report that we sold the lot to a fine nonwhite family who won the community to their side. We didn't. None appeared. The purchasers were a delightful family with three children who had no school "problems," since they were enrolled in a Catholic school. They built a handsome modern house, which has increased the value of the surrounding property and is a showplace in the area.

One crisis ended; others began. Since I had heard that many children attending Lincoln had working parents, we made the rule that our children should not visit their new friends until I knew the parents and knew that some adult would be at home. But we encouraged our children to bring anyone to our house at any time. They did.

Our yard began to overflow with children of color. This had a predictable effect upon our neighbors. You'd have thought we had smallpox, so studiously did most (not all) East Arroyo children avoid our yard.

At one point, I began to think that our new neighbors were right, for some of the events gave me pause. At first our eldest son, Niki, aged eleven, was so enthusiastic that he invited everybody and anybody home to play. All at once we had as nice a gang of potential juvenile delinquents patrolling our yard as you could find anywhere. They ganged up on the East Arroyo children and threatened them. They threw rocks and sticks at children in neighboring yards. When I was out, the young college student who lived with us had some colorful experiences. When she admonished them for stripping the branches from the tangerine trees, climbing the shaky trellis, and other misdeeds, they replied gleefully with a vivid string of four-letter words and continued unimpeded.

One afternoon the clamor of voices in the yard hit an unusual pitch. When I ran out, I stumbled into a flying squadron of East Arroyo children on bikes, skates, and foot rushing across our lawn. They were bearing a sinister assortment of lead pipes, sharp sticks and rocks. I trembled bravely up to the head of the column, where the leader confided in a serious of staccato shouts that they had come to beat up Niki and his gang in massive retaliation for the indignities they had suffered.

I summoned my general's voice and barked orders. The army marched home without losing a man. Later my husband and I reviewed Niki's troops. They all agreed to obey the regulations of our yard from then on and to discontinue any threats. That night I apologized to all the mothers of the neighborhood. The incident was not repeated.

Discrimination At Its Best

An astonishing event brought this sequence to a close. Once again voices rang through the yard. I went out to investigate. Young Niki was on the lawn. So were three colored boys. Our daughter Valley, aged ten, was in a tree. Niki, in a tone suited to a New York cab driver, was directing the three to go home and never come back. I was shocked at this display of inhospitality and I resolved to have an earnest little talk with Niki.

That evening he called me into his room. He had the earnest little talk with me instead. Pacing up and down, he said, "Mom, I've come to a decision. I've decided I like my friends because of their personality—the color of their skin has nothing to do with it. There are good guys and bad guys of every color. I didn't send those guys home today because they were Negroes—I sent them home because they were bad guys and I didn't want them following my sister home or fooling around our house. OK.?"

What could I reply but "OK"? He had made an important decision, had had an important insight. I was proud of him.

This was discrimination at its best, the kind it's important to practice.

A few weeks later, he asked me if he could join the Boy Scouts. After my affirmative reply, he hesitated and then said: "I'd really like to, but I don't know if they'll accept me." To my "Why not?" he answered: "It's an all-Negro troop. My best friends are in it, but maybe they don't want a white member."

Apparently his color was no bar, for he was soon invited to join.

Integration, But...

While my children were having skirmishes on the battlefront, I was busy trying to shore up home defenses. I felt confident that with patience, goodwill, and acts of thoughtfulness I could win my neighbors to my family, if not to their friends and associates.

The first year we gave a Halloween party and invited every East Arroyo child we knew—there were 33 in all. I carefully explained to our children that this was to be a "neighborhood" party. Since our neighbors were inexperienced (by choice) with people of color, they did not understand how we felt about them, and they didn't feel the same way. I said we have given our neighbors enough concern for now, and that I didn't think we should provoke them any further. Therefore, I told our children that they were not to invite any friends from Lincoln School. I thought I had made myself perfectly clear.

Halloween arrived, and so did thirty-three children, accompanied by nurses, governesses and other chaperones. Everything proceeded nicely; the children ate their sandwiches and carrot sticks, balanced cups of punch, and eagerly awaited the moment of the grand exodus for Trick or Treat.

In the midst of the gaiety, the doorbell rang. My daughter Valley came to me in consternation. She said that one of Niki's school friends had arrived as an invited guest. I went to greet him and discovered a tall, very dark Negro boy in a costume of somebody's too-large tail coat, waiting at the door. I tried to meet the moment by showing no concern, and invited him in. He accepted with pleasure, and no one was the least embarrassed by his presence. He joined the others in their rounds, and I awaited the moment to speak with my son.

Later I spoke with him. I upbraided him for violating my orders. I explained to him again my reasons for wanting only a neighborhood party. I explained them ad infinitum and made it clear that he had upset my grand plan. He took it all calmly, and when I had finished said, "Oh, so you don't want my Negro friends around."

I was aghast—he had laid my nicely hid prejudice bare. I wanted the best of both words. I wanted to "turn white" when it pleased me. It wouldn't work.

I never tried again to have segregated parties, though I did continue my efforts to attract neighboring children to our yard. We built a small swimming pool and invited everyone to use it. Only two ever did. Each invitation was received with a polite excuse: It was the cold season . . . It was the flu season . . . Johnny was dressed for company that day. But it doesn't take children too long to learn the hypocrisy of their elders. One hot day a small boy was standing by the pool watching the water-play hungrily. I urged him to join the others. He looked at me and replied flatly, "I can't swim in your pool. My mother says it's dirty." After that, I gave up.

The whole experiment was not without moments of doubt and worry. Our son Paul entered Lincoln in the first grade. After he'd gone to bed on his first day in school, I heard him sobbing softly. When I asked him why, he said: "Today, when I was sitting under the pergola, waiting to come home with Valley, two of those dark boys came up to me. The big one told the little one to hit me and the little one did hit me until a bigger dark boy came along and made him stop."

My heart sank—how deep would this wound be? What were we doing to our children—how much were they going to have to suffer for our principles? Would we mark them with distaste for people different from themselves? But my worries had no foundation. Young Paul made fast friends of children whose skins were a variety of colors.

One in particular was a small Japanese girl named Carol. Carol's mother was one of those exquisite people who can do everything. She included our Paul in all sorts of splendid adventures—picnics, swimming parties, art exhibitions, and frequent visits to her lovely modern home, perched high on a hill overlooking Pasadena.

Paul had only one dark day in his long happy affair with Carol. He came home one morning bedraggled and hollow-eyed from his first all-night visit to his six-year-old girlfriend's house. When I told him he looked tired, he sighed, "Well, Carol and I think we'll get married when our parents die. But I just can't sleep with that girl—she talks all night."

Our kindergartner, Erik, found friends too. One was a charming tiny dark girl named Ruthanna. Erik begged me to let Ruthanna visit him after school. So one day I picked the two of them up and drove to Ruthanna's house to ask her mother's permission. The sight of Ruthanna's surroundings sickened me. I had to pick my way through a yard full of rubbish to a battered old screen door. My knock was answered by a lovely young woman with a chubby baby on her hip. She invited me into the kitchen, which was a litter of dishes, half-used tin cans of food, and an open gas heater.

The mother gave permission for Ruthanna to visit us, and I took her home. There never was a gentler, a sweeter, more fastidious child than Ruthanna. She and Erik had many fine times together. She livened for me that ancient mystery—how does a pearl grow in an oyster—can an oyster learn from a pearl? When Ruthanna's family moved to another home some time later, I hoped it was the sort of house that would inspire her lovely mother to make a home that would match the beauty of her family. But I never went to see. It seemed better to enjoy Ruthanna and preserve the mystery.

Erik's other friend was of Japanese ancestry. He was a handsome, winning child named Donald, who was brought on his first visit by his mother. To my surprise, his mother stayed with him for the entire visit. We must have passed inspection, for after that Donald was permitted to come unescorted.

The relations our elder daughter Valley developed were deep and rich and lasting. Her closest friend was a Negro girl, whose name was Leonor. Leonor came from a remarkable family. Her parents were gentle people. Her mother was an accomplished musician, and taught her daughter piano for a year. It was she who took Valley to all worthwhile activities in Pasadena—to concerts, to the opera, and to their church. It was she who invited me to an arts-and-crafts exhibit of her women's club. It was she who reached across the gap between our two cultures and led me gently into hers. It was Leonor's father who called upon us when we first arrived to welcome us to the area and to Lincoln School.

And it was Leonor who gave Valley an example of responsibility. Leonor was a Seventh Day Adventist. Saturday was her Sabbath. While all other children were enjoying their day of freedom, she joyfully spent each Sabbath in her church and lived by its precepts on all other days of the week. She was permitted to play only in those hours that could be squeezed in between school and piano practicing. Yet it was Leonor whose rich gaiety made our house sing. It was she who gave Valley a lovely going-away party when we moved to the East Coast, and it is Leonor who faithfully writes Valley to help her keep in touch with the activities of her friends in the West.

Shortly before we moved, two East Arroyo couples expressed an interest in our experiences at Lincoln School. We invited them for dessert, coffee, and conversation.

After nibbling through the small talk we began chewing on the good red meat. The talk came to freedom of speech and freedom against self-incrimination. One of the men was loud in his protest against them. When my husband suggested that these principles were among the most important in our Bill of Rights, the neighbor said: "The Bill of Rights? Why that's a sacred document—it's— well, it's like the Bible. It's part of our precious heritage." He paused and then added, "The Bill of Rights is one of the world's great documents—but as for those first ten amendments, you can cancel them. Each and every one."

His wife was no less enthusiastic about the "American way of life." She told me that she had no prejudice—in fact, a few years before, she'd sent her son to a nearby parochial school. This, like Lincoln, was integrated—though nonwhites were in the minority. She described how her son had begun to bring home children of various colors and told of an unpleasant knife incident with a small Mexican-American lad.

Proudly she explained that she had not needed to set a course of future action for her son. She simply told him that he was never to bring anyone home whom he would not want his sisters to marry. From that day forward, no colored child ever darkened their door again.

The other couple was divided. The husband was a thoughtful man, perplexed by the good and evil in the situation which involved all of us. His wife was honest and open in her disapproval of any racial mixing on the social level. It was she who asked me the inevitable question: "Would you want your daughter to marry one?"

"My mother told me," I answered cautiously, "that some of her best friends are dirty, and they're not Negroes. My eldest daughter," I continued, "is only ten years old. I don't want her to marry anyone of any color. I hope she doesn't get married until she's at least eighteen. By then I don't expect she'll let me tell her whom not to marry any more than she'll let me choose her husband for her."

"What I hope," I said with some heat, "is that my daughters have enough sense to marry men who know how to love them and they will have learned by the time they're married how to love their husbands. I don't think it has anything to do with color."

I didn't convince the lady—but then, she didn't convince me. It was a proper conclusion to our stay on the East Arroyo.

Not long after, we sold our home and moved to another city. I had arrived in the East Arroyo with high hopes of converting our neighbors. Whether any conversions took place, I do not know. From what I do know, it looks pretty much like failure.

But someday some important questions will be answered. Will the experience protect our children from prejudice? Will they now avoid looking upon people of other races and religions as masses, stuck in categories? Will their eyes be open to see people as individuals with their individual failings and high potentialities? Will they be free to make in their hearts bridges across the barriers of color—bridges of love which will lead them into wider, richer worlds?

Let the Rage Uncoil

Liberation, 1967

Watts. It's an ugly word. It sounded like an epithet even before it became one.

Watts-squats . . . Who'd want to live in a place called "Watts"—even if it were as beautiful as Bel Air or Santa Barbara? Not I, and probably not anybody else. Watts, California 90002. Awful.

And there is an awfulness to Watts, at least on the northern border I visited one Sunday in December. It was ugly as only people can make a place ugly. In the gutter, on the sidewalk—trash. Nobody's trash, everybody's trash—and no street sweepers for it.

Dark-stained sidewalks, dark-stained buildings, gaping windows that opened on unlighted, dirty interiors. On the front of one building, posted like Martin Luther's Ninety-Five Theses, were packets of mimeographed sheets. "Boycott, baby. Boycott!" read one. "Let California Burn While Politicians Fiddle"—and there followed, in fine print, N-VAC's (Nonviolent Action Committee's) leftover 16-point program for candidates running in last November's election. Don't vote for anybody who doesn't support these valid needs. Another sheet, by Malcolm X, told "How I Got Out of the Draft."

The Revolution was spelled out in single-spaced typescript. It came on strong, baby, strong.

There were six of us who drove down from Santa Barbara to visit "Operation Bootstrap" that Sunday morning. Four were staff members of The Center for the Study of Democratic Institutions: W. H. "Ping" Ferry, Florence Mischel, Alan Butler, MD, and Hallock Hoffman. The other two were Dennis Dunn, writer and teacher in Santa Barbara's Work Training Program, and I, a sometime writer, full-time mother and wife.

In brief, Operation Bootstrap is Watts' self-help center. (Actually, its headquarters are not in Watts, but at Forty-Second Street and Central Avenue, in the Avalon district of East Los Angeles. But Watts is where Operation Bootstrap sprang from. Watts describes what Bootstrap is trying to overcome.) It's an educational project for, by, and of the people of East Los Angeles. They contribute funds to pay their teachers and overhead expenses. Industry has been asked to supply training, equipment and instructors. The Operation calls itself "A Systems Approach for War on Poverty." It's surely this—and much, much more.

Our presence there was part of the "more." We'd been invited to attend an all-day "race-relations session." We'd been told we would meet with and be challenged by leaders of the black community who represented a wide range of opinion, from extreme black nationalist to integrationist.

We pulled up in front of one of the dark-stained buildings and parked. Outside, spelled out in big, black letters, was "OPERATION BOOTSTRAP." On the window was the legend, "Learn, Baby. Learn." This was it.

Inside: cold cement floors, cold, paint-peeling cement walls. In one corner, three or four paint-new IBM punch-card machines (sole contribution of industry to Operation Bootstrap, up to then).

A small, very lively, very black man greeted us. His name was Robert Bailey. He's vice-president of Bootstrap. The meeting that day was his scene.

He introduced me to an aquiline-handsome young man, black in hair and beard, except for one tuft of white in his beard. He was dressed in black, which set off his amber skin, his piercing black eyes. I shook hands with Brother Lenny.

I asked for the ladies' room. It was freshly painted a deep peach. There was a sign on the mirror that read something like: "This is yours. Keep it clean." It was clean. But there wasn't any toilet paper.

When I came out, we were taken to a huge drafty room with chairs around it. About a hundred black and white people were sitting, waiting. We found seats where we could—separated. I first sat close to the door, but felt uncomfortable and moved next to a white woman whose hair was pulled back taut into a tiny bun. On my other side was my fellow Santa Barbaran, Dennis Dunn. I needed solidarity. People seemed to be shifting restlessly; I fleetingly wondered why.

The Inquisition

Bob Bailey introduced us. Ping Ferry apologized for our being so few. Then the meeting—no, the inquisition—began. Nothing had prepared me for what happened. We suddenly found ourselves "the target."

Hate, rage, anguish spewed out on us like scalding water. Mild-mannered Dr. Butler set off the first explosion by asking gently about health conditions in Watts, what services there were, what services were needed.

This was enough for Ernie Smith, a handsome, angry, articulate black man who represents a group called the "Anti-colonialists." His group feels the only way American blacks can free themselves from white colonialism is to be represented as a separate body in the United Nations and receive special funds and special aid as an independent people.

Ernie rose to his full stature and shouted furiously that the question was stupid, worse than stupid. Anybody who could read should know what health conditions were like in Watts—they were horrible, inexcusable—and what kind of a fool white man was Dr. Butler to come down and ask such damn fool questions?

I think I went into a state of something like shock at his response. I certainly didn't know what was going on. When I came to, Ernie Smith was still screaming invective. "Racists," he called us. "Reaganites, rich-bitch whites, apologists for the Jews—the Jews that sucked the black blood out of black bodies."

Another man, from the same end of the room, stood up to support Ernie Smith. He, too, was black-bearded, black-haired, with amber-colored skin. He spoke in a gently slurring voice, but his words were brilliant, clear. He was Ron Karenga, charismatic leader of a group called "US." His group wants to create a black identity and a black culture separate from the whites. I'm not sure he thinks the separation need be permanent after the identity is established, the culture is created. But I'm positive he's for separation now.

Although his tone was different from Smith's, his message was the same. Karenga's speech was emphasized by the presence beside him of a tall, young, black man who stood silent, arms folded. He was black-garmented except for the legend on his T-shirt which flamed in white: "Black Power."

Karenga finished. Smith began again, repeating his diatribe against the Jews, against the whites, against the privileged who used their privilege to subdue their darker fellows. The lady next to me kept crying, "Peace, brother. Peace." But Ernie Smith went on. And on and on and on ….

I felt anger uncurl in me. I waved my arm to speak. I didn't speak. I shouted, words spewing out. I denied his charges, denied them categorically, one by one. "I'm no Reaganite," I shouted, "no Brownite either. I'm with the New Politics—I'm *for* the

Revolution! And why do you include all the white folks sitting here with all the white people you hate so much? I'm not here to help you. I'm here to learn something. I'm here to learn how my kids can live in this society with you and gain from you and you gain from them. Don't beat me over the head because I came here. Come on, show me what I can do; show me how my kids can be friends with you!" And *I* went on and on and on . . .

Smith heaped scorn on me, reaffirming his charges—reaffirming them categorically, one by one. He exhorted me to give all my money to Watts and come live on roaches like the rest of them. I said I didn't see what good it would do my kids to reduce their opportunities. I wanted to find out how his kids could increase theirs.

My reply did not meet with an enthusiastic response. From another corner a man lashed out in anger that the blacks had suffered white hostility for hundreds of years and I could damn well take a little hostility on this one day.

Then Dennis Dunn spoke, saying he thought we'd come here for a dialogue, a two-way conversation, and this certainly wasn't that.

And behind and overlapping his words were random cries of "Get it out, brother—then we can talk. We got to get it out; then we can talk. We can't talk now. We got to get it out first."

Some pieces of the puzzle of what was going on began to fall into place. I wasn't ready to pay attention to it. I didn't want to fit the puzzle together yet. I was enjoying the fight too much.

I was enjoying the fight too much!

Here I was, treating black people like white people. Shouting out my resentment at their injustice against me just like I would have shouted at white people.

"My God!" The thought flashed, "We're locked in a real human encounter. This is great!"

I was so absorbed in this recognition I blocked out much of the next interchange. Then John Conyers, a young Congressman (black) from Michigan was introduced. I came to sharply when I heard him say, "It's good that lady said what she did. It shows how little she understands."

"Why that's me," I thought, "he's talking about me. He says I don't understand. . . ."

I listened intently, trying to understand. I did understand some of the things he said—about the years of oppression the blacks have suffered, about the dawning of their day, about Vietnam and how all black people should be peaceniks because the American dollars that should be helping them were being shot up in Vietnam. Gently he spoke, softly and gently, but with power. I heard him, too, talk about the need to "get it out."

About this time a well-dressed, handsome, light-skinned "black" man tried to say the black-power people didn't represent him. And whom, he asked, did they think they did represent?

The focus was off us. The force of attention was turned on him. Now he was the enemy. He, they shouted, had sold out "to the establishment." He was an Uncle Tom. He was hated as much as we whites were. He, too, was an outsider who "didn't understand."

"Sensitivity Sets"

Later I understood better what Congressman Conyers meant about "not understanding," for we broke up into small groups called "sensitivity sets." Mine was composed of five whites and four blacks. Our leader was a handsome, light-skinned girl who was highly educated, articulate and very hostile in a fine-chased way. She took command.

We were told to introduce ourselves. We did. Then our leader, whose name was Lynne, asked us what we wanted to talk about. Nobody else spoke, so of course I did. I asked why I'd been called "chauvinistic" in the big group. And precisely what did they mean by white chauvinism? It just didn't make sense to me.

My question was never answered but it gave Lynne her opening. From then on she needled us through the entire session, directing her particular enmity now at me, now at a very warm and very open man who was director of vocational guidance at a nearby college.

Lynne made her pitch. Without asking me a single question about myself, my life or my values, she explained in delicate detail that she didn't want to be like me, associate with me or live in "my" area. She wanted to live and be with people who shared her customs and her values—no integration for her. We whites weren't good enough to integrate with.

I made a few feeble attempts to say I was really on her side. I was "with" Stokely Carmichael's "Black Power" ideas, but I'd opted out of CORE since it had renounced nonviolence. I was for getting out of Vietnam and getting on with the needed revolution at home.

It was really funny. Whatever I said simply confirmed her previous opinions that the only level I could possibly operate on was hypocrisy and the words I used weren't worth the effort I made to say them.

She then turned her attention to the vocational guidance director, poor man. She undercut every effort he made to express himself about the difficulties of preparing nonwhites for high positions in industry. He tried to describe the problems he faced as an administrator—the reality of disparate knowledge, backgrounds and motivations.

His reality wasn't hers. She simply took him on as another contemptible white. Underneath her every response was the scathing blade of prejudice—and what was worse, dismissal. He was searching. I was searching. We thought the purpose of the group was to search for openings. But every time we found one, Lynne shut it in our faces.

It was really beautiful. Lynne was so poised and cool. We were so hot, uncomfortable and frustrated.

There were two other women in our group. One was Judy, a delightful, bright English girl who was apparently, a "regular." She was a sociologist from Claremont College and undoubtedly made some wise contributions—but I was so absorbed in Lynne's performance I can't remember what they were.

The other woman, Dorothy, was black. She didn't say a word. She just sat there and smoked. From time to time I thought she smiled at me, but I couldn't be sure.

The two black men talked of automation of jobs and their hopes to gain benefits from society as it is. It wasn't a terribly satisfying meeting. But I was enjoying the free-swinging encounters with Lynne. I felt good when we left for lunch.

Two doors down the street was the restaurant, where we ate in shifts. It was clean and bare. There were a few booths along one wall and a counter along the other. When I looked around, most of my group had vanished. I stood uncertainly, when I felt a tug at my coat. Dorothy, of our group, invited me to sit with her at the counter. I did. On the other side I found Judy, the British girl.

Dorothy

I had watched Dorothy in the group with some apprehension. Her face was flat, impassive. No expression gave me any clue to her thoughts. It wasn't sullen, exactly, just not responsive, except for those elusive smiles. She had none of Lynne's elegance. I wondered why she'd singled me out.

Judy told me I was naive and she couldn't understood why I'd asked so many questions. "You act," she said, "As though you came here to learn. It seems to me you already know the answers to your questions."

I said I had come to learn, that I didn't know whether the members of the group and I had the same meanings for certain words, and I surely did not know all the answers.

Then Dorothy began to talk—in slow, slurring accents, difficult to comprehend at first. She talked about whites who came down to Watts and pretended they did not understand what was going on. Shitty, she called them. She didn't *seem* to include me in that category, but I couldn't be sure.

The waitress took our order: chicken, salad and mashed potatoes; or spareribs, greens and yams. I chose the chicken; it was delicious.

Then Dorothy began to talk about herself. She disclosed she was a "Welfare Mother," a volunteer who helped her people in need. She helped those having trouble getting their welfare checks, went into homes when she saw kids outside without shoes. Her phone rang all the time, she said, always somebody in trouble. I told her I thought we needed an Operation Bootstrap where I lived.

She said I ought to get one going.

I said I couldn't. I was the wrong color.

"'Course," she said and added, "but I c'n help you. I c'n really git you in. Y'know, there some Negroes won' let a white near 'em. Scared t' death; clam up. But I make the way. After they git t' know me, I call 'em and tell 'em I'm sendin' a white over—they don't need 'a be scared. The white's O.K. Then they do see this white an' it works out. Tell you what, if you wan' ta work here, I'll git you in."

I was sorry to tell her I couldn't work there because I didn't live in Los Angeles. She seemed sorry, too.

She and I walked back to Bootstrap together. She told me she had to go to the laundromat that afternoon because her washing machine was broken. Anyway, she said, looking at the sky, it was raining and she couldn't hang her clothes out even if her washing machine did work.

I discovered she had eight children. She discovered I had seven. We compared notes. "How often do you wash?" I asked.

"Every day," she smiled.

I smiled back. "I wash every day too," I said.

What a lot of wash with such a lot of kids.

The Last Session

It was about 5:00 PM when we went to the last session. We were back in the big room, all sitting around. The volley turned on the Center again.

What had they done? What were they doing? What would they do for black people?

Ping said the Center's record wasn't very good in their terms. He explained it wasn't an action organization. It was, instead, a group of people trying to understand and write about the problems of living in the twentieth century. Then he described one of the Center's main projects: to draft a new US Constitution, one that reflected the new age we're living in, one that would eventually fit in with a future World Constitution.

There were howls of derisive laughter. How come you think you can write a constitution for this country when you don't have any blacks writing it with you? Blacks not good enough for you? What credentials do we need? Let's see if mine fit! How do I get into your egghead place? I'd like to come for a week—a month. How do I get appointed there? How'd *you* get in? What's so good about you? How come you don't have any black people thinking about those great big problems with you? How come? How come? How come?

Ping made no apologies. He said that the Center not only had no black people on its staff, it only had two women and no psychiatrists. In fact, most areas of our society went "unrepresented."

One person challenged him: "What if I write a black constitution, man, a real black paper? What would you do about that?"

Ping accepted the challenge with enthusiasm. "I'll read it," he affirmed. "I'll get my colleagues to read it. We'll discuss it with you."

Several people agreed to begin work on the black constitution. We agreed to proceed with arrangements for Operation Bootstrap to come to the Center at Santa Barbara with its contribution to a new draft Constitution for the United States.

At the last moment Ernie Smith asked Hallock if he thought the race question was the most important in the world.

"No," Hallock said, "I don't think it's *the* most important problem. I think it's *an* important part of a bigger problem— the problem of people trying to live with one another. I think it's a facet—not the whole."

Nobody cheered Hallock's reply.

As we broke up, Dorothy came to me and asked for my address and I took hers. We both knew we'd made some contact. This was a symbolic way of reaching out for more.

Lynne, the handsome leader of my group, didn't speak to me again.

And so we came home and the experience began to filter down. It was a remarkable one. Something important had happened to us all. I think I have a glimmering of what happened to me—at least in part.

Rage Needs Out

Only recently have I discovered how much rage and pain has been suppressed in my own children—how much has been suppressed in me. I've only just begun to see how our culture conspires to prevent us from expressing how we really feel because it "upsets things." It feels and is threatening, dangerous.

I'd been pretty proud of myself because we're beginning to express the way we really feel in our family. Most of the time we're able to recognize that our rage masks our resentment at not feeling accepted or loved, masks our inability to be honest and express our real needs and our real yearnings. More and more we've learned to express our rage at each other without being cut up by guilt and anxiety. With the rage discharged, we're able to be more tender. As I said, I thought we were really out front.

Well, Bootstrap is way ahead of me. It never occurred to me there could be such a procedure on public issues. And in my wildest dreams I couldn't have imagined it would be possible between blacks and whites.

It took me a while to realize what was going on at Bootstrap—but from then on, I was really with it.

Now that I've seen it happen, it seems the most obvious thing in the world. How can we possibly plan any future together until we unload some of our rage and pain on the people who are causing it—or the people who represent those who are causing it?

How can we give up our hurt and anger until we know we're really heard? Until something, somehow, happens to assuage us, to free us from our addiction to our pain?

It would be wrong if I left the impression that sessions like the one I've described are what Operation Bootstrap is all about. Bootstrap's main purpose is to train Negroes for skilled and semi-skilled jobs, but the leaders have discovered the training doesn't work until the feelings are free. No other group in the country enjoys a better success in job training than Operation Bootstrap. I think I understand why.

And I think I understand better now why nonviolent movements have lost ground. In the interest of a superficial love and unity, we clamp down the lid on a lot of reality. A big chunk of reality in all human relations, particularly between the different racial groups, is suspicion, hate, fear, and pain.

If we can bring this up to the surface and admit it to ourselves and to each other without guilt feelings—maybe the real caring might come.

Part III:
Breakdown and
Breakthroughs

"If you are looking for lay wisdom that pierces deep into what psychotherapy is all about," wrote Douglas Steere, Quaker theologian and educator, "you will be gripped and lifted by this autobiographical classic that is written in blood and tears out of her own life by Gene Hoffman, a gifted Santa Barbara Friend."[77]

Steere commends From Inside the Glass Doors *for its "ruthless honesty and its deep humanity." Carl Rogers, orignator of "client-centered therapy," said that he "couldn't put [this book] down."*

Gene had always tried to live her life according to her highest ideals. She had stood up for her political principles even when it meant rejection by her parents. She had confronted racism in herself and her society. She had tried to be the perfect mother, the perfect wife, and the perfect Quaker activist. These efforts cost her dearly. In 1959, after learning that her husband was having an affair, she suffered a nervous breakdown and was hospitalized with a diagnosis of "suicidal schizophrenic episode." Despite, or perhaps because of, this setback, she was determined to overcome her "illness," win back her husband, and save her marriage. But by 1969, despite extensive therapy, it was clear that her efforts to have a "normal" family and marriage had failed. After a severe emotional collapse, Gene signed herself into a mental hospital.

From Inside the Glass Doors *proved to be a journey of discovery that helped Gene to face her past and open up to new possibilities.*

She discovered that (as Steere puts it) there is no "major demarcation between the allegedly sane and the allegedly insane." In fact, as R.D. Laing once observed, "patients are better for patients than anyone else."

What Gene discovered in religious terms was that "there is that of God" in every one, including those labeled emotionally or mentally disturbed. "More and more, I have come to believe the patient capable of being responsible for his or her own growth and insights," wrote Gene.

Furthermore, she came to see a mental breakdown not as an affliction, but as an opportunity to realize fully one's human potential: "I feel that a person who has a breakdown may be closer to being able to be human than those who hold themselves in tight rein to meet the crazy demands... of our society."

Many of Gene's insights spring from what is called "humanistic psychology." This movement is based on the work of Maslow, Rogers, May, Bugental, Buber, Laing, etc. According to Tom Greening, editor of the magazine Humanistic Psychology *(which has published some of Gene's work), Humanistic Psychology is based on the belief that human beings are "more than merely the sum of their parts": they are conscious, make choices for which they are responsible, have goals and intentions, and seek meaning, value, and creativity. (In contrast, behavioral and Freudian psychological approaches tend to be reductive and deterministic.)*

Gene applied the principles of humanistic psychology not only to her work as a counselor, but also as a peace activist. This psychological and spiritual approach enabled Gene to become a new kind of activist—one whose work sprang from deep within, and was not simply a response to external circumstances.

FOOTNOTES

---

[77] *Friends Journal,* December 1, 1978.

From Inside the Glass Doors

On Thursday, July 10, 1969, I crashed. I abandoned the effort to function "normally" and gave up. I knew I could no longer be responsible for my home, my family, or my work.

These are the particular events that brought it about. At the end of May, another of my sons was arrested on a drug charge and I had to fly to Denver to cope with the situation alone, because at the same time, in the very same week, my husband was abruptly separated from The Center for the Study of Democratic Institutions, an organization he'd helped Robert Hutchins found some fifteen years before. He had been its first employee.

My mother (who had long since persuaded me she didn't want to hear anything about my personal life: "My doctor says I mustn't hear anything that will make me emotional") became acutely ill with Parkinson's disease. The number of my children who were in various stages of their teenage-mother-rejection period had increased to six. I had lost hope, felt totally abandoned, and completely alone.

I couldn't sleep or perform routine household chores. My circle of attention became narrower and narrower. I recoiled from our houseful of pets; swimming in our pool brought no soothing surcease. The flowers I had planted and tended blossomed, but not for me.

I alternated between total withdrawal and a flailing effort to continue in action. The three youngest of my children had left a few days before for a six-week trip to Europe. The others were scattered—I didn't know where. The house was very silent.

On that day a friend invited me to lunch. I pulled myself together to meet her. The lunch was a fiasco. Instead of eating, I wept. My friend was alarmed at my behavior and took me home. There she tried to explore with me possibilities for relief.

Could Stephen[78] and I go on a vacation?

No. Since he was in the middle of his own turmoil, he was unavailable to me. He spent his days being busy, his nights in his study, playing records, deep in what felt to me like a cocoon of cacophony. We were whirling in very separate orbits. A vacation together was out of the question.

Could I stay with a friend?

No. I didn't know one who was better off than I, and certainly no one who could give me the care I knew I needed.

Could I go on a vacation by myself?

No! The thought of sitting alone in a hotel room was appalling.

Every avenue, every escape from the intolerable present felt closed. I rolled up into a ball on the bed, wept uncontrollably, and sought some relief from my anguish by screaming.

I remember I felt as I had when I was in labor—searing gut pain. I locked my arms around my body and rocked on the bed, moaning for relief. Wishing there were someone who would take care of me, be with me, let me weep out all the stored-up tears... watch over me as I slept.

But there was no one. My tears had always frightened my husband and children, my mother and father, even my psychiatrist. They called me overemotional and I felt they were right. I did cry so much.

Ben[79] told me I suffered from too much emotionalism and it was "wearing out my glands." So the need to cry, coupled with the fear of crying, threw me into an insoluble conflict. My friend was deeply distressed by my behavior. I could feel her anxiety, which, of course, increased mine. She observed me helplessly for a while, then came up with another answer.

Some years ago, she had helped a psychiatrist, whom I shall call Dr. Arnold Forester, found a small psychiatric hospital in the Los Angeles area. She urged me to go there.

I was agreeable to anything if it meant being taken care of and not having to face responsibilities, nor the biting encounters with my family.

So she made all the arrangements, packed a bag for me, called Stephen, and about 3:30 that afternoon, he arrived to drive me to the hospital, which I shall call Brookhaven.

I don't remember much about the drive except that I was very quiet, very self-possessed, very distant. I know I thought I was going away "for a few days' rest"—just enough to reestablish my equilibrium.

Stephen and I talked about what I might learn at the hospital and how valuable it would be to keep notes of my experiences to share with my fellow counselors. I decided I would observe everything meticulously so I could write about it later.

On the ride down I semi-plotted my few days. As had long been my habit, I cut out the role I felt I ought to play and fitted it to me. It felt appropriate, and I was only half aware that underneath our "rational" conversation were volcanic sputterings—lava emotions seeking to erupt.

Part of my discipline as an actress enabled me to play it cool when I knew I had to. Hysterics—who needs them? As usual, I was in control.

So it was a calm, cool, quizzical Gene who arrived at Brookhaven. I observed that from the outside it was an anonymous looking place, but the admitting office was warm and welcoming.

A lovely girl greeted me and handed me some papers to fill out. As I wrote in the date, I realized for the first time it was our son Kristian's seventeenth birthday. My eyes filled with tears. The girls at the desk spoke to me reassuringly, telling me there was nothing to fear, and my tears stopped.

The only thing that came into full focus on the page were the words that I had to give 72 hours notice to be released if my doctor did not approve my discharge when I felt ready for it. I signed my name cheerlessly.

At this point I was called into Dr. Forester's office for a brief interview. He was not unfamiliar to me. I'd met him perhaps twice before at my friend's house. I felt good about him. He was very easy and supportive, open, friendly, fatherly—and very hurried. After all, he was the head of the hospital.

But I felt reassured. He greeted me warmly and called me Gene. He told me he thought a few days at the hospital would be just what I needed. He then explained to me he did not work on Fridays, Saturdays, or Sundays, but I could reach him by phone any time during the days he would be away.

He also said I was not a "regular" patient, but would be free to come and go as I liked.

Then, with a friendly hug and instructions to "get a good rest," he let me go with Stephen and somebody across a pleasant small patio to locked glass doors that looked in on an entrance hall with a glassed-in nurses' station on the left.

Our guide unlocked the doors and I was led to the nurses' station where I was asked to surrender my purse and suitcase to be explored (I learned later) for dangerous objects, breakables and drugs. This meant that any bottles, jars, pills, mirrors, scissors, etc., were confiscated I remember there were some people sitting at the end of the entrance hall. One in particular was an extremely fat, but pretty girl, dressed in white. I smiled at her. There was no response. She just sat there, staring sullenly ahead.

A nurse took Stephen and me to my room. She apologized, saying they would have another room for me tomorrow and in the meantime, I would be on the men's side for the night.

The room was cheerful, with bright colored walls and bright spreads on the twin beds. But the door was heavy, with a small grilled glass window in it. Outside the door was written the curious word "seclusion," while underneath, some wag had drawn the peace sign.

I stood there silently with Stephen, looking around at windows covered with protective grating and the vines tendriling around them—when I heard a male voice cursing loudly, feet stomping down the hall, and suddenly the blast of a kick on a door that felt very near. In about two minutes, the procedure was repeated—then again—and I became aware the male person was shouting in a hoarse voice: "Get me out of here; goddamn you. Get me out of here! If you don't get me out of here by 7:00 tonight, Dr. Forester, you will die and be in hell!"

I peeked out the door. The stomping, cursing person was a young man, about 20, with long blonde hair, dressed in handsome hippie gear, his beautiful face distorted by rage. I was surprised that I didn't feel the slightest fear of him.

Suddenly a slim, dark boy was in my room. He told me his name was Phillip. He spoke in a rather rapid, but friendly voice, telling me not to be alarmed. The kid who was screaming and stomping was Marshall. Marshall was on one of his weekly flip-out rages. He wouldn't hurt anyone—although it was wisest to keep out of his way when he lunged through the outside door.

Phillip explained to me that he and Marshall had the same "problem," but he, Phillip, expressed his differently. Phillip could neither stop talking nor sleep, while Marshall spent days in a more or less friendly mood, until the tension built up and he broke into one of these rages which relieved him for a while.

Meantime, the nurse returned with my depleted handbag and suitcase. Phillip left to bring me some books he thought I'd like. Stephen left. I was alone in the room.

But not for long. Phillip soon returned with another patient—a woman called Kit, who had long blonde hair and a childlike gaze. She and Phillip were very intimate. She spoke to him in a little girl voice, telling what I recognized was the latest installment of her impending divorce trial, describing the lost custody of her two adopted children, and how she was going to try to keep her natural son.

After this, she turned her attention to me, telling me how the hospital operated—where the washing machine was, all about the clothes dryer, hours for meals, and various other activities, concluding by saying: "You won't remember any of this, but sometimes it's comforting to be told." I think it was.

The nurse returned with my medication. Phillip told me if I had trouble sleeping any night, to come out in the hall; there was always someone to talk with, an aide or a patient.

I was given a massive sleeping injection which knocked me out for about six hours. When I awakened I lay tensely in bed until I saw the light and heard noises of people walking outside my door. I peeked out, wondering what to do.

There was Phillip who told me to get dressed and come to breakfast with him. I did. He led me to a colorful dining room, through the cafeteria line, where we chose melon, waffles, bacon, and coffee—a delicious breakfast. Then he described what to expect of the day.

At 9:00 there was Occupational Therapy (hereafter called OT); 10:30 snack; 11:00 group; 12:15 lunch; 1:00 OT again; 3:30 snack; 5:00 supper; sometimes entertainment or TV after supper; 9:30 more snack, and 10:00 bed. Some hour each day was supposedly set aside for a visit with my doctor (who also happened to be Phillip and Marshall's doctor as well).

I didn't go to OT that morning. I wandered around, looking at the facilities. There was a spacious lawn with chaises and umbrellas (littered with gum wrappers, cigarette butts, and plastic coffee cups). There was the OT shop, where all sorts of crafts were available with young, fresh-faced students eager to teach them. There was an exercise room, and a teenage hideaway for listening to records.

This latter had some beat-up old couches—the inevitable litter, and poster-covered walls. Most of the posters were made by patients. In each was the ubiquitous peace sign, and messages such as "I shall be released." [Folksinger Bob]Dylan was certainly there.

In fact, patient-artists had daubed the peace sign everywhere—inside and outside the building. Most, if not all, the teenagers were peaceniks. I have since wondered about the relationship between their political radicalism and the fact they were there. As I reflect, mine made me unacceptable to my parents, and their deep disapproval was certainly a factor in my uncertain self-esteem.

Then I explored the main hospital. It was a U-shaped building with rooms for 30 people. Everyone's door was open and faced on a wide main corridor. The long-term patients had decorated their rooms, each in his own fashion, with paintings, sculpture, weavings—some with yarn poodles—and various other items they'd made in OT.

The rooms were bright and each looked out on a lawn or special garden spot. In addition to the patients' rooms, there was a lounge or TV room where one could play cards, read, meet with other patients to talk—if someone didn't insist on having the TV going full blast. This was also the Group room.

Somewhere outside, I was told, was a swimming pool, where patients could go in groups with a leader, or, in rare instances when they had all privileges, alone.

Surrounding the pool were the doctors' offices.

At 11:00 I joined the other patients for Group. It was a talky meeting. I didn't get much out of it except that I saw most of the adult and young-adult patients for the first time, as well as many of the staff. (This group was closed to teenagers, who had their own.)

I also had an opportunity to examine the leaders and learn that they were almost indistinguishable from the patients; each was called by his or her first name.

I discovered our main leader was a social worker whom I shall call Sara. Sara was unmarried, friendly, nervous. She always seemed to me to be on the verge of tears. She smoked nervously and incessantly, lighting each cigarette with trembling fingers as she sought to put us all at ease and control the more recalcitrant members.

As informal co-leader, she had Gerri, the hospital dietitian, a vital, warm, opinionated, much loved black woman. (I thought Gerri the most sensitive of the group leaders, although she frequently let her authoritarianism get in the way.)

Sometimes we had a nurse named Prudence. Prudence was 38ish, rather plump, with an attractive high-cheek-boned face, tilted eyes, and gold-rimmed specs. She was tender, firm and earnest, also opinionated, but strong. The patients really depended on her.

Some patients sat way in the back at the card tables and didn't participate. Others, like I, sat in the front row circle, ready for action. There was one who didn't sit at all.

That was a girl named Pam. She walked around restlessly, chain-smoking, her head hunched between her shoulders. Somebody told me she'd come in a couple of weeks ago after an O.D. (overdose) and had been on a suicide kick ever since.

She'd smashed four or five huge hospital mirrors, had slashed her wrists with the broken glass, and was in a deep depression. She was also 58 years old, though she looked to me like a dissolute 30. Group ended and we queued up for lunch. It was delicious (as were all meals at Brookhaven). That's when I learned about privileges, met other patients, and discovered some of their habits.

For example: Marshall always sat in one particular corner and heaped up food around him. He would collect everything he could, surround himself with plates of food stacked high, and keep up a battery of shouted charges against the institution and everyone in it all during meal time.

No one sat near him, for, as Phillip explained, Marshall got nervous when anyone came too close. He would usually eat about a fourth of the food, mixing the rest in the most unpalatable combinations to be left for others to clear. No one was upset by his stream of imprecations, nor by the fact he didn't bus his own trays as the rest of us were told to do. It all became part of the landscape.

As to privileges: patients were obsessed with privileges. These included telephone-out privileges, telephone-in privileges, sometimes both, and visiting privileges. Teenagers were allowed to see their parents only once a week (more than that caused them too much anxiety). Other patients had individual arrangements.

Then there were passes: group passes, which meant you could go out with others, chaperoned by Engali, a student from Turkey, who was also the Recreational Director. There were weekend passes, special passes for a particular limited time, i.e., one or two hours, and ad-lib passes, the most desirable, which meant you could come and go as you chose. There were a wide range of rewards, ardently wished for.

I discovered that Phillip and Marshall had no privileges and no passes. Phillip, because he'd left without permission the week before, and Marshall, because he was considered too psychotic to be allowed any.

Leaving without permission was a common experience. The hospital was low security and the kids were always literally going over the fence, and always—while I was there—returning after a few hours or a night away.

I tried to learn what privileges I had, and discovered none were marked on my chart. I calmly explained to the nurse that Dr. Forester had said I could come and go as I pleased, that I was an optional patient who had come for rest and care.

The nurse was very friendly, but noncommittal, and said she'd try to reach my doctor to confirm this, but since nothing was written on my chart, I would have to wait until she heard from him.

This really frightened me. I was locked in. I couldn't call out or receive calls. The nurse, I realized, did not believe what I had distinctly heard Dr. Forester say, and she didn't know when she could reach him, because he usually went sailing on weekends and they had to call him at sea.

Paranoia set in. Although I knew Stephen was out there and would ultimately take care of me, and that I was sane, I began to wonder... since nobody confirmed my self-knowledge, what was really true?

Without confirmation, I discovered I couldn't really be sure *what* Dr. Forester had told me the day before; I knew I had been pretty far out of it. It got scarier and scarier.

I found myself sitting silently on my bed, unable to read, beginning to doubt everything. Although the hospital was bright and cheerful, and everyone was warm and friendly, panic set in. I controlled my panic by going to snack and talking with the other patients.

I didn't really know how scared I was until that night, when I was called to the nursing station and told by the nurse, who'd reached my doctor, that I had all privileges, including an ad-lib pass.

It was an enormous relief. But the one paralyzing day of being cut off from everyone made me realize how crazy-making it must be to be committed to an institution by a public authority, with no recourse to friends or family who will testify to your sanity. Where no matter how much you protest that you're sane and have been mistakenly treated, your protestations only confirm the opinion of the staff and other patients that you're delusional.

It was wonderful to be able to call Stephen and hear his reassuring voice telling me he would come the next day to take me out to dinner at 5:00.

By Friday night I learned to go to the nurse's station for my night medication, and stood in line with the rest of the patients who were waiting for theirs. Then I went to bed.

That night sleep would not come. The medication had the opposite effect—it stimulated me. I returned to the nursing station and explained this to the head nurse. She said she could do nothing until she cleared it with my doctor, and it was too late to try to reach him. So I spent Friday night trying to keep calm, and the next morning rose haggard and weary.

Fortunately, I had things to occupy me. I was to be moved from what I discovered was a first night observation room for nonviolent patients, to my permanent room, and the nurse promised me faithfully she would reach Dr. Forester and get the medication changed.

All morning I spent moving to the room on the women's side. It was exactly like my previous one, except that the walls and bedspreads were of different colors, and it had no bars on the windows, and no peephole in the door. And now I had a roommate.

She was a precise, gentle, distracted little woman who hardly spoke to me. Her name was Emily. She was very friendly, but distant. She was pleased to discover I was neat. It portended well for us both. In my new location we shared a bath with two other patients who were out on weekend passes. We had the only tub in the hospital, which I later discovered made us very popular.

Meantime, Marshall was going his rounds, cursing at the top of his lungs, curiously pausing when we met to smile and comment on my purple-framed glasses. We both knew we'd made some contact. From time to time I would encounter Phillip, but by now he'd lost interest in me. I felt very isolated, very alone.

So I decided to use my ad-lib pass. Having learned quickly, I took orders for cigarettes and candy from those less fortunate than I. I walked for miles up and down the nearby boulevard, wondering "What would passersby think if they knew I was an 'inmate'!" I returned to the hospital just in time to get ready for Stephen's arrival.

Stephen arrived punctually. Since it was early and the evening was warm, we went to a nearby park and watched the children play. I longed for him to hold me—but he didn't. I sensed he was afraid. This made me terribly afraid.

After describing the hospital and some of the people I'd met, I found nothing else to talk about. Stephen felt very threatening to me, very distant, very uninvolved. This froze me up. I could hear his words, but couldn't feel any warmth in them, any welcome. They were so rational and precise—so detached.

Fear curdled in my belly and seemed to run like poison through my intestines. But outside I was frozen, anxious, out-of-it, but cool—oh very cool.

Part of my reason for coming to the hospital in the first place was because I was out of communication with Stephen. And now I was even more separated from him than ever, not only by emotional distance, but by physical distance as well. My home was behind the glass doors.

As we sat together in the car, waves of despair, like nausea, rose to my throat, and it was with great relief I returned to the hospital and heard those doors locked behind me.

I found it warming to return and be greeted by the ever-present welcoming crew, the door-watchers, with "Hi, Gene. Did you have a good pass? How did it go?" I had a vivid sense of belonging somewhere—at least here.

10:00 rolled around and I went for my medication. The nurse had not reached my doctor. My medication had not been changed and I gloomily looked forward to another sleepless night. I was also scared. Hadn't Dr. Forester promised me I could reach him any time during the weekend—hadn't he?

That night it really hit. I panicked for real.

I hadn't slept. I hadn't been able to communicate with Stephen. No warmth or love flowed from him to me. I felt betrayed by my doctor. I was locked in a hospital with a lot of strangers, all of whom behaved with various degrees of oddity. None of my children called or wrote. I felt they were relieved to be rid of me. Phillip was in a different mood. When I greeted him by touching his shoulder, he wriggled away and snapped, "Don't touch me." Emily was mutely reading a book she said bored her but which she felt compelled to finish because she'd started it. The interminably smoking door-watchers looked so dreary to me under the harsh, overhead light. . . just like pictures of crazy people in hospitals, with nothing to do but line up against the walls.

I lay in my bed, getting tenser and tenser. The medication had absolutely no effect. Emily was sleeping. From down the hall came sounds of an uproar. Phillip and Marshall were fighting, telling each other to fuck himself at the top of their lungs. There were scufflings and shoutings; someone said, "Into Seclusion," and I lay in bed, terrified; fear curled my insides into a solid lump.

Then I remembered Phillip's first night advice: "If you can't sleep, come out by the nurses' station. There's always somebody to talk to." So I put on my robe and ventured out.

Sure enough, he was right. There were beds lined along the hall wall. Various patients and aides were sitting on them, talking. Someone was coping with Phillip and Marshall. I huddled up on an empty bed and waited. I felt I'd better talk to somebody soon because I knew I was fading farther and farther out of it.

Pretty soon a young boy came up to me and said, "You look like you're in pain." I admitted I was—that I was panicking. This struck a responsive chord in him. He sat down with me. He told me his name was Mark and that he was 17. Then he asked me if my panic made my arms all numb, as if the life was draining like blood out of my fingers. I responded, "No," my panic hit me in the stomach and felt like a knotted ball and it really hurt.

Mark was very sympathetic. He held my hand and began telling me how he got there. He'd taken an OD of every pill in his mother's medicine cabinet, after a series of hair-raising accidents and troubled involvements. He comforted me for a while, then left.

Then Marshall appeared, calm and mostly unruffled. He was unable to circumnavigate the building because the outside doors were locked at night. He took one look at me, sat down on the bed, and put his arms around me. We didn't need to talk. He brought me coffee, candy, cigarettes, nuts. Then he told me his story.

He'd been "busted" in Santa Barbara where he'd worked at an eatery. He'd roughed up somebody in a pool-hall fight. Then was thrown into County General Hospital instead of jail, and had finally been brought here.

He told me he had a child named Martha-Mary, an ex-wife, and a girlfriend he needed to get back to and would—because "they're going to get me out of this place tomorrow." (This last, I later realized, was Marshall's security litany.)

Then he wanted to know my story. I told him in a few brief phrases some of the problems that had caused my breakdown—

the barbed chasms between me and my kids, my husband's distance from me, my fears that I wasn't an attractive woman and would be abandoned.

He promised to pray for me, assured me I was "beautiful and better believe it," and began explaining his mystical theory of life, which was a mixture of astrology, the Maharishi, Krishnamurti, Christianity, and hope that this really *was* the Age of Aquarius and a new life was about to begin.[80]

Marshall sat out most of the night with me until I finally went back to bed about the time they unlocked the outside doors and he could begin his circular stomping again.

I don't remember Sunday much. From then on, all days seem to melt into one another. I can't speak of consecutive experiences, just vivid happenings and impressions and sharp awareness.

But I no longer felt isolated. My Saturday night vigil, and the patients who helped me stay with it made me an initiate. The Saturday night of released terror, and the companionship of people *who were not afraid of me and who had plenty of time*, seemed to begin some mysterious reconciling process.

Dr. Forester was never reached that weekend and I spent another wakeful night. But Monday morning my real—which means my more aware—life at the hospital began.

On the way to breakfast, I heard screaming from one of the rooms down my hall. I assumed somebody was in trouble, but also assumed somebody else was taking care of it, so went on.

How right and wrong I was, I learned at breakfast, when Kit, of the first night, came in white and shaken. This is what had happened: Kit had awakened, just before I walked by her room, to discover her roommate, Pam (of the hunched shoulders, broken mirrors, and slashed wrists), hanging by the neck from the fire extinguisher fixture in the ceiling. Her sheet was her noose. Kit held Pam up and began to scream for help. At last someone came in and cut Pam down. Pam, Kit told us, was barely alive.

The reality of this was somewhat blurred for me. But as the day wore on, and I walked by seclusion and saw Pam on the floor on a mattress, surrounded by aides, the reality finally broke through. She *had* nearly died.

After that, Pam's doctor ordered that she be "specialed." This meant she had an aide on duty with her 24 hours around the clock. She was allowed to go nowhere without the aide, not even to the toilet.

Pam was the cause of my first dissent. Rumblings began among patients and staff—"a spoiled brat—who does she think she is?" It rose to my fever pitch when Pam and I stood together at the nursing station one night and the night nurse said sarcastically: "Well, you finally got just what you wanted, didn't you, Pam, total attention, someone you can lead around by the nose."

Adrenalin rushed through me—I was furious, and blurted: "Don't you dare criticize her. She knew what she needed. She knows her own truth. If it takes a month of aides around the clock to help her get over her fear, it's worth it. Don't you understand? She knows what she needs, and thank God, she can get it!"

The nurse dismissed me with a curt "Here's your medication," and both Pam and I went to bed.

Pam's room was three doors down from mine. After her attempted suicide, she spent most of the days and nights playing her guitar and singing in a sweet plaintive voice—mostly antiwar or Hebrew songs. (Pam's first question of anyone was: Are you Jewish? If the answer was yes, she felt a deep satisfaction.)

Her favorite song was an eerie one in which the heroine hangs herself by a winding sheet, and when her father finds her, he also finds carved upon her breast the words "I died of love."

She took a special delight in repeating this song over and over again, and it echoed down the halls and reminded us over and over again of that Monday morning.

Lured by the guitar, I began to sit in Pam's room and listen. Sometimes she would nod in my direction; she wasn't ready to talk yet. I came to know the aides who "specialed" her. They were mostly students from a nearby college majoring in psychology. I also came to know Kit.

Kit presented multiple personalities. She came on direct and strong when we talked about politics. She was an avid KPFK fan.[81] She was as wise as anyone I know when she talked about her young son. She was seductive with the aides. She would turn childlike in a moment, with wide-wondering eyes. And she could be distant, suddenly not there at all, or wild with fury. She was unpredictable. I liked her a lot. I felt uneasy with her, but fascinated.

She'd been in Brookhaven twice, and had had a disastrous experience in the County Psychiatric Unit once where she'd been taken after she'd shot herself in the stomach. Her history was horrifying. The hurt that brought her to the hospital this time was that her husband had turned middle-aged flower child and had left her for a hippie girl.

I spent many hours in Pam and Kit's room, arguing the merits of various forms of therapy. One aide and I became particularly close. He was Bernie, a graduate student. Bernie and I found we agreed on almost everything. We were both directed toward Humanistic Psychology and kept arguing the merits of Rogers, Maslow, Jourard, and Skinner. (He was pro-Skinner.)[82] Both of us were enthusiastic about Ronald Laing. Both of us questioned many hospital practices.

Little by little a group gathered around us. In the beginning it included Phillip, Pam, Kit, Mark (who was sure I was a social worker in disguise until my Saturday night flip-out), the aides, and me—with Marshall popping in from time to time. Kit called us the Key Club, but anyone could join because keys were free to all.

And pretty soon others did. The one-time death room became a center for discussions, jokes, laughter, and song—with Pam sometimes sleeping, sometimes waking. And I no longer used my ad-lib pass to walk by myself.

From time to time, Engali, the Recreational Director, would poke his head into the room, urging us to "go for ice cream"; or "go to a movie." I resisted his blandishments for a long while, until one day I ventured into OT.

There I met Doris. Doris was about 20. I'd seen her in group, suddenly standing up and moving center to weep or make some startling statement, usually returning to her chair angrily, or rushing out of the room because the leader intervened, trying to force her to "make sense."

Marshall called her "the zombie." Doris was tall, with close-cropped hair she said she hated, a rigid body, which sometimes lapsed into surprising grace when a record was playing and she danced—heedless of those around her. Then—she would freeze again.

In OT, Doris was drawing with pastels, very surrealistic things. I showed an interest. (One is very cautious about this in a psychiatric hospital, because patients are indignant at being patronized—and they should be.) She welcomed it and began explaining what she was drawing.

She then took me to her room and showed me others of her drawings. Most represented Marshall, with whom she was in love, and who hurt her terribly because he couldn't bear to have her around. In her pictures, Marshall was almost always a Christ figure—but sometimes he had little knobby horns peeping through her drawings of his flowing hair.

She told me she was diagnosed schizophrenic. It seemed reasonable to me. One moment she would be present in a "logical" conversation. Then she would suddenly stiffen and veer off and begin speaking in an obscure metaphoric language.

I listened attentively and discovered I could decipher some of it and speak back to her in similar terms. This was a joyous moment for us both. We could communicate on a deep level. A bond developed between us. We knew when we were speaking in the different language. Once I described it to her as "the language of the immediate perception"—completely uncensored, unscreened.

She delighted in this term and wrote it down. She frequently referred to it as we slipped in and out of the "straight" language. She recognized she used the language of the immediate perception when the straight language wasn't elastic enough to encompass her emotions, or when she was too frightened to be direct.

Little by little she told me some of her "secrets," that she had been present as a little girl when her mother killed her baby brother and herself, how guilty her father felt; how guilty Doris felt; how much she disliked her stepmother; how she loved her motorcycle; how much she loved her fiancé....

One afternoon I invited her to look at a book of modern paintings with me. She was enchanted.

Once we began sharing, *I* was enchanted. Her remarks about each picture were original, unpremeditated, direct. On one page was a Duchamp photo-collage—a metronome with a huge eye in the center of it. Doris studied it for a while and then said, "I believe that!" She looked long and carefully at each picture. Of one Picasso portrait of a woman she said, "She hates men; she's a witch." Of a Gauguin landscape, she remarked, "The cloud is a man; God, maybe, striding over the hill."

When I showed her a photograph of my son Kristian, her response was: "Oh, he has marks!" I didn't understand what she meant until she pointed to the moles that dotted Kristian's neck and arms. "I call them stars," she said solemnly, then twinkled, "stellations—constellations, really, but he doesn't need the 'con.' He's really with it!" And we were both delighted with her pun.

The relationship with Doris developed toward the end of my first week in the hospital. I found I was enjoying every day. New people would come sharply into focus for me, and as I came to know them, whole new universes would open. I became greedy to know more and more.

By this time, my medication had been changed and I'd begun to sleep. One night, as I dozed off, I heard shouts and laughter down the hall and remarked sleepily to Emily, "It's really weird, I don't remember having so much fun since I was in the dorm at the Pasadena Playhouse. I haven't laughed so much." It *was* weird—and it was true.

After the Saturday night vigil, Marshall was my friend. He was too restless to sit for conversation, but every time I saw him, he had a welcoming remark in *his* unique language. Often it would be "Hail Mary, you are the moon, and the moon stands for love." Or again, he would stomp by and roar "justice—JUST ICE. That's what it is." Or he would flash a smile and aver, "I'm going to get out of here 8:00 tonight, and you'd better believe it." Then he would continue his endless, angry rounds again.

As he saw my friendship with Doris develop, he stopped cutting her so cruelly. He would pause by the door and remark: "Good, Doris, stay with. She'll show you how to be a woman."

One day Marshall showed an interest in my book of Van Gogh paintings. I suggested we look at it together. I'd enjoyed the experience so much with Doris that I wanted to repeat it with Marshall. He agreed. We sat in the yard, in the blazing sun, looking at the blazing Van Gogh paintings.

As we turned each page, Marshall became more and more tense. He began to crumple and tear them, turning them faster and faster. When we came to the end of the book and he read the paragraphs about Van Gogh's final madness and suicide, his face clouded. He became enraged, threw the book on the ground and fled to his room.

Later that evening, Marshall attacked me for the first time. He called me a filthy bitch and refused to have anything to do with me. However we did exchange glances, and in them was our mutual recognition that I deserved the treatment. Through the book, he'd come face to face with his deepest fears and I had to be punished.

Next day he was friendly again, and a week or so later he referred to the afternoon, asking me if I remembered the time I'd "made him so angry."

His move toward reconciliation was to invite me to his room where he showed me his paintings and read some of his writing to me. Some of it was pure poetry. Most was incomprehensible. Then he invited me to choose one of his paintings and gave me a moving sculpture he'd made.

This was the beginning of my discovery of the patients' need to give. Among most of them was an unparalleled generosity. In fact, it was an overwhelming need.

One of the common bonds among most of us was that we hadn't met the expectations of key persons in our lives—usually our parents. We each felt they had wanted us to be somebody else, be different, and none of us had been able to do that. Although we'd tried—and trying, damn near died.

It was tentative at first, this giving—the sharing of a letter or a book. But it moved on to other things: "You like my ring? It's yours—take it." Ultimately confidences, deep, inchoate communications, brief glimpses into the others' tightly-held, fear-ridden world. Gifts of self. "*Look at me—Love me—Take me as I am.*"

Marshall thanked me for spending the afternoon with him and hugged me.

When I arrived, Marshall was in his "middle period." I learned that when he entered the hospital, he was in quite good control—bright, handsome, full of jokes and laughter.

But little by little, the rage uncoiled. When he arrived, his paintings were more or less realistic. In this middle period they were abstract. As time went on, his work became less and less coherent, and toward the end of my stay, he was daubing mud and clay and tying snaggled stones together, while describing their deep mystical meaning.

But Marshall's deeper level of sanity came clearest to me on the night the astronauts landed on the moon. All of us spent the evening in the TV room. Through the hours of simulation and waiting, we giggled as we recognized our kinship with millions of people all over the globe who were staring into black boxes at phony copies of the real thing.

Marshall couldn't bear to sit with us. He would crash in and out. At last, the time arrived when the first astronaut lunched drunkenly on the distant moon surface. At this precise moment, Marshall burst into the room shouting: "God, all of you— come on outside. Come look at the sunset. It's *for real*! Greatest thing *you* ever saw!. . . . Christ Almighty, come on out—you'll never see anything like it again. Come on, all of you!"

Then, when there was no response, he turned on his heel and shouted: "The hell with black and white!" And strode out, slamming the door behind him.

I was the only one who followed him, and he described to me the mystical signs in the sunset—there was Mary, there was Jesus, there the Father, there the Holy Ghost....

It *was* something I'll never see again; it can't be rerun.

Bernie, my favorite aide, and I cared a lot for Marshall. Most patients felt Marshall was getting worse. Bernie and I didn't. We both recognized brief moments of leveling Marshall hadn't been capable of when he first arrived as the big Hippie jokester.

For example, one day I found him sitting yogi-like in his room, staring. When he saw me he cried, "Oh God, I'm the loneliest in the world." And he was. . .

Both Bernie and I felt the more Marshall flipped out in this protected place, the more hope there was for him. Bernie described it in these words: "He's getting better because he's getting closer and closer to the terror that's driving him." We were consumed with hope.

But then came the underground rumblings. Marshall, it was whispered, was due for Shock. Neither Bernie nor I could believe it. We were dismayed. So was Marshall.

He became very distraught; he begged me, since we had the same doctor, not to let it happen. I told him I was a patient, just as he, that I was helpless, but since I didn't believe in shock, I would bring it up in the next staff-patient meeting.

Staff-patient meeting was a weekly occurrence. The idea was a good one—that patients could participate in the running of the hospital, bring up their gripes, get them settled, make suggestions and perhaps have them followed.

At previous meetings, we'd talked about conditions in the hospital, supplies for OT, a new washing machine, whether we could get a yoga teacher, and protested the use of grapes in the dining room. (All outspoken members, including Dr. Forester, were for "*La Raza*."[83]) It was light and gay and fun.

This time I came in determined to talk about the use of shock. I asked why Marshall was to be given shock, indicating as strongly as I could my disapproval of it.

I got nowhere. Dr. Forester told me it was an inappropriate subject for staff-patient discussions. Marshall sat hopelessly in his corner. The subject was closed.

Next morning, the hospital was very, very quiet. Marshall was in the shock room, getting his treatment.

When he emerged, he, too, was very, very quiet. He was pleading and plaintive and confused. He recognized us and tried a bit of his old bravado, but it didn't come off.

Only a few days later did he rise to his old heights of rage and anger, and because of it, we all knew he'd have shock again.

Meantime, my second weekend rolled around and I planned to go out on my first weekend pass. Just before I left, I acquired a new roommate. (Emily had disappeared the day before without saying a word of goodbye to anyone.) The new patient was a small, frenetic redhead who introduced herself as Connie.

By now I knew the standard entrance syndromes. One of them was to come in very high, very talkative, very eager to prove they were all right. Very anxious, very "wired." It didn't bother me at all anymore. It was "normal."

Everyone knew that in about three days the new patient would come down, begin to be unscared of the place, and ready to admit to the distresses that had brought them there.

Connie exhibited more wired admission syndrome than anyone I'd met before. She was not only high—she was flying. She was a nonstop talker and a nonstop smoker who had the room in total disarray two minutes after she got into it.

Before I left, an intuitive caution prompted me to write a note in bold letters and paste it on my side of the bureau saying: "This painting and this sculpture belong to Gene Hoffman. Please do not move." Then, with great relief, I left, hoping the weekend would give Connie time to come down.

The weekend out was really weird. I'd seen Stephen almost every other evening at supper since I'd been in the hospital, but I hadn't driven away from its protective area.

This time we stayed at my vacationing parents' home. I felt very fragile, very crystalline, as though I were waiting to be shattered. I longed for something—something—what was it? It didn't come. I felt totally vulnerable—my relationship with Stephen seemed senseless—laced with pain.

Outside reality was so different. I couldn't cope with it. I'd become so accustomed to hospital language, to the directness, the uninhibited quality of it, that it was almost impossible to get my bearings in the straight world.

I couldn't get into any satisfying contact with Stephen. My conversation kept veering off to a spaced-out language, a kind of free-association. I felt unreal. All the familiar places, even the furniture, felt transparent. Although Stephen and I slept in the same bed I was terrified. I felt so isolated. The body that had planted five children in me was there—but not for me.

I could hardly wait for the weekend to be over.

By this time I'd given up the notion that I'd come to the hospital for a few days' rest. I didn't know how long I'd be there, but decided to play it day by day. I described myself to myself, and to others as an "Optional patient" (which was true). I didn't know why I was there—I only knew it felt safer than anyplace else. I was glad to get back.

When I returned to my room after the weekend, it was in chaos. I found Marshall in a fantastic fight with Connie. When she saw me, she leapt out of bed, heaped high with pillows, (including mine), went to the closet, flung open the door and asked me poignantly: "In reality or in fantasy, aren't those clothes mine?"

I looked at the rack of clothes I'd left on my side of the closet, found them on Connie's side, pushed them back and said: "In reality *and* in fantasy, they're mine. I left them here yesterday."

Then she turned to Marshall's painting and sculpture and said, "'The Colonel'" (her name for Marshall) "says these are yours, but I think they're mine. Whose are they?"

I gave her the same reply, "In reality and in fantasy, they are mine."

This appeared to satisfy her, except for one article of clothing—a yellow tennis dress of mine she decided really *was* hers (though it was about six sizes too large). Because she liked it so much, she was sure her husband had bought it for her. (Her husband had brought her some clothes, but she had distributed them through all the closets in the hospital.)

I denied the yellow sun dress belonged to her, and a tug-of-war began. Nothing I said persuaded Connie the dress wasn't hers, so I had it locked in the nurse's station. I also requested either a change of room for her or me. I knew we couldn't survive together. Connie was moved. I put the tennis dress back in my closet.

That afternoon I went swimming. When I returned, in my closet was the sole article of clothing Connie knew she possessed—a tiny turquoise mini-dress. She was outside, wearing my yellow tennis dress. Ultimately it was given back to me, but I never understood why it was so important to her (or to me, for that matter).

We were all sympathetic to Connie. She joined the Key Club rap sessions and began distinguishing somewhat between reality and fantasy. We were all excited about her progress and listened to her endlessly.

Suddenly, like Emily, she, too, disappeared. We were told her husband decided the hospital wasn't the right place for her and took her out. We were desolate. Connie was beginning to make it, we felt. She was talking with less circumlocution. We exchanged some direct sentences. She was beginning to differentiate between "reality and fantasy." She seemed on the verge of being able to talk about things which terrified her. Then—she was gone.

About this time I was beginning to experience the validity of ideas I'd formerly only read and believed. One of them was Dr. Ronald Laing's opinion that patients are better for patients than anybody else.

I must have had frequent sessions with Dr. Forester, but I can't remember any before this time. What I do remember is the directness, the sensitivity, the empathy, and honesty among the patients. We were healing to each other because we didn't say yes when we meant no—we didn't mystify each other with diagnoses, interpretations, or advice. We didn't treat each other as sick and dangerous. We dealt with the immediate realities in our relationships, with the third-eye quality—listening because we knew it brought relief. We were tender with each other, too.

Meantime, Pam, of the broken mirrors and near suicide, and I became very close. She felt to me more like the me of 18 than I did myself. She looked like I did, wore her hair cut in the same fashion, and, when they thought it safe and returned her glasses to her, we discovered we'd chosen the same style frames. Her brown ones were replicas of my purple ones!

We spent a lot of time together and we talked long about her fears, her love-hate relationship with her parents, and her need to prove herself through performance. Every night she would come to my room to have me rub her back and to talk.

It was through Pam I got in with the "kids." She was moved out of Kit's room into the adolescent room—a dormitory with beds for four, fantastically decorated, with walls and doors painted by the occupants. Some of the adolescents were long-term and had school passes. Others had passes for dates. The atmosphere was like a college dorm with many watchful housemothers. Pam, at that time, had no passes at all.

The back rubs began to take place in the adolescent room, as did the talking. One by one a new group formed, comprised of the kids and me. Most of them were OD cases. One was a former heroin addict. Most were the victims of multiple marriages—one boy had five "fathers"—or parents locked together in a hostile-dependency relationship, who acted out against the child. In one case, the girl was adopted by professional parents whose expectations she could never meet, and who never had time for her. Their work was more important.

Pam was an exception. She came from a close-knit Jewish family who wanted togetherness above everything else.

But whatever the reason or the background, they all seemed hungry for an understanding, accepting "adult" relationship. They began to invite me on their outings. We went to the beach at night in the hospital bus, with Engali as chaperone. We walked on the moonlit sands, running in and out of the water, stopping for ice cream on the way "home." During these times of freedom (Engali usually waited near the bus), the kids would gleefully talk of splitting—but they didn't.

They included me in their parties, taught me new dance steps, invited me to their rooms to listen to their records, to look at their family photographs, or the things they'd made in OT, to play cards, and asked about my children.

We got one thing straightened out early. When they referred to themselves as mentally ill, nuts in a nut house, I cracked down hard and fast. I told them I didn't believe any of us were mentally ill. I knew we were hurt and confused, but I also knew we were not sick. I felt we were solving our life problems.

I also suggested something I feel to be true: I said I felt we might be mutants, breaking the barriers of our conditioned consciousness.

The latter made little impression on them, but they really dug the former. And from then on, the seriocomic chant was: "We're not sick; we're solving life problems!"

My theories were severely tested a few nights later when a new adolescent was admitted. His name was Tracey. Tracey was on a real trip. He introduced himself as a singer and guitar player who had an appointment with his agent in the morning, and was only spending one night in the hospital.

Tracey was one of the most unattractive kids I'd ever met. He was 15, fat, sweaty, pimply, openly homosexual, and weepy about it. He was an incessant smoker. He would have at least two cigarettes going at once and would plead with other patients for more. I wondered how anyone could get close enough to him to work with him.

A few nights later, I learned how. Tracey, Pam, and I were in the adolescent room. Pam's guitar was beside her bed. Tracey asked if he could play it and sing to us. Pam reluctantly agreed. So he picked up the guitar, plucked at the strings, and began to "sing." Pam and I looked at each other. He couldn't do either.

Pam leveled with him: "You can't play or sing, can you, Tracey?" He responded with a weak "No." "You don't know the Monkees [a popular American rock group] and you don't have an agent, do you?" Another weak "No." "It's all made up, isn't it, Tracey—all about being a performer on TV and all that shit?"

This time he responded with muffled sobs. I went over to him, put my arms around him and held him for a long time while he wept noisily.

After that, we were friends. There were no physical or psychological barriers between us.

Meantime, I chose my next roommate. I asked for Heidi, a dark-haired, blue-eyed girl, who was serenely beautiful, with a very childlike face. Heidi and I had met over meals and had an empathy for each other. We'd talked, but not deeply. I wanted to know her more.

She was agreeable, although she kept warning me, saying, "You won't want me with you when you know how sick I am. I'm the sickest person in this hospital. I'm too sick to be here. I'm only fooling you like I've been fooling everyone else."

Heidi spoke truly. How truly I only learned later. She had a new baby, an ambitious husband, a big home in an expensive suburb, and, for financial reasons, two weeks allotted to her to "get well."

She had been brought in because of a suicide attempt. . . after months of withdrawal, when she hid behind the drapes of her beautiful house and tried to disappear.

Heidi and I talked for long hours. I hardly ever left the room because she was afraid to be alone. She kept repeating a phrase I only half understood at the time. It was: "I know she didn't mean to and couldn't help it, but I want to tell my mother it's her fault I'm here."

I knew both halves of the statement were true for her—as they were for me. I didn't know what to do about it. So I listened, and we tried to understand what the compulsion meant.

I discovered a strange thing happened to me in my relationship with Heidi. I felt I had to be very careful to say precisely what I meant. My speech became very slow, cautious, and considered.

I realized later it was in response to my feeling that Heidi needed an honesty as absolute as possible. She'd been deceived by life and people—not in any malicious way—but apparently because her family felt (like so many of us do) that truth was too dangerous to be used among them.

And truth can be dangerous—hard to come by, hard to face, and harder still to tell—for it often contains so many hurts, so many paralyzing fears.

But no matter what Heidi told me, she would usually conclude with "There's so much more I want to say, but I can't. If they knew the truth, they'd throw me into seclusion or give me shock."

So Heidi continued to "control herself," while retreating farther and farther from relationships, hiding under the covers, and refusing to go to meals or OT.

It was then I decided to learn all I could about seclusion. This was the room I mentioned before, where Pam lay the morning after her suicide attempt, and where patients were put if they became violent, or out of control.

I went in. There was no furniture, no light switches, no light fixtures—nothing but a bare room, with battered holes in the walls where frenzied patients had pulled off plaster with

128

their bare fingers, trying to get someone to pay attention to their plight. A room with a heavy door—a door without a peephole.

Sometimes the patient was in restraints (a straight-jacket), sometimes not. Sometimes he was left there alone, locked in, in the dark. . .

I'd heard a variety of opinions about seclusion. One patient who had arrived in a self-destructive state told me how much it had meant to her. She frequently said it felt like a very friendly place. She was put in it with the door open and an aide by her side.

Mark, my 17-year-old companion of the first Saturday night, told me he'd felt most secure in the straight-jacket, that when he first arrived, it was the only place and way he felt safe enough to fall asleep.

Then there was the day Pam lay on a mattress on the floor, and the night of the fights and scuffles and "into seclusion" with Marshall or Phillip.

None of us felt reassured. The threat of seclusion hung over us all. Worst was, the guidelines weren't clear. We didn't know precisely what would make us candidates for it, so we proceeded warily. Seclusion was a mode of control and all of us kept ourselves reined in. We all wanted help to exorcise whatever demons had brought us here. Letting the demons out did not seem an acceptable way to the hospital authorities.

I have since come to believe that seclusion could be the most important room in the hospital. But—it must be used as an opportunity, not a punishment. Punishment is the last thing a distressed person needs. He's probably distressed because he's already had too much of it. I agreed with Menninger that any kind of punishment is always a "crime."

I think there would, optimally, be two kinds of seclusion rooms. One would be a safe room, where patients could yell, scream, shout, and pound on the walls. This room would be the anger-venting room, probably with padded walls and ceilings and thickly carpeted floor. I think it should be light and bright and invite the patient to do just what he or she needs to do with explosive feelings.

The other seclusion might be a beautifully appointed, warm, inviting place, with soft lights and cushions on the floor. A place where people like Heidi could go with someone and literally break out of their tremendous emotional pressures—go safely through their fear and grief, experience the necessary catharsis so they can move to the next stage of understanding. (All of us really have these pressures. They're just more upfront with some like Heidi and Marshall.)

The patients could be told when they arrive at the hospital that such rooms are available and they may go in them with informed, listening people, who are ready to stay with them lovingly, attentively, non-judgingly, while they go through their needed experience of pain and anguish and anger.

I think—at least for myself—it's repression of emotion that causes breakdowns. I also know it's inappropriate to dump anger and hostility and grief on others, on innocent bystanders (or one's children!)—that we're all seeking appropriate ways to get it out. Seclusion in a hospital would be an appropriate place, providing there were aides (or even other patients) as companions and guides as patients went through their mazes of fear.

If seclusion were transformed from a control center, an alien and scary place, it could be the most important facility available to help patients on their journey toward emotional equilibrium. And I believe patients could quickly learn to help others go through these trips.

Patients really understand each other better than anyone else. They're already "there." And, most important, they're not afraid, although their anxiety level about themselves is very high.

Heidi's other repressive fear was of shock. I inquired about her doctor's position on shock and learned, with relief, he was the one member of the staff who absolutely refused to give it, had never given it, and disapproved of shock for anyone. I was reassured and reassured Heidi, as did his other patients in the hospital.

And Heidi became more open—both with me, and so she said—with her doctor. Her longing to go through whatever was weighing on her was so intense. She gave so many hints.

One night she began to regress. I stayed up with her through her regression into infancy when she described in a tiny voice how small, weak, and helpless she was.

I sat with her for three or four hours, just listening, and encouraging her to go on. Finally, I was exhausted, went to the nurses' station and asked for an aide to come—telling him Heidi was on a bummer.

A young man responded immediately, brought a chair, and sat by her bed. Heidi continued and began describing herself as "nothing but a vegetable."

The aide's response was totally different from mine. He spoke to her statements directly saying things like "You don't look like a turnip to me," or "I've never heard an artichoke say the things you do"; and, "I know a carrot can't think like you can. . ."

I began to giggle. I put my pillow over my face to muffle the sounds, but the giggling was contagious—that it was also healing, I began to learn. Heidi began giggling too, and the next I knew, it was morning and we'd both slept.

I thought Heidi was beginning to make it. But the next day, against her doctor's orders, against her husband's pleadings, she signed herself out, and we began to wait out the 72-hour hold.

All of us rallied around her, but nothing we said dissuaded her. She just kept repeating over and over again—"I'm too sick to be here. If they *really* knew, they'd throw me into seclusion or give me shock."

131

The only clue I had to what Heidi was afraid they'd find out was that she longed to freak out, to scream and yell at her mother and tell her—against "all reason" that her mother "had done it to her."

But nobody heard this, and nobody let her, and the next weekend, when I returned from my pass, Heidi was gone.

But not for long, for on Monday Heidi returned, wan and chastened, ready to try again. She lived in a constant high level of anxiety about shock. We all continued to reassure her it couldn't happen, and begged her to be more open with her doctor.

Not long after Heidi's return, I was discharged, comforted in the knowledge that she was still in the hospital, safe from the outside world, and the threatened shock.

My comfort was short-lived, for when I returned to the hospital for my weekly appointment with Dr. Forester, I learned that Heidi had set fire to her hair one night, and her doctor had been persuaded, by whatever hospital forces there were, to give her shock.

I felt terrible, not only for Heidi, who had again been deceived, but that I had played a part in her deception. What will happen to that beginning trust I saw developing I could not know. I would say the prognosis is bad.

I've seen both Heidi and Marshall since I left the hospital— when I returned to visit them. Heidi recognized me and called me by name. Marshall hugged me, then stood back, rubbed his forehead and said wearily, "You're one I *do* remember; you're the one with the purple glasses."

I've thought about and explored different views on shock treatment since then. I'd like to share some of my opinions with you now.

I know all therapists should pay more attention to their patients—in fact, I think they should reduce the number if they can't give the ones they have enough time and attention.

I feel confident Marshall and Heidi would not have needed shock treatment if there had been enough people around enough of the time to stay with them during their "psychotic episodes." Or even if they had been able to count on seeing their doctor regularly, every day, at a time agreed upon in advance.

One of the problems in the hospital was that the doctors were so busy the patients never knew when they would see them, and this uncertainty left us all confused and bewildered—and very, very anxious.

Usually I found I could cope, hold myself together, if I knew there would be a particular appointment at a particular time. But I never knew from one day to the next if and when I would see my doctor—although I had been told when I arrived I would have an appointment with him every day. The irregularity heightened my anxiety.

Marshall had no set time to see his doctor. He would go for days without an appointment, and would plead with me, who was more fortunate, to try to make an appointment for him. Heidi's doctor was about to go on a vacation when she entered the hospital, and she knew it.

I know that when we're in such a desperate condition that we must go to a psychiatric hospital, we're in no condition to tolerate added frustration. I know a reasonable expectation would reduce the severity of wide mood swings. But easier than that— if each patient had two or more therapists, the dangerous dependency would not develop. The doctors would be freer and the patients would feel more secure.

I believe shock treatment and drugs are substitutes for deep, caring human relationships. I also believe it is the responsibility of the therapist to see that patients are supplied with plenty of nourishing, caring relationships, and for the patient to be able to count on them for as long as he or she needs such intensive ones. I feel shock and drugs are dangerous substitutes for these relationships.

I believe "psychotic episodes" are the return of repressed hurts or trauma we have suffered. They give us an opportunity to work out unsolved difficulties of our early life. I believe shock and drugs abort this process.

I do not believe we can cope with such episodes alone. I think it's people who can give us the caring attention we need, not electronic or chemical substitutes. Patients can give this attention to other patients, especially if taught and encouraged to do so.

My friend and favorite aide, Bernie, talked long about Marshall and Heidi. He was disconsolate. He felt that Marshall had been destroyed, and Heidi was on her way to it.

However, we both found some small comfort in the knowledge that the effects of shock don't last forever, and perhaps someday, somewhere, Heidi and Marshall can flip out in a safe, protected environment, and no one will abort the journey through grief and fear we feel each of them needs to make, to heal.

By now, my own healing process required I face a new reality.

After I had been out of the hospital a few times, I could no longer persuade myself that I was in for a few days' rest. I realized I had problems to work on.

One day, in OT, I watched Doris draw. I picked up a pastel and began to draw, too. I didn't know what I wanted to do. I just gave myself up to the mood. I found myself sinking deeper and deeper into some unknown recess of myself. I drew with feverish intensity.

My first drawing turned out to be a "Psychological Portrait" of my father—a picture of flame, snarled all over with barbed wire. I then drew one of my mother, infinite regressive squares, with pale, diminishing colors. My eagerness and the depth of feeling increased. I wanted to draw Stephen. . .

What emerged was the outline of a face, but instead of features, random smiling lips covered it, hung together on delicate chains. The excitement was almost unbearable. I moved on to my son Paul. His portrait was composed of brilliant colors, precise, geometrical, crystalline shapes, which coalesced into the shape of a cross. My youngest son was next. Tears stained the page as I feverishly drew a vivid yellow sun whose rays penetrated every corner of the paper I had shaded a clear green. When I wrote its title: "Small sun shining," I was drained, exhausted, I could do no more.

Next day I eagerly waited for OT to open. I went straight for the pastels and began to draw. My eldest son, Nikolas, was next—many-hued spheres filled the page. I called it "The Many Worlds of Niki." Then Nina-Kiriki, my youngest daughter—a luxuriant blossom, half-opened, against an intense green sky. It was the most sensual of all the drawings, all female and celebration.

I barely finished one of my son Kristian—a multicolored surrealistic violin—when the call came over the loudspeaker that it was time for my appointment with Dr. Forester.

I held the picture of Kristian between two fingers and walked into his office. Tears streamed down my cheeks. He looked at it absently as I placed it on the couch and then sat in the chair to begin the session.

That was the afternoon of a breakthrough. For on that day, in his office, I relived some important part of my "emotional" childhood.

In our previous "head-trip" sessions, Dr. Forester told me I had a vast amount of anger to get rid of. That in the straight world, I had to play the straight person, and save all my emotional upheavals for the privacy of his office. My relationship with Stephen should be light and gay and fun—with no serious over or undertones.

The theory was right—perhaps. The practice, under the old modes of therapy—i.e., a week between one-hour sessions— impossible. Mainly because no doctor can see anyone as often as he/she needs being seen in those early periods of uncapped distress.

On this day I had a vision of what might be possible—if there were world enough and time. For in the safety of his attentive presence, I regressed without fear or inhibition into infantile states.

They were intense, vivid, re-creations of a state I had experienced once before when I had unwittingly eaten food laced with either hashish or LSD.

In Dr. Forester's office I had hallucinatory visions of myself as a small golden-haired child in a circle of golden light, at the bottom of a black well. (At first I thought the child was my son Paul—then I realized it was I.) I was holding a long-stemmed multicolored flower whose crimson and purple petals reached up to the well's opening. I described everything as I perceived it to Dr. Forester in minute detail.

Suddenly the vision blacked out, and I heard my voice, small and piteous, telling him, "They've taken away the trust..."

Then I began my journey through a Dante-esque hell which I continued to describe to him while tears flooded the words. Old angers and fears I thought were long since exorcised by my "reason" rushed out through the feelings into words.

I re-experienced a moment when I felt my father rejected me as I was—a girl, wild, untamable, one whose "spirit" they could not break. But god, how they tried! I repeated over and over again: "They said they had to break my spirit. They said they had to break my spirit." Then, a moment of triumph, "But they didn't!" And Dr. Forester smiled his assent.

I experienced the excruciating pain of being abandoned, isolated, alone—was I in a crib? In a huge house alone? I don't know. Only the fear and pain felt real—yet unreal, for I knew all the while I was in Dr. Forester's office—I was "really" safe.

I relived a moment of old anguish when my father beat me psychologically, attacking me with his relentless "logic," while my mother sat in the same room, impotent, and I silently pled for her help.

Time had no reality. I moved in it freely, without boundaries.

I experienced my own birth and told Dr. Forester that I saw, and at the same moment was, a bleeding, bruised newborn, crushed by forceps and dry pelvic thrusts.

I told him "they" were crushing my "real self," that "I," the real "me," was abused, unwanted, mangled, all but destroyed.

Suddenly Stephen appeared on my psyche's horizon: cold, icy waves seemed to emanate from him, spears of hostility. I buried my head and wept, "He hates me. Oh, he hates me," I cried. And through this onrush of horror I heard Dr. Forester's calm, undisturbed voice, "No, Gene," he said, "he doesn't hate you. He is only afraid."

Suddenly, in the calmness of that moment, it seemed as though all the forces of self-hatred and self-destruction that had been determining so many of my actions exploded into my felt consciousness.

"He doesn't hate me—he's afraid! Why should he be afraid of me?" I knelt in Dr. Forester's office, my fingers gripping his desktop; I wept and screamed over those early sundering experiences, over my grief that I was some monster who brought fear, not love, to my husband and children.

Dr. Forester didn't have to encourage the explosion, my need was so great.

So many things I'd *talked about* in years of therapy, so many things I "knew" in my mind, I felt through in his office. I went through this "trip" with Dr. Forester as my Virgil, and came through cleansed. I experienced the depths of a state I'd only known about intellectually before: catharsis.

For the first time in my remembered life, I had been permitted to go through an intense emotional experience with someone else and wasn't stopped. Nobody said, "You frighten me." Nobody said, "You're a big girl—or a grown woman—you don't need to cry." I did need to cry—and I did.

Nobody explained away my parents' behavior, telling me how much they had suffered. (I always *knew* how much they had suffered and had tried to balance my own pain against theirs.)

Nobody said, "They've done so much for you—why aren't you grateful?" In that moment, I *owned* my own feelings! (And I wasn't leveling them at my parents.) It was all right for me to feel the way I did. For the first time, I didn't have to worry about *their* sufferings—I was permitted to experience my own— without guilt.

When Dr. Forester said anything, he encouraged me to experience there, in his office, all the hate and rage I'd felt (but never dared admit even to myself) since I was very young.

He didn't interpret; he didn't analyze; he was just there. And for the first time, when I was experiencing an emotional hurricane, I was fully conscious that I was *not* crazy, not evil, not destructive, not bad. Nobody wrote me off as irrational. And I wasn't.

I was more completely sane and rational than I'd ever had a chance to be before in my whole life. I *had* been hurt, terribly hurt (as all of us are in this culture), and it was *rational* to be angry and full of grief.

At last the session ended. Dr. Forester told me I had a lot more pain and rage to feel, and I should feel it in his office. He also told me I must, under no circumstances, let it spill over into other relationships—particularly with Stephen.

I was a good actress, wasn't I? I could act happy and pleasant with Stephen, and bring all the anger and grief to Dr. Forester where it wouldn't hurt anyone else.

I felt a flood of gratitude and resolved to do as he advised. Perhaps I should have; I'm not sure. It felt phony to me. Perhaps I could have, had he had time for me. But my appointments were erratic and short. There were so many patients waiting to see him. My sessions were constantly interrupted by telephone calls, which were more important to him than my need.

Often he was late and hurried, or had to cut a session short. I was also aware that I was privileged—I could see him when Phillip and Marshall couldn't—and I felt them outside—waiting....

Often I was aware of the ticking of the inexorable clock and the limit on his time. "Time—nobody ever has enough time for me," metronomed through my head, as I tried over and over again to experience my hurt and rage.

Sometimes the thought flashed through me: "I have to pay him $50 an hour to get what someone who really loved me would give free. I have to buy love!"

And this thought would freeze me. My feelings of deprivation would close me up. I felt again in my glass prison, observing him at a distance through the window of some new hurt I felt *he* had authored.

I knew I wasn't really important to him. No matter how skilled he was—and he was very skilled—I was just one among many, and this knowledge became a further hurt and a defense against him.

Irrational? I thought so then, and mentally tried to flog myself into line. But now I don't think I was irrational. I now know I needed and deserved many spans of someone's undivided, loving attention.

Dr. Forester had the warmth and understanding necessary—but he didn't have the time, nor the awareness of my need for it. He couldn't resist the insistent demands of the "important" people in his world. More, one therapist simply isn't enough, (now I know it isn't necessary to limit myself to one), and so, I closed him out.

But even with these impediments, through my sessions with Dr. Forester, I gained enough awareness to perceive more clearly the needs of persons in such distress as the other patients and me.

I'd like to share some of these perceptions now.

Buttressed only by my knowledge of the work of Ronald Laing, Dr. John Perry, Julian Silverman, Carl Rogers' Client-Centered Therapy, of course, Dr. Benjamin Weininger, and a few other adventurers into the mysterious land of the psyche, I came to the hospital aware that my overwhelming present-time fears carried the freight of innumerable past fears and hurts with them.[84]

This is why they appeared to be, and were, irrational.

I learned through Dr. Forester's ministrations how to begin to separate present-time fears and hurts from those of the past. I knew I had to determine whether a present-time fear was truly relevant to the present, or whether some experience in the now was reminiscent and was triggering the old world of past terror into being, flooding the now with anguish and fear and anger which were inappropriate to the present moment. I learned a direction—but I didn't learn until much later how to follow it.

But here are some things I did learn in the hospital:

The hospital was really a remarkable place. There was more loving, hugging, and caring there than almost any other place I've ever been. It came mostly from the patients, the staff, and the aides.

Most staff members were there because they wanted to be. They must have been selected for their capacity to listen and empathize, because most of them did so with healing ease.

They were open in their delight about being privileged to work there, and about their own self-discovery in the process. They listened to learn, and I was often affirmed by their learning process.

There was no verbal censorship, and surprisingly little behavioral censorship. That was a novel experience. It was OK for anyone to say whatever came into his/her head, and most of us listened for the import.

One old lady, Emma, was completely wandering and senile. Neither her mental nor bodily functions operated well. She suffered from chronic diarrhea (a common symptom of fear). The need to defecate would invariably overtake her at mealtime and she would stand up and shout anxiously (both hands clutching her intractable buttocks), "I have to go to the bathroom. I have to go to the bathroom!" Anyone near her, young or old, would guide her to the bathroom where she relieved herself. No one minded. No one resented her. Everyone knew she was worthy of and deserved our attention.

The patients weren't discouraged from helping and caring for one another. We did it automatically. But nobody on the staff, nor even among us, realized how capable we were. So our helping and caring didn't receive either the direction, nor the recognition it deserved. By caring for each other, we emerged, at least momentarily, from our own self-concern, and this was an important part of the healing process.

One small example of patient care: I was drawing in OT when I began to cry, involuntarily. Ethel—until then a rigid, withdrawn woman whom I hadn't seen relate to anyone—came over to me, put her arms around me, and said, "Go ahead, Gene, cry; sometimes you *have* to cry." And I did. It felt good, and my vision was clearer when I finished.

Another time, when I sat in a corner, wrestling with an overwhelming sense of pain and withdrawing rapidly, Doris, the girl diagnosed as schizophrenic, took me by the hand and asked me to walk through the garden with her. I did, and we paused at each bush and tree, examining the flowers and leaves. Suddenly it flooded through me that I could see a lemon leaf again! And I cried.

How long had it been, I wondered, since I had seen a lemon leaf, or was aware of its spicy odor, released by the sun. A sense of great joy and wonder coursed through me.

It was Ethel who later told me why the hospital felt so good to her and why she had returned to it again and again, each time for a longer stay. "There's freedom in here," she mused, "Freedom to be as we are."

Engali, the Recreational director, described the potential if not the reality of the hospital one night when I overheard him tell a new patient, "You don't have to be afraid here. Here any kind of behavior is accepted. Outside, you have to be careful how you act, but not here."

These statements were less than wholly true. There *was* a wider area of freedom for unusual behavior in the hospital. But we all knew there were limits. These limits prevented our getting well, for they kept us in fear, and part of the pervasive fear was that we didn't know what those limits were.

The hospital continued the old authoritarian attitudes between patient and doctor, between group leaders and patients. One of the gravest problems, as I see it, was that people didn't know why they were there, or what they were to accomplish. And nobody really knew what to do for us.

In fact, I wonder if the greatest problem about almost all therapy is that nobody really knows what it's about.

For myself, I came to the hospital because I was wounded— both in the present time and in the past—possibly even before I was born. My distress had reached such a degree that I could no longer function. It was far greater than my awareness of the world around me or the potentialities for a decent life which lay in myself. I was overwhelmed with seemingly insoluble problems. There simply seemed to be no exit.

What I needed was to be listened to, to scream and rage and cry. To be attended to, cared for (not sympathized nor empathized with, nor advised and interpreted). At this stage that's all I was ready for.

Laing's experiments with patients, encouraging each other to flip out—to go through their needed trips unimpeded, while helped and encouraged by the attention of other patients—seems to me just right. It was not encouraged in the hospital.

We had to be "in control" or we were subject to the last resorts: seclusion or shock (viz Heidi and Marshall.) Even in a psychiatric hospital, it's not permissible to "go out of your mind." The same controls we had to exercise in the straight world were imposed on us, only to a lesser degree. But even this reduction, with its accompanying acceptance of us, was healing.

(As I write this, it seems unbelievable to me that it's not considered right and sane to burst into uncontrollable tears anywhere at any time if I feel like it. What's so "crazy" about crying, when there is so much pain and hurt in ourselves and in the world?)

I'm not saying patients should be permitted to act out their destructiveness in ways that would harm others, either physically or psychologically. I don't think they have to.

I agree with [archetypal psychologist Carl] Jung's three stages: catharsis, interpretation, then education. I think we have to tune in to where the patient is—and if he/she's in need of catharsis, let them/her go through it. I've come to believe that a person could come through his/her episodic need for violent action if there were someone, unafraid of him, who would stay with him during this period and encourage him to scream, shout, pound, tremble, and verbalize what he's feeling.... all the while reminding him/her that he's safe, is in the company of someone who's listening, and that expression of painful emotion is part of the self-healing process.

Then, as I see it, freed from the blocking of unreleased emotion, we are ready to begin to interpret what's happening to us. After that comes the great opportunity for education, learning new and more viable ways of living, moving ahead toward living consonant with our Spirits—as I see it, that of "God within us."

In the initial stage, the stage of catharsis, I think any psychologically talented, fearless, understanding person can help. That's why I believe that if patients were instructed and encouraged, they could do this for each other.

Later, through the stages of interpretation and education, I think we need a congruent guide, someone who, optimally, has been in the patient's space and moved through it to living a rich, well-balanced life.

This leads me to the place of therapists. Ideally the therapist would be a warm, attentive, caring and nonjudgmental person. Many of them are, and in their warming presence, with their confidence and encouragement, many of us have come a long way toward fuller realization of our potentialities, whether he/she is a psychiatrist, psychoanalyst, counselor, or aware friend.

What I see as possible is further implementation of healing therapy, when I suggest that aides and patients can facilitate the healing of hospitalized people.

Outside the hospital, I feel therapists should be more aware of their own condition and motivation. Most important, I think they should constantly examine themselves to see whether they "need" the dependency of their patients. I perceive therapists as people who can help another through a troubled period until the other can go on his or her own—much like taking a child by the hand until the child can walk by himself.

This means constant growth on the part of the therapist, constant scrutiny of him/herself, and the direction of setting the patient free to function from his/her own resources. This probably requires self-sacrifice on the part of the therapist. Having someone dependent does, for a while, give one a sense of value which frequently leads to ideas of omnipotence. I am beginning to think that, after the first unloading of distress, therapy should be brief and intermittent.

Unless therapists are in the process of continuously healing their own wounds, they (like the rest of us) often project them on the patients, and deal with the patients in irrational, nonloving ways. And the patient has no recourse, for he/she is the disintegrated recipient of attention from a supposedly integrated person.

In the logic of nature, this cannot always be so. Therapists have suffered, too. The line between their rational responses and their irrational behavior is pretty much the same as the rest of us. I do not believe anybody can be considered either sane or insane; everyone has problems with which he or she must cope, problems which frequently interfere with an appropriate response to the present. People just become overwhelmed by their life problems at different times.

There are moments of disequilibrium in each of our lives when we cannot live without help. When these distresses surface, we must be healed of them to live. In this effort, we will often do bizarre things. We call this "mental illness"—that's true, of course. Great upheavals in consciousness are taking place. But really, in my opinion, and certainly in my own case, the suffering person is simply calling for help from someone who, at that moment, isn't suffering as much as we are.

Therapists suffer just as much as anyone else—perhaps more. Many that I've talked with say that they became therapists in an effort to work through their own life problems. Some of them recognize when their difficulties impede their capacity to work with some patients. When the patient and the therapist have the same problem, it's almost impossible for the therapist to keep that emotional distance needed for the patient to feel safe.

Sometimes therapists are suffering too much to work at all. Because of their need to earn a livelihood, few suspend their practice when their personal problems become great. This is a terrible double-bind they live under and something should be done to alleviate it.

I found the aides at the hospital acutely aware of this, and when we talked about it, we often discussed ways it might be handled. For example, one idea that came up was that therapists should continually be supervised by their peers, and their colleagues would help them become aware when their personal problems were affecting their practice negatively. The consensus was that no one therapist should be the final authority for any one patient—that team therapy was more protective of the patient.

Obviously, if this were put into effect, some cooperative arrangement would have to be made so therapists could survive, both financially and psychologically, while they took time out to become congruent. And, there should be no loss of self-esteem, or the esteem of others. Getting and staying congruent is, as I see it, a continuous life effort for all of us.

Another need that became obvious to me is that the therapist must recognize the validity of the patient's truth, of his/her knowledge about him/herself. As a counselor, I was often quick to diagnose for my client and then try to fit his/her unique situation into my diagnosis. I now know I was wrong.

I know, through myself, that the patient is the only one who knows his/her own needs, who can analyze his/her condition, and act upon the new insights. The therapist is simply an enabling person, one who makes the patient feel safe enough to come to new understandings, to make the painful discoveries, and then have the backing and confidence to act upon them.

The greatest help I've received from therapy is the opportunity to unburden myself of my "secrets" in the presence of an accepting "other" so I could gain the strength to recognize my irrational behavior, my delusions, my illusions, my idealisms, and break old destructive patterns—then to discover alternative ways of living.

I don't even think it was important that my therapist understood what I was talking about. Whenever I was listened to respectfully, I came to my own understanding and could often communicate more fully to my therapist. Often I couldn't communicate directly—it was too threatening. So I used inverted ways. But whenever I was not corrected, invalidated, dismissed, or condemned, the very telling become part of the healing process and I could move from it to straighter communication.

I learned something else: when I was in a state of low self-esteem and the therapist drew analogies between his experience and mine, it confused me. Often I would try to operate from my therapist's experience, not recognizing that he was a different, totally unique person. Then I was overcome with guilt when I couldn't follow his prescription.

Even if his interpretation, analysis, and advice was right, it was still an impediment. I could know intellectually how I "ought" to act, but was still not able to act on it. The therapist's timing is critically important: there are times to use analogies, but the right time must be felt intuitively.

More and more I have come to believe the patient is capable of being responsible for his/her own growth and insights and is healed by the therapist's confidence that he/she can and should assume this responsibility.

Another point I feel important is that the therapist must try to make sure—over and over again—that the patient recognizes limitations of time and attention.

I know my initial experience at the hospital would have been far less destructive had Dr. Forester told me the day I entered: "I may not be available this weekend. Call me if you need to, but if you can't reach me, I know you're strong enough to wait it out."

Better yet, he could have told staff members exactly what his schedule was and have assigned others to help me through the anxiety of waiting. It would have been very good if a substitute doctor could have been available for such changes as my medication and privileges.

Instead, I was led to believe that I would be treated in a certain way and when these expectations weren't met, I lost trust, felt betrayed and very frightened. When I finally did see Dr. Forester and protested my treatment, he responded with "Well, a little frustration is good for you."

First of all, it wasn't a "little frustration." It was sheer, debilitating terror. And I didn't need any more—I'd already had so much frustration and terror it had catapulted me into the hospital. We are all so much more vulnerable than either we or anyone else imagines.

I also gained some new perspectives on groups in the hospital. I've always been concerned about groups. I've been in a few and I never could understand the therapeutic value of dumping hostility on a stranger, nor of having it dumped on me. So I became very wary of them—with cause.

I know we all long for community—a group of people with whom we can get connected, with whom we can relate on a free and open level. I guess that lots of people are like me and want an extended family.

I think Group Therapy has become so popular because it holds this promise. But groups, like families, can have the opposite effect. Like families, they can be healing and crazy-making at the same time.

The group in the hospital had both these qualities. I will write *only* of what I consider its crazy-making side.

There was no malice in the leaders, no intentional cruelty, absolutely none—instead, there was a reaching out and an eagerness to help. But because of what I consider an inadequate understanding of our nutty society, the group was in great part an extension of the crazy-making patterns of our put-down society in concentrated form.

I saw operating in the hospital group, among leaders of good intentions and goodwill, an amount of mystification and condemnation which really upset me.

First, the group leaders kept themselves completely separate from the patients. They were the "leaders." They did not refer to themselves, or any possible life difficulties they might have. Any similarities between us and them were purely coincidental. They reminded me of my parents whose dogma was to present a solid front to me, even though they knew (and so did I) that one of them was wrong.

In the old authoritarian system (of which they were also the victims), to admit error was to lose control. The group leaders—so it seemed to me—felt they really needed control. They explained to us all, when confronted, that they got their therapy (if at all) elsewhere, and group was solely for the patients.

Many group members, including Marshall, saw through this. Few had the courage to voice their perception. Marshall did. He recognized some of the anxieties and hang-ups of the leaders and pointed them out in strong terms.

He was consistently put down for describing the reality he saw. The leaders either laughed and discounted what he said, which made him lose confidence in himself, or they became defensive and out-argued him. Marshall could out-shout them all, but he couldn't live outside the hospital. Both they and he knew it. So he lost doubly.

Group in a hospital is different from one outside. Many of the patients had been forced to come there. They didn't feel self-confident enough, "sane" enough, to challenge the leaders who were allowed to live in the straight society. Fear was in the saddle here, like everywhere else.

Since I was luckier than most, and had confidence in my own perceptions, from time to time I would support Marshall. Then I found the other patients were freed to express themselves more fully. It appeared to be good for the patients, but very threatening to the group leaders.

One afternoon I went to Sara's office and talked with her about my concerns. I asked her if she didn't feel she could benefit from our concern for her as much as we benefited from her concern for us. Her response was, as I described previously, "Group is for the patients and I get my therapy elsewhere."

I then tried to talk with her about her habit of trying to force Doris to talk in the "straight" language when she launched into one of her tangential monologues. I suggested it would help both her and Doris if she'd learn Doris' language.

Sara said she had no intention of doing so, and it was up to Doris to communicate in a way she, Sara, could understand.

I then asked her if Marshall could be allowed to take over the entire group, at least once. I said I felt he needed our loving attention and I'd like to see what would happen if we gave it to him. He usually crashed in and out of group, shouting non sequiturs, stamping around the room, turning lights on and off, attacking the leaders for "not getting him out of his [sic] place." It *was* terribly disrupting and difficult, almost impossible to cope with.

She agreed, and the next time, we devoted our attention to Marshall. It had a startling effect; he behaved in a new and remarkable way. Of course he tested us for a while, but when he discovered we really meant it, he stopped shouting and began to speak in a hushed voice of his wife, of his fears for his baby, and of his girlfriend he wanted to get back to.

It really worked, just as I'd read in Tom Wolfe's book *The Electric Kool Aid Acid Test*, where he described a process of Ken Kesey's Merry Prankster Commune. When someone in the commune was on a bad trip, all other group members gathered around in love and concern to, as Kesey phrased it: "Feed the hungry bee."

Well, on that day, we gave Marshall the honey of our attention, and he was able to communicate with us and with himself in a new and wonderful way.

But Sara was unmoved, and she returned to her old method again, saying that she and I came from "different disciplines." I guess I really wouldn't have cared what her discipline was if I hadn't felt those two elements of condemnation and mystification in it.

The other two leaders, Gerri and Prudence, were, for the most part, warm and wonderful. In many ways this made it even worse, for the patients accepted more easily their right to accuse patients of game-playing, attention-seeking, and crazy acting-out.

I found one of the worst aspects of group was being accused of "game-playing"—a favorite term at that time. Telling a hospitalized patient he or she is playing a game is almost the ultimate put-down, a near perfect crazy-making device.

It's true, the patient may be repeating some pattern of behavior which is destructive to himself and to others. But he/she doesn't know it. And calling such behavior a "game" just makes him continue to feel crazy and mystified and attacked. So he/she retreats further and further into his psychic prison.

People don't *want* to play games, to mystify, to confuse. They want to be heard. I think we should listen to the emotional condition of the patient, not the verbal behavior.

So I learned not to be frightened of "chaos." Whenever a group member became "chaotic," rambling, incoherent, violent, or tearful, the leaders would usually stop and try to "bring the patient around."

One day I protested this, asserting that the rambling, the incoherence, the tears, even the violent, angry outbursts might be valuable—that there was some logic behind it or they wouldn't do it. I even made a speech in group, saying we shouldn't abort the process, but should listen closely to try to find that thread of hidden logic the patient was trying to express. And even if we couldn't find it, I thought we should accept the patient's need to be—at that moment—rambling, incoherent, violent or tearful, and support him/her during it.

This suggestion was not well received by the group leaders. They accused me of enjoying chaos for its own sake. But it had an interesting effect on some of the patients. A couple of them dared go farther in their free-associating in group than they had before. They even cried and laughed a little longer before they succumbed to the stern, "That's enough of that now. Tell me clearly what you mean."

I've come to think what we call chaos is just our efforts to sort out our undifferentiated distress. I think it's an important condition on the way to healing. Expressing undifferentiated distress is part of the process and has a lovely order behind it. Because, after we get that undifferentiated distress out in the open, in the secure and loving presence of a group or of another caring, listening person, we can begin to be selective about those areas which need particular attention.

My hallucinatory experience in Dr. Forester's office was certainly chaotic. But out of this splitting up, out of this freedom to ramble, to shout, to laugh, a new clarity of vision and ease of spirit emerges. It was short-held, to be sure, but it was a free view of what I now know can be.

I believe more and more that the process of deconditioning ourselves, of breaking out of old patterns only *appears* chaotic. I think we each know precisely what we need to do to heal ourselves—and what we need most is encouragement to do it, and sometimes, some precise directions about how to stay with what we know.

I do not think chaos, nor the sense of being totally lost, is bad—not if there is someone with us during that period and we are conscious that someone is with us. Sidney Jourard wrote we have to "go out of our (conditioned) mind to find it" (our true one).[85] I know this was true for me, and I think it's true for others as well. Experiencing and coming through this inner chaos feels to me part of it.

I do not think a breakdown is a bad thing. In fact, I think it's presently necessary. Perhaps it's the only way we can get relief from intolerable repetitions of destructive relationships and destructive behavior. I feel that the person who has a breakdown may be closer to being able to be human than those who hold themselves in tight rein and meet the crazy demands of our crazy-making society.

I've really come to the end—almost. I'm at the point of leaving Brookhaven. I had both internal and external reasons for it. My internal ones were that I'd gone as far as I could go in Brookhaven—I *felt* what I needed next and Brookhaven didn't provide it.

My external reasons were that our three youngest children were returning from Europe and I wanted to be home to greet and care for them.

So, on the afternoon of the night they were due to arrive I packed my bags, and Stephen arrived to take me to the car.

I went around to say goodbye to everybody. There were tears and long hugs. I missed one boy, a withdrawn fourteen-year-old named Noel. I found him cleaning the barbecue unit in the patio, weeping, with his nose running. I handed him a napkin to wipe his nose and he turned toward me and said, "Gene, what shall I do? I can't feel. I can't feel. I never could feel."

Then he threw himself face down on the floor and sobbed. I knelt down, uncertain what to do. At that moment, Gerri came in and found us. She ordered Noel to stand up. He did so, resentfully.

As I walked out the door, I heard him shout at Gerri: "I. . . Hate. . . You!" It was a moment of triumph. Noel *could* feel!

Just before the glass doors were unlocked to let me out, Mark came up and hugged me, saying, "Good luck out there in the real world, Gene." Then he paused and reflected, "Hey, maybe this is the real world in here, and that's the fake one out there."

I smiled through my tears and replied: "You'd better believe it!" And left.

Epilogue

This was the end of my experience behind the glass doors. It was not the end of my instability, my emotional fragility. Despite an initial remission—our real pleasure at all being together again—relationships among our family soon reverted to old destructive patterns.

It was not an easy time. The fact that I had been in a psychiatric hospital was somewhat frightening to my children and to my friends—to Stephen, too. So I wrote a paper about it for the counselors at the Night Counseling Center. This paper was distributed widely and appeared to ease many.

Stephen had not found any rewarding work after his separation from the Center. Our differences became more apparent. I was plunged back into old familiar terrors and I no longer trusted Ben to help me. Instead, Stephen and I joined a group of people in a—to us—new therapeutic process called Re-evaluation Counseling. It was being espoused with enthusiasm by Quakers across the country and we attended classes at Friends' Meeting.

This support group—where we learned how to co-counsel with different members of our class, seeking to enable one another to experience catharsis—was very helpful and healing. We were taught to listen to one another and care for one another in new ways, and we belonged to a network of people who were all seeking self-healing through this peer counseling process.

As I perceived it, Re-evaluation Counseling was a gift of caring that people could give one another—a ministry of love. This was part of its great appeal to me, in addition to some of its inherent truths about our need for catharsis, and the capacity for ordinary people to help each other heal themselves by means of aware, attentive, safe, caring listening.

Then Stephen found a position at the California Institute of the Arts and we moved again—this time back to Pasadena. With the aid of Re-evaluation Counseling and by enrolling as a student I had enough energy to sustain me through the next year. I knew Stephen was more distant, but I thought we would somehow come through, for I was still doggedly determined to have my marriage endure and bring us all into the sweet harmony I had long ago envisioned.

I earned my BA degree at Cal-Arts. When it moved to Valencia, California, we moved back to Santa Barbara, where we remodeled our house with what I thought was the intention of beginning a new life together in our beloved Santa Barbara.

But this was not to be, for on another August day of 1971, Stephen left.

He told me that since our children were leaving, he was afraid to live in the house "alone with a woman," and he moved to an apartment in Valencia near his work. A week or so later I received a letter from him telling me he did not "want to feel married for a year or two." A month or so after that I received another letter, telling me he had decided to live with a young girl who had been a schoolmate of one of our sons, and whom at one time I had sought to help through a period of adolescent distress.

I felt completely isolated, but I knew I would live. I would not go the suicidal trip again—not even the hospital trip. That was progress!

I tried calling friends—no one responded. After the trauma of Stephen's dismissal from his work with Robert Hutchins, no one from that organization reached out to us.

I called Ben, and he responded that he had "told me so, over and over again"—that my needs had always been too much for Stephen, and I had deluded myself in thinking he had wanted to be married to me. That, indeed, Stephen had stayed with me on sufferance for a long time.

This truth was so painful I did not call him again for a year. The last thing I felt I needed was to learn I had been so foolish and unaware, and had wasted all that time and life and effort.

No one from Stephen's large family contacted me, and the only relative I had was my mother who, at this time, was so ill she could not even recognize me.

So there I was, a woman in mid-life, with seven distressed children—abandoned, suddenly flung into orbit with what felt like no one and nothing to lean upon.

Even though all the old feelings of being abandoned and helpless assailed me, I was neither alone nor helpless. It took another four years to move from being overwhelmed by the feelings to living within the reality of the surrounding love and affection. It wasn't a straight line—if I made a graph of my days, it would be advances and regressions, exultations and total despair.

There were wide fluctuations of mood and behavior, which, as I look backward, appeared bizarre and out of character. But this behavior taught me much that I needed to learn. And through it all, I was guarded and guided by loving friends who believed I could again be whole and fully functioning.

On the day the last letter arrived, there was, in my home, my longtime friend, spiritual sister, and "co-madre" to my children. At this point, she went into action, loving me, sitting with me in the afternoons so I could sleep, calling me each day to answer any need, reminding me of how much we had already experienced together and that I "was going to make it."

Then my neighbor let me into her heart—always ready to listen to me, at whatever time I needed. She was also ready to watch over my children, perceiving they "were making it" too— when I felt totally lost from them and they from me.

I was still involved with Re-evaluation Counseling (which I had brought to Santa Barbara when I was Director of the Night Counseling Center), and co-counselors were ever available, coming often in the middle of the night, sometimes sleeping with me when I was too terrified to sleep alone. They became my new family, performing those necessary acts of love and caring which enabled me to keep some sort of equilibrium.

Timidly I returned to Quaker Meeting. Friends greeted me warmly, even those who could not openly greet my pain. I think they may have felt they would interfere with my privacy. What I needed was sharing and support and confidence in myself.

These they gave me as they could. All, I know now, gifts of grace. They came and brought with them their own unique and irreplaceable gifts of love and caring and listening—and meaningful work for Meeting.

There were many others, others who gave me a true vision of myself, unwounded, whole, and beautiful. Those who confirmed me in [Jewish philosopher] Martin Buber's marvelous I-Thou way.[86] People, like hands of ministering angels, came. Men and women who loved me and confirmed me as friend, confidant, mother, artist, desirable woman, spiritual, intellectual being.

Then came opportunities to use my talents again—opportunities to write for [Quaker publications such as] *Friends Journal* and *Friends Bulletin*, to teach a writing class at La Casa de Maria [a Catholic retreat center near Santa Barbara], to go to Pendle Hill [a Quaker retreat center near Philadelphia] and rediscover the power of the Spirit.

I began silent worship each morning—so restive and tentative at first I could maintain the quiet for only a few moments at a time. Then, as the Spirit moved me, for longer periods. Sometimes with a book to help center me, sometimes with my journal and pen, frequently, feverishly writing of new openings as they came pouring in. And, I could write poems again! Sometimes just sitting silently, open, expectant, waiting—outside of time, timeless waiting—timeless responses.

So many welcomes! No longer was I living in isolation, in an isolated house, in an isolated mind.

And my children—at last they recognized me, telling me they loved me, writing me they loved me, wanting for me and giving me beauty and richness and love. Sharing the gifts of their deepest selves with me. Trusting me, being open—at last feeling safer with me.

So many gifts, so much cherishing—even to my co-madre designing and making special clothes for me so that I would walk in the grace of color and fabric and flowing lines—and then, nursing me through a serious illness and telling me it was one of the great experiences of her life.

Then Ben came back into my life. One day I called him and he was there for me, present and aware. He said he had waited, that he knew I was not ready for him, but that we would resume our relationship sometime—when I *was* ready. And we did. He poured his wisdom on me like ointment, anticipated my needs for wider relationships, a wider view of the world, and he offered me all he could from his bounteous store.

In December 1973, Stephen and I were divorced; a week later he married his present young wife. Since his marriage we have had little relationship. He has all but disappeared from my life. But I keep open to any possibility. I do not have any hope for any particular outward relationship, nor do I "work" toward it. I believe all whom I have loved, all who have loved me, live on in me—even though they may no longer live. I have my own inward relationship with them. I seek only to meet that which addresses me with understanding, acceptance, and (I hope) love.

Out of this journey back has come a deep recognition.

"God" manifests "himself" to me in whatever way I need. I needed pain to learn from and pain came. I needed to shatter old structures of belief, old patterns of living, and they were shattered. I needed certain experiences to learn that nothing human was alien to me. I had those experiences. I needed despair to learn I could come through it. I needed doubt to learn it is a necessary companion to prevent closure and limiting beliefs. I needed my conditioning—indeed I bless it—and I no longer seek to exorcise it; I have made friends with it. For I know that my conditioning is my particular gateway to growth and love and understanding which is peculiarly mine.

I needed people—and the people came. I needed to make sense out of all that happened to me, and I began making sense, meaning—satisfying sense; satisfying meaning. I needed love—and love came. I needed books—and books appeared. I needed letters—and letters came.

Most of all, I needed to learn to place my trust not in a particular person, a particular relationship, a particular situation, but in life (which is synonymous for me with God). I needed to trust the process—to welcome whatever happened to me as though I'd prayed for it.

My needs were filled—not in ways I could have planned or controlled (as was my wont), but in totally new and unexpected ways. Ways that enabled me to trust again.

Today, November 3, 1976, the sun is shining and I feel "in love with life"—which Ben says means I have been healed.

I recently completed my master's program with Goddard College in Religion and Pastoral Counseling. I have been given new work to do on the psychiatric unit of a Santa Barbara hospital. I lead a creative writing group there which is extremely rewarding. I have been asked to produce a video documentary film for the unit, and feel privileged to be a healing presence for those who are going through shattering experiences similar to mine.

I'm returning to the world of old enthusiasms, such gardening, theatre, music! Last summer was spent in Japan and so many new possibilities for relatedness opened to me that I am studying Japanese to broaden my horizons.

From time to time the old patterns ensnare me; ambition to force changes rears its head—old fears grab me again. But now—I greet these difficulties. I am aware of their presence, that they are temporary and the anxiety they bring in their wake will subside. I wrote a poem on the unit the other day. It seems a fitting way to end this narrative—

> "In the midst of darkness
> Light persists."
> Mr. Gandhi said—
> I'm beginning to
> See that pinpoint
> Of light after
> Some time in darkness—
>
> And it all comes clear—
> I don't have to be a sun
>   or a moon
>   or a planet
> Not even a star—
> Not even a flashlight!
>
> Just can be—
> That's enough
> And being—perhaps
> I can shine enough
>
> To light my own way
> And perhaps—
> For a moment—
> Yours

FOOTNOTES

---

[78] A pseudonym for Gene's husband Hallock Hoffman. Unfortunately, neither Gene nor Hallock could recall the name of the hospital or of the therapist referred to a s "Dr. Forrester."

[79] Ben Weininger, her psychiatist/guru, see p. 22.

[80] Krishnamurti (1895-1986) was "discovered" by Theosophists who saw him as a "World Teacher," but he dissociated himself from all organized religions and philosophies, and sought to raise awareness by talking to people not as a guru but as a friend (see http://www.jkrishnamurti.org.) Maharishi Yogi was a popular guru of the 1960s best known for "Transcendental Meditation" and his appeal to celebrities such as the British rock group, the Beatles.

[81] A progressive radio station associated with Pacifica Radio. Pacifica was the one of the first listener-supported stations in the US. It was founded in Berkeley, California, in 1949 by Lewis Hill, a conscientious objector and Washington, DC, newsman who was fired from a mainstream radio station for refusing to misrepresent the facts. Another founder of Pacifica Radio was Robert Schutz, a Quaker who edited *Friends Bulletin* in the 1980s.

[82] B.F. Skinner was one of the founders of behaviorist psychology, which holds that all behavior can be explained in terms of stimulus and response to pleasure or pain. For a brief description of Humanistic Psychology, see p. 98.

[83] A Spanish expression used to refer to those of Mexican background or, in this case, Cesar Chavez's movement to organize farmworkers in the Central Valley of California in the 1960s and 1970s.

[84] Julian Silverman was a psychologist, educator, and research psycho-physiologist in the areas of consciousness, psychedelics and schizophrenia. Carl Rogers (1902–1987) is best known for his views about the therapeutic relationship. These views revolutionized the course of therapy. He took the radical view that "the client knows what hurts, what directions to go, what problems are crucial, what experiences have been buried" (Rogers, 1961, pp. 11-12). R.D. Laing, author of the *Divided Self* and *Politics of Experience*, was a controversial figure whose approach has been dismissed by most psychologists, but was widely accepted by psychiatric patients. He believed that the therapist should, like a shaman, enter into the mental state of patients, exorcising illness through mutual catharsis. John Perry was a Jungian psychologist whose most famous work is *Trials of the Visionary Mind.*

[85] Sidney Jourard (1926-1974), humanistic psychologist best known for his classic work, *The Transparent Self,* first published in 1964 and completely revised in 1971.

[86] Martin Buber (1879-1965), Jewish theologian/philosopher, published his seminal work *I and Thou* in 1923. In this book he argues that we often objectify people, relating to them as we do to things ("I-it" or "I-them"). He notes that it is possible to be truly open and vulnerable to another human being (or to God) when we entered into a relationship based on "I" and "Thou." This connection enlarges a person and makes true dialogue possible.

Our Children Are
Guests in Our Lives

The Church Woman, February/March 1978

In his book *Reaching Out*, Henri Nouwen wrote: "Our children are our most important guests. [They] enter into our home, ask for careful attention, stay for a while, and then leave to follow their own way. Guests," he reminds us, "are carrying precious gifts with them which they are eager to reveal to a receptive host."

I have borne seven children—five sons and two daughters. Only now, 34 years after the birth of my first child, am I beginning to be able to treat them as guests, give them the careful attention they deserve, recognize their gifts, and let them go.

Why wasn't I able to do this before?

Ignorance.

I'd like to describe some of the ideas and events that kept me ignorant. Then I'd like to share with you some of the gifts my children have given me. Finally, what it means to me to let them go.

To begin: I was a sheltered, privileged, "only" child who was educated for a career in the theater and as a writer. My life was absorbing and self-centered. I lived in a half mystical, half fantasy world. Part of my fantasy was that I could *be* a mother to anyone, let alone to seven children.

I welcomed each child with joy. And there was much to be joyous about! They were exquisite babies with perfect tiny hands and feet, tender, fragrant bodies to be caressed; tiny persons to wonder over, to delight in. "You come, little son," I wrote of my fifth child, Kristian, "to teach us of ourselves and of the Eternal One who sent thee. . . ." And I was right.

But it wasn't enough.

I knew these wondrous things about them.

But I didn't know they were real.

And I didn't know my husband was real.

And I didn't know my life was real.

So I felt my children would be with me forever, were mine to create, to mold. And I was very busy, trying to create and mold them, busy trying to maintain a relationship with my husband, busy saving the world in one way or another.

All these "important" details so absorbed me I didn't pay attention. Their childhoods slipped by partially noticed.

I had lived so much of my early life alone that I didn't know how to be with anyone—so, of course, not with my children. I was superb doing *for* them. I could create fantastic playrooms out of boxes and crates. But I never played in them. I made remarkable schedules of chores, careful to recognize abilities and interests, but I never worked with them. They felt used and unappreciated.

Another crucial thing I didn't know about was pain in life, that pain is not only acceptable, it's as necessary to our growth as water to a plant, and should be welcomed and lived through. *House Beautiful* didn't mention pain, nor did my parents—my right was to life, liberty, and the pursuit of happiness. Pain? What had that to do with me?

So when pain came—and lots came (my husband couldn't respond to all those children, or to me, so he disappeared emotionally a few years after our marriage, and physically 25 years after it; he needed a very active professional life and the home life of a recluse)—I thought there was something terribly wrong with me. To correct that wrong, I tried to "work it through" with therapy, reading, talking; or escaping through work, or being sick, or going crazy. I was willing to do anything but face the reality of a marriage that wasn't right for either of us and living out the reality of being a single parent.

Now one of the great things I learned is: we get a second chance. Some people call it karma and think of it as punishment for making mistakes. I see it differently. I see getting another go-round (and another and another) as a gift. I'm making a lot better use of my second chance with my children than I did with the first.

Sometime after my husband left (eight years ago), I realized my task was to get in touch with each of my lost seven and try to compensate for the deprivations they had suffered.

But where were they? My babies with the wide, wondering eyes and the tenderly curling hair? My red-gold-haired daughter with almond blue eyes? My youngest, the small sun shining?

I found one lost in the jungle world of drugs and sex, then prison. I found another in Haight-Ashbury, living the street life from a van. Another would not return to visit me except for an hour or two a couple of times each year, seeking in stony places the love she missed. Another anguished over the dawning recognition of his homosexuality, and no place to go, no one to talk with ... Another was trying to make it in the world of rock music, singing himself hoarse in smoke-filled nightclubs. Another lived in her room, 100 pounds overweight, thinking herself ugly, eating herself ugly. My youngest, only 14, lost in the world of motorcycles and anger and loneliness—such loneliness ...

But—

At this same time, one was making music, such music! Ballads and songs of wished-for love. Another was making films, important statements about life, and weaving tapestries that could grace a cloister wall. Another was painting and creating his inner world in silk-screen for all to see; another became a conscientious objector and served his time without complaint, working in a convalescent home for the elderly, and as janitor in a YMCA. Another was illustrating children's books with such vision, and anger, and beauty, I wept to see it all. Another wrote journals and poems, sonnets to stars and mud and to the promptings of her spirit, and made music. Such music! While my youngest moved slowly toward a life in harmony with music and the earth and contemplation.

All these gifts they brought me, heart-offerings. All these riches they brought to me, sometimes in violent anger, sometimes in tears, sometimes in defiant indifference, sometimes in withdrawal, sometimes in warmth and openhearted grace.

And I began to pay attention, to live in the wonder of each moment, and I began to see the gifts my children brought to me.

One son and I were united; the pain I sought to exorcise through therapy and books, he sought to exorcise through sex and drugs. We were not "different"! We both could grow!

My almond-eyed daughter gave me confrontation, at last the courage of confrontation, then, tender, the beginnings of reconciliation. She showed me how I sought unneeded, but momentarily comforting "love" in stony places. Through my homosexual son I learned that each of us is born to learn to love, and he was chosen to learn this way. My conscientious objector son taught me that creativity is not the goal, but living is, living with integrity and simplicity, in touch with the work of one's hands. My fame-struck son taught me that sometimes we must go away, far, far away to come home again to our own truths, and we must trust the wanderer in ourselves and others. My daughter of the sonnets and the mandolin taught me of the hidden jewel in each of our consciousness, and the pushing toward our own wholeness, even though the route may seem devious. My youngest taught me of the slow rhythmic cycles of growth and the long patience needed to bring the flower to fruit.

These gifts, and many more, my seven beloved guests have brought me. Gifts of understanding, growth, learning, joy and faith.

And now I begin to feel their love—not infant swaddling love, but their caring by being Who They Are with me. Daring to speak thoughts to me. Daring to differ. Daring to respond. Treating me as a mature person, worthy of their wisdom and my own.

Yes, each came home, asked for my careful attention and received it; even brought an inimitable gift; each stayed for a while and now each is leaving to follow his or her own way.

And now I can let them go, for I see each has begun to forgive me.

And how do I know I am forgiven? Well, as in the old Hasidic story, I know I am forgiven my sins when I no longer need to commit them.

Photographs

Above: Left, Gene with her mother Valley. Right, Gene at six months.

Below: Gene at age twenty (1939). Right, Gene with her baby Nikolas.

Gene in various roles and
guises as an actress.

Top: Gene playing the role the ideal mother.

Below left: Clockwise from top: Kristian, Nick, Valley, Gene, Kaj, Paul, Nina, and Erik. (Ca. 1958)
Below right: Clockwise fromtop: Kristian, Valley, Gene, Kaj, Nina, and Erik. Photo by editor, 2003.

Left–right: Karen Dugas (niece), Marie Christiansen (Gene's adopted sister), Paul Hoffman (son), Valley Hoffman (daughter), Valley Mary Knudsen (mother), Thorkild Rostgaard Knudsen (father), Hallock Hoffman (husband), Gene, Neil Christiansen (nephew).
Bottom row: Kristian Hoffman (son), Nina Kiriki Hoffman (daughter), Jason Christensen (grand-nephew), Kaj Hoffman (son).

Beginning at top, left to right: Kristian, Hallock, Niki.
2nd row, Kaj, Gene, Valley.
3rd row: Nina Kiriki, Paul, Erik.

All Possible Surprises
GENE KNUDSEN-HOFFMAN

All Possible Surprises is not just a collection of poems, but a chronicle of a woman's education. Using her spare, reverent, melodic style, Gene Knudsen-Hoffman offers us lessons from a wide variety of experiences —the complex relationships of motherhood and marriage, the raw intensity of love and hate, the baffling simplicity of a seed—all these are explored and celebrated within these pages. This book urges us to learn and dares us to remember.

From Inside The Glass Doors

Gene K. Hoffman

Cover of Gene's autobiographical books

Below: Photo of Gene in the 1970s

172

Top right: Gene Hoffman with Yasser Arafat during a meeting sponsored by the American Friends Service Committee (see "After the Peace Accords—What?" p. 296).

Below: Gene's father Tom Knudsen, at the airport with Pat and Richard Nixon, whom the family supported politically and regarded as "the son they never had" (see "Reflections on Meeting with Richard Nixon," p. 191).

Above: "Welfare Mothers" demonstration in Santa Barbara during the 1970s. Gene is standing next to Mary Selleck, an activist/artist who was imprisoned for her convictions.
Below: Gene Hoffman with Leah Green, founder of The Compassionate Listening Project (see pp. 317–325). Photo courtesy of Linda Wolf.

Part IV:
Peace-making
From the Inside Out

"Gene is a Quaker mystic. Her calling was to carry pastoral counseling out of the pastor's study into public life."

—Dennis Rivers, a communication skills instructor
from Santa Barbara, California

As Gene sought to integrate her spiritual and psychological practices with her peace activism, she came to believe that the traditional methods of peacemakers were not working. Rallies, conferences, and confrontation ("speaking truth to power") did not address the underlying causes of violence. Nor did peace activists confront the subtle (and sometimes not so subtle) internalized violence caused by unresolved psychological conflicts.

Because of these conflicts, peace activists were often unable to influence those most in need of their message. She diagnosed the problem by saying "we were trying to heal ourselves from the outside....We didn't understand that inner healing had to take place first."

The essays in this section range from inspirational talks to a scholarly article written for the Journal of Humanistic Psychology.[87] *In these articles, she reaches out to an extraordinary range of people, even Richard Nixon, who tells her in an interview that "war is evil...If five percent of the expense of world armaments could be cut, we could end world hunger." Her most moving pieces are those concerned with meeting the* hibakusha *(victims of the nuclear blast at Hiroshima and Nagasaki) and her encounters with Vietnam veterans at a retreat led by Thich Nhat Hanh, the Vietnamese Buddhist peace activist. This article about healing the wounds of war ends with the prophetic words: "It was then I realized that I was in the underground peace movement, the movement of transformation. We were quietly transforming our lives and could practice war no more."*

FOOTNOTES

[87] See p. 182.

A Peace Pilgrim's Progress to Inner Healing[88]

Awakening, February 1990

During my lifetime I've worked with many peace people and peace groups. Rarely were the people I worked with peaceful. Perhaps I was the least.

In the peace movement I found wondrous people, people who sacrificed themselves, who often turned the other cheek, who could write eloquently of compassion, forgiveness, love of the enemy. I found those who hungered for righteousness and were on their way to it.

I found, too, that the seeds of all society's ills were also in us, often hidden or disguised. Few of us recognized or admitted this to ourselves. We felt exempt. But the anger, the anxieties, the jealousies were still in place, camouflaged. Peace people, I found, weren't all that different from non-peace people except that we had found a humane goal to work toward.

Like our counterparts in the military, we thought of ourselves as the righteous ones, while those "out there" were the ones to change. We wanted to touch their consciences, bring them with us into the light.

We didn't change anyone, except in rare cases where people were on the edge of being persuaded. Our ragged band of rebels was still that—a ragged band of rebels. We weren't meeting with the opposition; we weren't in dialogue with them or listening to them. We didn't have a notion of what their hopes or grievances were. We listened mostly to ourselves.

One day I saw that we felt the same as our opposition. We just used different methods. We still wanted to win; we still wanted to change others so they'd be like us. We still denied we had anything in common with the enemy; indeed, we often denied we had enemies.

We were trying to heal ourselves from the outside. We had great teachings and thought we could live them by reading and talking about them. We didn't understand that inner healing had to take place first. Recognizing this, I began to look for new routes to become inwardly nonviolent, non-judging, non-controlling. I sought ways to integrate what I knew in my head with my behavior.

I first looked to my Quaker meeting, where I cherished the pregnant silence, the sometimes eloquent ministry, and the monthly queries. I began to see that Quakers, as a body, rarely expressed a need for personal reform except in prophetic terms. We used most of our energies to "change the world." We didn't share the intimate details of our lives with the group, and so we cut ourselves off from feedback that we so desperately need.

I began years of psychotherapy, believing that if only I talked about my problems long enough, I would be able to solve them. This was an important step and I learned a great deal. One day, however, it dawned on me that talking things out was, as Joseph Havens wrote, "a pale reflection of the high adventure of actually taking the path."[89]

So I explored various groups. Each taught me something I needed to learn, although they were as unfinished as I was. One deep exploration was into Zen Buddhism. In the teachings of the Vietnamese Buddhist monk, Thich Nhat Hanh, I found "engaged Buddhism" which embraces social action. He wrote, "It is the individual who begins to effect change. But . . . to effect change, he or she must seek the kind of lifestyle that is free from destructiveness.

"Recovery happens always in relationship. The illness and the healing exist in relationship. It is our sick relationships which sicken the world—relationships to one another, to the earth, to possessions, to the self, to God. Healing of relationships helps heal the world."[90]

Zen became my focus. I pursued it at home and abroad, delighting in its literature, developing a solitary practice, and attending numerous workshops and retreats. Whenever I was in a group (or *sangha*) I did very well. I gained precious insights and wisdom. But where I lived, there was no *sangha*, and few with whom I could discuss the process and growth through Zen. I had some difficulty with its "Oriental" practices, for I learned I was a Western Quaker activist, heart and soul.

The discovery that I am the grandchild of alcoholics—as well as the dynamics in my family—led me to the indigenous American spiritual program known as "The Twelve Steps." I am in Al-Anon, the program for friends and relatives of alcoholics. The Twelve Steps encompass some of the best of Quakerism and Zen with its emphasis on original goodness, meditation, active listening, and the belief that each person has direct access to their "higher power"—whether that be in the form of the spirit, wisdom, life force, or God.

No one in a Twelve Step program may speak for any other, so whatever I write is my own perception of the program. Basic to the process are regular meetings, held once or more each week, where we share the fruits of our daily study, prayer or meditation, and the new behavior which grows from our experience. These meetings focus on positive aspects of our learning and we are discouraged from playing the role of victim.

I keep a journal to record new insights and ways of bringing them into being. I also record newly discovered flaws so I don't repeat them, as well as new ways of coping. During my crisis (even without a crisis) there are members to call for help. They never give advice; instead they seek to enable others to deal with the crisis in terms of the Steps.

The uniqueness for me of the Twelve Step program is that I no longer need to deal with a mass of undifferentiated distress. Instead, I proceed at my own pace, in small increments and in my own unique way. I might deal with my habit of blaming or a need to detach lovingly from one I love. Each difficulty is examined in relation to *my* behavior, not another person's. This strengthens my recognition that the only person I can change is myself. Today the goal is egoless service within the Twelve Step program. Tomorrow I hope it will mean service, anywhere.

In her stunning book *Everyday Zen*, Charlotte Joko Beck writes, "All of us feel we are separate from life; we feel we have a wall around us. The wall may not be very visible . . . but (it) is there. As long as we feel separate from life, we feel the . . . wall . . . That wall has been keeping us out of touch."[91]

I believe Interhelp[92] has the seeds to help break down this wall, through groups around the world using Despair and Empowerment models. [Buddhist psychologist/peace activist] Joanna Macy feels that when we transcend the isolated ego self, we perceive our true self-interest and our connection with others. In Interhelp we understand the survival skills of listening and reconciliation. What remains to be done is to create processes and forms for ongoing groups to help them move toward wholeness, using Interhelp philosophies.

Many of us have given up or lost our families of origin. We learn, through these small groups, that everyone can be a part of our family, and we can regain some of the security we have lost. I have come to call these pockets of mutual caring the underground peace movement, for none of these avenues can be pursued without our becoming clearer and more serene; without transforming our lives and being unable to practice war any more.

This small group movement is one of the most hopeful signs today, and I find it essential to my inward peace. It's happening wherever people are willing to share the truth of their lives, feel their feelings, and examine themselves for damaging behavior. It is wherever they make amends, take the risks of honest "carefronting," and accept one another as teachers.

Such groups are essential for peaceworkers. They appear to me to be sources of new revelations for our peacemaking, our life-making. And, their reward seems to be the peacemakers' desired fruit of nonviolence of heart and mind and hand.

FOOTNOTES

[88] The title alludes to John Bunyan's classic work, *Pilgrim's Progress*, as well as to Mildred Norman Ryder, another famous "Peace Pilgrim," who walked tens of thousands of miles for peace between 1953 and her death in 1981.

[89] Joseph Havens, author of *Yoga and the Fifth Relationship*. Wallingford, Pa.: Pendle Hill Pamphlets, 1951

[90] Thich Naht Hanh, *Being Peace*, Parallax Press, 1988.

[91] Charlotte Joko Beck. *Everyday Zen*. Harper and Row Perennial Library, 1989.

[92] Interhelp is a Buddhist peace organization associated with Thich Nhat Hanh.

No Conflict,
No Reconciliation

Journal of Humanistic Psychology,
Vol. 29 No. 3, Summer 1989

The fields for reconciliation are vast. Few of them are seeded. Reconciliation seems always something we are going to get to—tomorrow. I see conflict as the hidden wound of today. Wherever I have worked, wherever I have lived, there has been this secret sore, unacknowledged, draining our energies.

Personal conflict means people see things differently and both people feel they are right. Other times people are in different predicaments and have opposing needs. There is no single cause of conflict, but it usually results in anger. I think anger is a message that something is threatening us and we feel helpless. Conflict is not the threat, although how we handle it can be. It can be either energizing or debilitating. Conflict can be a significant teacher. Through it we may come to reconciliation. Reconciliation is the bringing together of that which has been sundered, set apart. How might we resolve conflict? How do we bring separated people together again? Here are some ways:

First we need to understand that there is often a deep fear of exposing differences and admitting conflict. The admission of differences and conflict in a relationship often shakes our comfortable assumptions. How often do we stay with the hurtful familiar instead of daring the unfamiliar? A common response to feeling hurt, rejected, or ignored is to continue in an uncomfortable denial, doggedly proceeding without resolution, smothering feelings, seeking to make things right by being nice. Often we peace people are so disturbed at being angry that we refuse to acknowledge conflict and try to appease. It does not work.

Sometimes we try to reduce the anxiety by quick forgiveness, thinking it's necessary to forgive and forget as rapidly as possible. This does not work either, for we deny the unresolved issues. They remain and continue to poison the relationship.

Sometimes we try confrontation, which is a healthy move. But if we do not take into account the condition of our opponent, if we do not understand his/her fears and anxieties, if we do not speak carefully to his/her condition—reconciliation does not take place. Our opponents can easily feel their share of truth is rejected, and the conflict persists.

When I have these first intimations of differences, discontent, or resentment, I need to honor them. I must not discard them as mean, petty, or shameful. I feel these are messages telling me something is wrong and I must look at it. I believe my first responsibility is to seek to change myself, to deepen my understanding, to examine my motives. Sometimes a shift in my perception can accomplish the healing.

If this is not enough, then I must take it to the person with whom I am in conflict and seek to settle it by "care-fronting," telling the other person what is going on in me as carefully as I can. If this doesn't resolve the difficulties and the anger continues, it is time to ask someone to mediate the differences. An outside person who cares for both of us and does not take sides enables me to be more responsible for what I say. Both of us can try to talk without inflicting hurt upon one another. Using a mediator enables us to look at unpleasant, possibly unwelcome, perceptions without feeling the compulsion to act on them. The mediator's presence can enable each to listen with less fear blocking the communication.

If the conflict cannot be resolved by these means, the next step could be to have the mediator meet separately with the conflicting parties, interpreting each to the other. Thich Nhat Hanh, the Vietnamese Zen master and peacemaker, has suggested this process:

Reconciliation is to understand both sides, to go to one side and describe the suffering being endured by the other side; then to go to the other side and describe the suffering endured by the first side.

Of course the desirable outcome is to have both people acknowledge their differences, come to a new resolution of them, and emerge more loving than before. If this does not happen, they probably must separate and work individually to forgive and understand the other and themselves.

I believe the time is here when peacemakers need to focus on reconciliation. We are surrounded by conflicts in our lives and in the world. I find many of our efforts to resolve them are adversarial, which simply means they set a person or a group against another person or another group.

I have been looking at Central America. It seems to me that most of our peace actions there have been against US policy and against the Contras [violent opponents of Sandinista government in Nicaragua]. I wonder if we could have done something besides oppose. (Peace Brigades and Witness for Peace did much to stand with the Nicaraguans and Guatemalans in their suffering and guide people to safe places.) Perhaps focusing on building the new society in the United States instead of attacking the old might have begun a transformation. Perhaps we need to be the changes we want to see in others (Nhat Hanh, 1988). This is much harder than asking others to change, but it might reduce the fear that often leads peacemakers "to attack the forces of death directly and to underestimate their power ... Then the same fear that leads the war makers to war starts to affect the peacemakers; the strategy of war and the strategy of peace become the same and peacemaking has lost its heart" (Henri Nouwen, 1982).

Here I want to share with you some of the thoughts of Adam Curle (1981), British Quaker and long-time mediator in Third World countries, from his stunning booklet called *True Justice*.

He drew inspiration from this biblical quotation: "True justice is the harvest reaped by peacemakers from seeds sown in the spirit of peace" (James 3:18). I find it inspiring, too.

"I begin," he writes, "with a concept of human nature based on the belief that there is within each of us a divine element ... and this God within is ever available, awaiting our call to help us restore the harmony ... Our access to this deep mind [of God] is blocked by the rubble of prejudices, fears, memories of hurt, confusion, humiliation, likes and dislikes. And above all, by misinformation about [the Divine presence]."

Adam Curle sees three present obstacles to peace that are our various stages of development. One is the quiescent stage where the oppressed are unaware. Next is the revolutionary stage where people are aware of their oppression and want to throw it off. Last is the conflict of equals—conflicts between neighbors, businessmen, and nations. "Today," he says, "we are in the stage of revolutions."

How do we approach these conflicts?

Believing that reconciliation is the only true basis for peace, Adam Curle recommends that we act "from awareness of the good in others [so] we will promote the expression of the good." This, of course, springs from remembering the divinity that exists within each human being. In the mediation sessions we must practice "the absolute necessity: attentive listening." We must be "inwardly still and as receptive as possible [so we can] hear exactly what is said."

If we listen in this way, "we not only 'hear' the other person, but we communicate with him or her through our true nature." And "we must remember that this true 'nature' exists in members of the other side, those we oppose." As Paolo Freire [Brazilian educator concerned with raising consciousness among the oppressed] wrote of unjust people: "they, too, are maimed by what they are doing. They, too, must be rescued."

The primary purpose of the peacemaker is to liberate the victim and to free the oppressors from the degradation in which they are trapped as well. "Peacemakers [need to] affirm that they are on the side of all who are caught in the trap of war, whether as civilians, soldiers, or political leaders. The only enemy a peacemaker may know is the belief that human problems can be solved through violence."

Here I shall leave Adam Curle and consider protest and resistance versus reconciliation. I believe protest and resistance are important. They are not reconciliation. They can be preludes to it. Protest is a way of announcing that an injustice is being committed. Protest says "Look! Help! This must change." It can be an act of courage that stands bravely against the violence of unjust deeds. Resistance, like protest, is a way of saying "no." It is a call to awareness; it can be a first step toward nonviolent action. All through history, saying no to an unjust power has been an act of supreme courage. Many have died for it. Both of these may open ways to reconciliation.

The question before us is: "Do we soften the heart of our opposition by protest and resistance?" My response is: rarely. Softening the heart of our adversary seems to require other actions. I believe that to soften the hearts of those opposed to us, we must approach them with loving concern and an effort to see things from their point of view. In this way we may, perhaps, invite the healing presence within them into the world. Of course we may fail, but Gandhi taught us that it is not ours to determine the fruits of our actions. It is ours to trust that we may have planted some seeds on fertile ground, but we do not know when, if ever, they will be harvested. "No matter how small a thing you do," Gandhi reminds us, "it is very important that you do it."

Many of us have dealt with hard hearts—often our own. Many of us have despaired of ever changing them. Here I want to share the attitude of John Woolman, the Quaker abolitionist who lived in the 18th century. As Daisy Newman said, "Unlike his predecessors in the anti-slavery movement, Woolman did not condemn the slave-holders. He spoke to his hosts out of such tenderness and deep humility that they could take no offense, for it was clear that he sympathized as much with them as with the slaves."

Now, for a last thought. There is a Buddhist saying, "If you feel anger and aggression against someone, give that person a gift." What kinds of gifts might we bring to the Contras or [controversial retired Marine Lt. Col.]Oliver North [who helped the Contras during the Reagan administration]? Is there some kind of service we might perform that would acknowledge our connections instead of our separation? Is there something we could do that would show them the humanity we wish they would show others? Understanding? Respect for their divine potential? Inviting their concern for others because we express our concern for them? Listening? Perhaps these are gifts we can give—even to those whose actions we oppose.

To feel connected, encouraged, of value, with meaning— these are gifts we can give one another. They can help restore our sanity and hope. This is the substance of reconciliation.

None of this will come to pass if we do not put reconciliation into practice, moment by moment, day by day. If we choose to be reconcilers, then we must choose to study and practice this work. And then we might be given the gift of transformation we are longing for.

This is a revised version of an article published in the May 1988 issue of Friends Bulletin. *Reprinted with permission.*

REFERENCES

Arnett, IL C. (1980). *Dwell in peace.* Elgin, IL: Brethren Press.

Curle, A. (1981). *True justice.* London: Invicta Press.

Gandhi, M. (1964). *Gandhi on nonviolence.* New York: New Directions.

Knudsen Hoffman, G. (1983). *Loving the stranger.* New York: Fellowship.

Knudsen Hoffman; G. (1988a). *Spiritual base communities in the USA.* Madison, WI: Interhelp.

Knudsen Hoffman, G. (1988b). *Ways out, The book of changes for peace.* Santa Barbara, CA: John Daniel & Co.

Nhat Hanh, T. (1987, Winter) Techniques of reconciliation. *Buddhist Peace Fellowship Newsletter.*

Nhat Hanh, T. (1988). *Being peace.* Berkeley: Parallax Press.

Nouwen, H. (1982). "The spirituality of peacemaking." *Fellowship Magazine.* Nyack, NY.

A New Approach to Peace Speaking Truth to Power

Friends Journal, October 1, 1981

"Speak truth to power" became a resounding call among us Quakers in the '50s. It brought with it a sense of vast possibilities. It is still a significant call and demands courage and presence in its practice—but it's only half the equation.

Recently I've been thinking about and experiencing the other half: "Listen to power to discover the truth it speaks."

Within the past year I have made two pilgrimages. One was around the world, visiting peace centers and peace people in troubled areas. The other was across our nation, for the Fellowship of Reconciliation, to speak of what I had learned. I carried with me a talisman from Thomas Merton: "We have to have a deep, patient compassion for the fears and the irrational mania of those who hate."

On both journeys I met with people who feared, people who I thought had irrational responses to dangers today, people who expressed what felt like hatred—and they were people of power.

One example must stand for all. This experience took place at a Jewish temple where the majority were political Zionists. I described the peace movement in Israel and the conditions among the Palestinians which had created it. After my address I was met with abuse, excoriation, threats, certainly fear, and naked hatred. (There was also courageous support.)

I had never met with political Zionists before, and all my reading had not prepared me for the fear and grief that had sealed some of their minds against knowledge of realities between the Israelis and the Palestinians. I had not listened long nor deeply enough.

This contact has led to a meaningful correspondence with the rabbi of the temple. I feel we meet as human beings across the wide spaces in thought, philosophy, and belief between us. Way is open for us to continue to explore each other's approaches to life.

My experiences have persuaded me that some of us must begin thoughtful acts of listening to people in power *with no thought of trying to speak our truths.* And I believe we must meet them on their home ground.

There are so many we can meet with. We can meet with the pro-nuclear people, with those who live down our street. We must get out of our safe forums and our seminars and sit down face-to-face with our opposition—with those who manufacture Trident submarines, with people from Westinghouse and G.E., with military people—with whomever God sends our way. This is how we will know there are *people* on the other side of these terrible questions, and so will they.

Then we must listen. We must listen and listen and listen. We must listen for the Truth in our opponent, and we must acknowledge it. After we have listened long enough, openly enough, and with the desire to really hear, we may be given the opportunity to speak our truth. We may even have the opportunity to be heard.

For no one and no one side is the sole repository of Truth. But each of us has a spark of it within. Perhaps, with compassion as our guide, that spark in each of us can become a glow, and then perhaps a light, and we will watch one another in awe as we become illuminated. And then, perhaps, this spark, this glow, this light will become the enlightening energy of love that will save all of us.

Reflections on Meeting with Richard Nixon

Friends Journal, November 1, 1986

It's long been my opinion that we who work for peace should listen carefully and respectfully to those we consider our opponents. I have had a unique opportunity to do just that. Through events too complicated to describe in this brief article, I was appointed a member of Richard Nixon's International Foreign Policy Roundtable in April 1985. My first meeting with him was a private briefing in New York in December 1985 (the original meeting had been canceled). The second was with the entire roundtable in California in March 1986.

I want to share the highlights of these meetings, and I have focused on areas of agreement, some of them surprising.

On December 17, 1985, a black limousine picked me up at my hotel at 9:45 a.m. John, the very friendly driver, snaked his way through dense New York traffic, and we arrived at Federal Plaza in the financial district precisely on time.

I was surprised how at home I felt upon entering the outer office. It could have been the home of any peace center across the nation. On the walls were huge posters of many lands visited by the Nixons. Three people were at desks, busily typing. Strewn about were cardboard boxes of incoming or outgoing materials, a variety of Christmas decorations, and a welcoming young woman named Dolores, who asked me to wait a few moments.

The few moments passed and I was taken into a spacious office with wide windows and a huge desk. Presidential mementos and family pictures were scattered around. Two comfortable black leather chairs faced each other. I sat in one of them and waited.

The former president entered. He sat down easily opposite me and asked if I cared for coffee. It was promptly brought to me.

Richard Nixon looked amazingly fit—grayer, of course, than when I had met him in 1959 at the White House on Pat Nixon's 47th birthday. The conversation opened with warm reminiscences about that occasion; about my father, who had contributed to all his campaign funds; and about my mother, who had chaired his campaign for governor of California and had been a deeply involved leader in all his campaigns. We spoke of the high regard in which my parents held him and how I had been present when my father had given the Nixon Chair of Political Science to Whittier College [in Whittier, Caifornia].

We talked about my work as creator of the US-USSR Reconciliation program for the Fellowship of Reconciliation (FOR), and how I had become a Quaker. We spoke too of my first Meeting, Orange Grove in Pasadena, of his affiliation with the East Whittier Friends Church, and of friends we had in common.

I then said I'd brought questions; could I ask them? He agreed I could. Here are some of my questions and his responses:

Gene: How can we of the FOR cooperate with President Reagan's cultural initiatives with the Soviet Union?

Nixon: Commend him for his new stance. Take note that exchanges with the Soviet Union have been sharply curtailed. Last year we had 15,000 students from China, and only 100 from the Soviet Union. This was not only the fault of Americans; the Soviets are very particular whom they permit to visit us.

Recommend that he suggest to the Soviets that they broaden the age range of people who come here to include college and high school students.

Gene: How can we promote change in our relations with Eastern Europe?

Nixon: You must have contact, not lack of it. We must have peaceful change. The military option is out. Nuclear weapons have made the use of force obsolete. We must seek peace without victory.

Gene: How did the remarkable breakthrough with China come about? What can we do to create a similar one with the USSR?

Nixon (*with a wry smile*): Exchange 15,000 students! (*then more seriously*) It took a long time. Preparations began in 1969. That's when I wrote my first memorandum to Henry Kissinger that a new relationship must begin with the People's Republic of China. We cannot afford to have over one billion people living in angry isolation. We began moving on four fronts—economic, sports, cultural contact, and travel.

Gene: What do you think might be done about terrorists? It is they who might easily spark World War III.

Nixon: We must be more honest about it. We are against terrorism only when terrorists are against the things we like.

Gene: I feel people become terrorists when they feel they aren't heard, will never be heard, and their grievances will not be addressed.

Nixon: I agree. But the real problem is that there must be a whole change. In World War I, 15 million people were killed. In World War II, 55 million people died. That is when we began bombing civilians—the fire-bombings of Dresden and Tokyo. Since then, anything goes that will break the morale of people. War is evil. The idea of unconditional surrender, which we insisted on in 1945, was totally wrong, catastrophic.

Gene: Do you believe it is necessary for the superpowers to cooperate to prevent smaller countries from using their nuclear weapons? How?

Nixon: Absolutely! It is to our common interest to have nuclear nonproliferation.

Gene: How do you think that will affect other nations that have nuclear weapons, like Israel and India?

Nixon: We must keep local conflicts from escalating. Some 900 billion dollars are spent on arms each year. One half of that sum comes from the United States and the Soviet Union. It is ridiculous for India and Pakistan to be armed against each other. Duane Andreas has written that if five percent of the expense of world armaments could be cut, we could end world hunger.

My next meeting was with the entire roundtable at Nixon's former home, Casa Pacifica, in San Clemente [California]. It was an exquisite affair. The house is beautiful, low, and Spanish, faithfully copied from its original in San Sebastian, Spain.

Before dinner, Richard Nixon gave us the briefing. In reporting on it, I shall focus only on areas of new information, agreement, or just new opinions. Questions came from the group. The briefing was held in the loggia overlooking the pool. Richard Nixon stood in front of the fireplace while we all sat comfortably facing him. He first spoke about China.

Nixon: There's been a profound change in China, in their agriculture. The Chinese can now feed one billion people and export food as well. The business section is, alas, full of corruption and inflation. The Chinese are open and honest. They urge people to "tell us how we can improve."

Q. Could you describe [Mikhail] Gorbachev [former leader of the Communist party in the former USSR who initiated sweeping reforms and was deposed after several years]?

Nixon: Zia of Pakistan says Gorbachev is a thoroughbred Communist. He is vigorous, intelligent, will live through five presidential terms, is dedicated and tough minded. He is moving toward the Chinese; that's why we have a stake in Chinese efforts.

Q. Does Reagan have the right chemistry to work with Gorbachev?

Nixon: That's not the question; the question is: do Gorbachev and Reagan respect each other? We are adversaries; we must have respect. Without respect we're not going to avoid the miscalculations which will lead to war.

Q. What about our going along with Gorbachev's proposed [nuclear] test ban?

Nixon: The test ban is a volatile issue. The Soviets went on a crash testing program. Now we feel that we need one, [to test our weapons] for accuracy.

Q. What do you think of their offer to get out of Afghanistan?

Nixon: Getting out of Afghanistan is a public ploy. The Soviets are concerned about the preponderance of Moslems in the Soviet Union. They can overtake the revolution. That is the Soviets' fear.

Q. What about the Philippines?

Nixon: That's a hard-to-govern country. There is immense corruption. [Maria Corazon]Aquino [who won the election against Ferdinand Marcos and became first woman president of the Philippines after a popular uprising] must move on several fronts. [Fidel] Ramos is honest, clean, a professional. He will deal with insurgency. But Aquino must not turn to a bigger government. She must break up state monopolies and turn to private enterprise. We must aid Aquino economically and militarily; we must not give a blank check. We must give aid but, for her own good, with strings (attached). She must be led into right economic policies.

The Catholic Church must be credited for the bloodless coup, as well as the militarists who defected. [Ferdinand] Marcos played a critical part as well. He called an election, invited inspectors to come and observe them. They swarmed in and he didn't repress them or the Catholic Church. He did not use force. We can't intervene without leverage; we don't have leverage now. Now we must let the Philippine people handle their country.

The next part of the briefing was hit or miss and covered a wide range of subjects. Nixon maintained that Nicaragua was a "Soviet client state, and Central America is nothing but an incident on the road to Mexico. Mexico needs a peaceful revolution. The Middle East offers the greatest danger to US-Soviet confrontations, and no nation or individual at the present time is strong enough to make peace. Enemies grow stronger as time goes on." He reiterated that the Moslems are growing in the Soviet Union and the Moslem revolution competes with the Communist revolution and that it is a rebellion against Western culture.

Q. What about the United States?
Nixon: We must get American diplomacy out of the "high posture." We must play a subdued role. America has too many missions; we must practice quiet, tough, economic, diplomacy.
Q. What are you for?
Nixon: I'm for increased contact, increased trade with everyone.
Q. What about the next summit?
Nixon: Summitry reduces miscalculation. There is a possibility of nuclear war when our interests collide. Terrorism is the number one danger. [Libyan President] Qaddafi could get the atom bomb; all small nations can build them now. We must do something about terrorism.

Nixon then made his final statement. He was fervent about it. "In my view," he said, "a signed test ban should be supported by the administration. We don't need affection between leaders. The important thing to have is respect. It is important never to press the president to reaction. The cause is real peace."

I was convinced by these two meetings that it is more important than ever to listen to those we consider to be our adversaries. Reconciliation, it seems to me, is bringing together those who have been set apart. I found wisdom in much of what Richard Nixon said. There was much I disagreed with— and more I did not understand—but there were areas to build upon, corners where small trusts might be established. This, I believe, is the attitude we should carry to all people.

Disarming the Heart

Friends Journal, November 15, 1982

Our life is love and peace and tenderness—and bearing one with another—praying for one another, and helping one another up with a tender hand.

So wrote Isaac Penington, Quaker, in the year 1667. Our life today seems far from that. On all sides there are cries of anguish. If we listen, we can hear them from El Salvador, from Calcutta, from Moscow, from Seattle, and from Santa Barbara.

All around the world children starve for food and hope, while we plead, "Choose life, so that you and your children will live." And all around the world, and in Philadelphia, we choose death—because we are afraid.

Fear which lingers, fear which lives on in us, fear which does not prompt us to *wise remedial action,* becomes engraved upon our hearts, becomes an addiction, becomes an armor which encases us. This fear guards and guides us and determines our actions. It leads us directly toward that which we fear. And it is fear which is leading us into the chambers of the nuclear holocaust.

How can we know the dreadful truths about our world and not fear? How can we know of the thousands of weapons poised to exterminate us and not fear? How can we listen to our leaders' threats and counter-threats and not fear? How can we know of the wars we have caused, are causing, and not fear?

I don't know how "we" can know. I know a little of how I can know, and I don't think I can live without fear. I haven't evolved to that place yet. But I have learned to handle my fear better, learned to stay with it to discern what message it has for me. I've also learned to use my fear to guide me into appropriate action, action grounded in some Truth which heals.

And I know something else. I know that the Presence—the mystery we call God—is bigger than our world and all its nuclear weapons. I also know that within each of us is an Informing Spirit which enables us to know, at each moment of our lives, in small and whispered ways, good from evil and to follow the good.

Another thing I know is that by following the promptings of this Spirit as each of us perceives it, we become empowered with a strength we did not know we had, and possibilities are realized we could not have even dreamed.

There are many examples from the lives of saints and sages: Saint Francis and the building of his church at San Damiano, his larger building of a group of people devoted to poverty and reverence for life. Mother Teresa and the homes for the dying which now dot the world. Jim Douglas and his companions at Trident submarine base, wearing away the rock of military pride with the waters of love.

Anywhere love takes root in the heart, we can find the talents and the energy to express it, and a little bit of God is released into the world—a little bit of transformation takes place.

I know there are many ways of manifesting this connection with God, with the Source—as many as there are human beings in the world. For I see that each of us is given unique talents to use in our life task which [Jewish philosopher] Martin Buber described as "bringing God and the world together."

Gandhi's perception of this Truth was described by the author Pyrelal:

> Even an infinitesimal of an individual, when (she or) he has realized the ideal of Ahimsa (harmlessness) ... becomes filled with its power, to which there is no limit and before which all opposition and hatred must cease.

Many of us think of ourselves as living in an end time, an Armageddon time, a holocaust time. All these may be true, and certainly become true if we choose them.

But I see it in another way. I see this "end time" as a time for ending old ways of being and acting. As a time for ending old fears that there's not enough to go around, a time for replacing competition with cooperation, a time for choosing simpler ways of living, a time for giving instead of getting, a time for keeping our hearts open to new truths which can lead us out of the nightmare reality.

I see this time as our opportunity to explore and experiment with this law of spiritual change in our own lives, beginning with little ways, infinitesimal ways, which will lead us to the larger, broader ones. Because I see Truth, God, is ever opening out to possibilities—new possibilities that are infinite in scope. There are infinite possibilities for us, for our nation, for our world.

And what has all this to do with disarming the heart?

I think it has to do with the faith and understanding and experiential living that will enable us to turn our fears into courage. To do this, our hearts must become disarmed and open to new understandings of mercy and compassion ... love. This love is not sentimental. It does not pretend that evil in events and persons does not exist. It offers a way to deal with them.

And it begins here, in our own lives. It is here we can seek to respond with compassion no matter how erratic the behavior of our friends and adversaries. It is here, in our own lives, we can stand by and seek to become healing presences. And it is here, in our own lives, we may begin to perceive the loneliness and fear in those who would resort to such vast violence in the misguided notion that through it they can save their children and themselves—for surely that is what they seek, too, and not the earth's extermination.

For underneath, like a crocus beneath the snow, we need to be aware that a quality of holiness undergirds all life. I tried to describe it in a poem. It's a variation on a theme by [British peace activist] Muriel Lester –

> *The job of the peacemaker is*
> *to know there is no enemy.*
> *What we fear are fear-masks*
> *worn by ourselves*
> *and the "other side."*
> *and behind each mask*
> *— the hooded Klansman*
> *— the complacent housewife*
> *— the marble-faced general*
> *— the weapons-maker*
> *— the rich who seek more riches*
> *— the smiling president*
> *is something trembling to be born,*
> *something pure in eclipse,*
> *some love waiting to be released*
> *a person —*
> *deserving reverence*
> *and faith. . . .*

Hope from Hiroshima

Fellowship, July/August 1982

Anne Morrow Lindbergh once wrote: "If suffering made one good, the whole world would be good." I read that many years ago and have wondered about it since. Why does suffering sometimes transform us, help us to grow in compassion, become inspirations to all around us? Why does it sometimes twist us, shrink us into unrecognizable creatures, devoid of compassion and inspiration? There seems to be an answer to this mystery in the words of some of the *hibakusha* [victims of the nuclear blast at Hiroshima and Nagasaki] and others whom I interviewed in Japan. Perhaps it is because of them that some call Hiroshima "the Nest of Peace."

* * *

Paul Sekiya is a Quaker, a gently balding, thoughtful man. He was fighting in China when the Bomb was dropped. He is not a *hibakusha,* but what he has to say relates to them.

"War is the enemy," said Paul, "How great an enemy is shown in Hiroshima. In the old days, war was fought between soldiers; now it is against civilians: women, the old, the children.

"There was never any official apology from the US for dropping the bomb and the government of Japan agreed it would never ask for one. The Japanese government took responsibility for the war.

"There is a religious basis for this," he continued. "As a Christian I see our *hibakusha* as an atonement for the whole nation. Many Japanese see the bombing of Hiroshima and Nagasaki as a baptism, even as we look upon the crucifixion of Jesus as a baptism: an experience of spiritual purification and renewal. Hiroshima is a metaphor for sacrificial suffering for our nation and the world."

It is important for us to understand what a Japanese person means by sacrificial suffering. Here are two examples:

There was a nuclear physics professor in Tokyo who was deeply concerned about the safety standards of nuclear power plants in Japan. He worked in every way to have them improved, but no one listened to him. So he killed himself, leaving a note that said he had failed in his responsibility to his students and his community. After his death, the changes he had called for were made.

The women who act as conductors on Japanese buses led a strike for better working conditions and higher pay; the strike failed. So seventeen of them, holding hands, walked into the volcanic crater of Mount Aso on behalf of all their fellow workers. After their deaths, the reforms they had sought were made.

This is the background from which Paul Sekiya dares to say that "Japan might be the Peace Center for the world."

* * *

Dr. Tomin Harada is one of the most influential men in Hiroshima. A Buddhist, his life is dedicated to preventing nuclear war. He, too, was a soldier in China during World War II. As he remarked, "I actually thought I could go to war and still do good and pursue truth. I learned differently. War experiences made me stronger in spirit, but the presence of so much death made me insensitive to evil."

Being in China when the bomb was dropped did not shield him from its effects; his sister was one of its casualties. Before she died, she returned to her home, calling his name. Her family

203

did not know who she was, she was burned so badly. Her last words were, "Don't you recognize me? I am your daughter."

Harada is a strange, mystical man. "The condition of the peoples of the world, and our need to help presses in on me," he said. "In the old days, the nobility took the treasure for themselves. Today our treasure is in instruments of death. The people revolted against the Emperor's storing up of gold and jewels. When will we revolt against the government's storing up of weapons?"

In 1950, Harada was brought to the United States as a student surgeon with the Hiroshima Maidens, *hibakusha* who were brought here for plastic surgery. Back in Hiroshima, he became the leading plastic surgeon for atomic bomb survivors. "There is no spirit of revenge among the *hibakusha*," he said. "They are a very humble people. They have the Buddhist stoicism and resignation in the face of suffering.

"The *hibakusha* saw hell. They knew it was too sad to be experienced by human beings. Their message to us is 'Let us not repeat the sin. Forgive me, you who were killed by the atomic bomb, for surviving. I will do my best to prevent another war. I won't let this happen to anyone on earth again. Use our bodies for peace.'"

* * *

Reverend Tanimoto is one of the persons John Hersey interviewed for his book, *Hiroshima*, in 1946. He is white-haired and vigorous, a remarkable man who became a Methodist minister even though his Buddhist father disowned him and erased his name from family records. At the time the bomb dropped, he was three kilometers from the hypocenter, standing in front of a rich man's house with a bridal gown for a friend. He saw a great flash—even in the brilliant morning sunshine—and was thrown to the ground. Somehow, the strength of the house protected him, even though the building was demolished. He climbed a nearby hillside and saw the city in smog and flames; destroyed, erased. There was no sound, no vibration.

Tanimoto dashed toward his church, where he encountered a long line of naked people, their hair gone, the skin peeling off their bodies. There was no expression on their faces; it was a procession of ghosts. Cries for help came from everywhere. As he tried to answer them, he wondered where his wife and baby were. Out of a desperate need to find them, he left the injured, feeling that they wondered how he, a minister of God, could leave them. He has never forgiven himself for abandoning those people in favor of his own family.

"The people in Hiroshima," said Reverend Tanimoto, "do not blame anyone else for their suffering . . . only themselves. I saw my race fighting against humanity, fighting in selfishness.

"The bomb burned hatred and greed out of us. Because of the total destruction, it crushed any hopes based on war. An evolution has taken place. The survivors have evolved. . . .

"I saw that war makes people crazy to fight. War itself prohibits making war. War is a crime."

Tanimoto suffered from radiation sickness, but he survived. Why, he does not know. The years since have been filled with working for the victims, working for peace, working for the poor, working for the suffering. "After Hiroshima," he said, "I found a burning spirit in my heart to overcome tremendous pain."

This spirit has led him to his new career, which is to help young people understand nuclear war so there will never be another.

* * *

Dr. Tomin Harada took me to the A-bomb hospital, built in 1957 and painted in shades of dark green and blue. Only survivors who were directly exposed to the explosion are cared for there. The average age of the patients is about seventy. Dr. Kuramoto, the head surgeon, a slender, sensitive man with crisp gray hair, was eager to answer all my questions. All funds for the care of *hibakusha* are donated, I learned; there is no government aid. In fact, the government would prefer not to acknowledge their existence.

To qualify for care, patients must carry a green card that identifies them as the true *hibakusha*. Every patient in the hospital suffers from a serious illness. Among the aftereffects of the bomb are diabetes, malignant tumors, cancer of the thyroid, brain damage. I asked Dr. Kuramoto how he felt about caring for terminal patients, ones he knew could never recover.

"It is very complicated," he said, "but I perform this service as an act of compassion. The aging survivors have so many troubles, but they do not complain. Their attitude makes it possible for me to continue my work."

* * *

Arthur Booth, a British sociologist, published some interesting findings in his study of A-bomb survivors. In most cases, the atomic bomb destroys our humanity. When the total environment is vaporized in one instant, it is almost humanly impossible for most people to respond in ways they would like to. But some people did not lose their humanity. These were people who believed that their own lives were less important than caring for others. Some were ministers, doctors and soldiers who had been trained for action after attack; some were teachers. These were people who had made prior choices to "be human," whose choices stayed with them through a terrible period when the entire fabric of their lives vanished.

* * *

Hiroko Takahara lives in Nagasaki. Like all other *hibakusha*, she carries the "green card" which identifies her as a victim of the atom bomb. Unlike other *hibakusha*, she is married, to Dr. Makoto Takahara, a cancer specialist and surgeon. Like other *hibakusha*, she goes to the Atomic Bomb Casualty Commission for regular checkups. She still has shards of glass embedded in her skin. The possibility of cancer is very real to her. Through her war experiences, she "learned that human life is very precious." Quietly, she told me how it was after the bomb was dropped.

Her family's home was repaired before others and became a shelter. Many survivors came for help. There was no medicine, only cooking oil to spread on the burns. It was Hiroko's task to remove maggots from the wounds. Nobody knew what kind of bomb it had been or how to deal with the effects. Her hair fell out; there were blood patches on her skin.

No answers were given to the victims because "our government did not want the people to know what kind of bomb had been used." For a whole year, nobody knew what had happened to them.

Hiroko feels no spirit of revenge against the American people. Her anger is directed at war, whether it is fought by Japanese or Americans or Russians. She feels that very few people understand the nature of atomic bombing; she thinks they should come to Japan and learn. Hiroko hopes that the voice of resistance against nuclear weapons will become louder and louder, that we will hear it in our hearts.

"The way to honor the war dead," she said, "is to make a world without war."

I wonder—with this vision of the survivors before us—dare we do less?

Thich Nhat Hanh:
The 'Nam Retreat

Friends Bulletin, July 1989

"I feel full, abundant with a dose of love that remains after the Thich Nhat Hanh Healing and Reconciliation Retreat." – Art James, Combat Vet in Vietnam.

Art was one of forty-two people who met in April 1989 at La Casa de Maria, a retreat center in Santa Barbara [California], for the "'Nam Retreat" led by Thich Nhat Hanh, the Vietnamese Buddhist monk, poet and peacemaker. Twenty-two participants were vets and nurses who served in Vietnam; twenty were non-vets, either caregivers or people with a deep concern for the Vietnam War and its aftermath.

It really began in the summer of 1987 when I visited Plumb Village, Thich Nhat Hanh's retreat center in France. I spoke to him of my concerns about the Vietnam war, the Vietnam veterans, and about Americans who were in denial about what had happened. I felt we Americans needed help. My sense was that until we could acknowledge what had happened in Vietnam, we would repeat the escalating violence until the whole earth and all its peoples were destroyed. I asked him if he could help us. He listened and agreed to come to Santa Barbara to lead a retreat with Vietnam vets in 1989.

Two years later, with the enthusiastic support of Denver Mills, Director of the Santa Barbara Vet Center, and Don George and Stephanie Glatt, Director and Assistant Director of La Casa de Maria, it happened.

The retreat was Buddhist in form and content. It lasted five days. We meditated in La Casa's spacious hall morning and evening. Our acts and thoughts were guided by the "bell of mindfulness" which rang at unsuspected moments—bringing us back to our true selves. We walked in silence with Thich Nhat Hanh each morning, through fields and orange groves. We sat under a tree to listen to his messages of love and healing. We had daily "Dharma talks" when Thich Nhat Hanh helped us expand our thoughts and understanding by describing the compassionate universe of Buddhism and the practices helpful toward living in it. We also shared poems, stories, music, and told one another who we were. We ate silent (and sometimes not so silent) meals together. We laughed. We sang. We hugged. And we learned about loving. Perhaps some fragments from the dharma talks will enable you to experience and understand some of the impact of this retreat.

"We must take good care of our pain," said Thich Nhat Hanh. "Sometimes we do not love it. We must let our pain nourish us."

"If there were no impermanence, how could we grow up? We believe the planet and people are permanent, so we do not take care; we do not practice impermanence [an awareness of our own mortality and of the degradation of the planet by humans]."

"Anger is a zone of energy. It makes us suffer; we burn. We want to let it out. We can cause lots of destruction by expressing anger, and that doesn't solve the problem. We must solve the problem of roots. Transformation is the way. We do not have only our memory of the war, we have had relations with our family, with our nation, with our world. Often as we express anger, we become more angry. Breathe on your anger. Don't always express it. Keep the garbage. It can be transformed into a flower.

"When you go to war, you go for the whole nation. You are not totally responsible. Your hand is not yours alone. It is the hand of the whole nation. They cannot shout at you, 'You have done it.' That is not true; it comes from the collective. If you go to war to save your people or 'the good,' it is not your thinking alone. It is the thinking of the nation. You are a light on the war-candle of the whole nation. The healing of yourself is the healing of the whole nation. If you understand this; if you accept this, you will transform hatred into compassion.

"My suffering hurts others. How do we heal? We must face the painful things in our life with courage and not seek to blot them out with alcohol or sex or violence or other distractions. You must find a 'practice' to help yourself through the pain. Get in touch with nature. Hug a tree for a month. You will get better.

"For years we have gone on a journey to find what is wrong. Now look for what is right. Find what is right—what is more pleasant, more kind. Seek the loving support of groups, therapists, friends. When you are sad, your immune system doesn't work. Practice joy. Create joy. You do not have to touch one another's wounds. Help your body and the body of your group by smiling, by creating joy. Offer one another support, love and understanding.

"If you seek a community, remember the best is where people are recovering and are strong and healthy enough to welcome other people. Put sick people in a joyful community. Offer an environment that is healthy and joyful.

"When you came home you found people cool, neglectful. Remember, they knew nothing about the war in Vietnam.

"You can understand and have compassion for them.

"Your experience can enable you to become very important in awakening people. You can be a new light on top of a new candle."

These were some words that guided us into healing and reconciliation. And there was more. We met two days in small groups of eight or ten to tell our stories. In all groups we non-vets asked the vets to go first. We felt they had suffered the most. One of the vets disagreed and he said so. This caused a great controversy. The argument rose to a high pitch. At the end of the day, after the non-vets told their stories and we learned, among other griefs, that one was an incest victim and one was an incest perpetrator, there was an undeclared consensus that no one was willing to trade his or her suffering for another's.

In each group were Vietnamese people. There were exiled monks and nuns, some boat people, and a Naval officer who fought for South Vietnam and had killed his own people. Americans asked forgiveness of the Vietnamese, and the Vietnamese, through Sister Phuong, declared "There is nothing to forgive."

There was Winnie, the American nurse who had thought of the Vietnamese as "Gooks." She took care of American soldiers dying from indescribable wounds. She hated the Vietnamese, hated America, and yet loved both while she cared for a napalmed Vietnamese baby. There was John who threw his helmet on a grenade and then stepped on it to save his buddies. The grenade ripped his body and he almost died. He won the Medal of Honor for this act. He showed it to us and asked how he could make it into a peace medal. Today John is planning to develop a retreat house where vets and others who suffer can come to healing. There was Jim, who never fired a rifle and was ambushed with his whole company. He lay, immobile, during the attack, his poncho over his head, holding a grenade close to his chest. He determined to use it if the Vietnamese used bayonets on him. The ruse worked. The Vietnamese left him.

When they were gone, he learned he was the only one who had survived. Today he is director of a Vet Center in Indiana. There was Jeffrey, who was ordered to strafe a village from his helicopter. Moments later a radio call informed him the pilot saw only "dogs, chickens, women and children." He felt reprieved when the answering radio call ordered all helicopters to cease fire. In a burst of fury he recalled that the commander later informed the helicopter that an air strike would be called, bringing even more destructive weapons down on those same women and children. This week Jeffrey leaves for the Insight Meditation Center in Massachusetts to spend two months in retreat with U'pandita, the Burmese master.

We all referred back to twenty years, to the '60s. That's when these vets were fresh-faced 18 and 19-year-olds ready to save a beleaguered "little" people from Communism. That's when they performed "unspeakable acts." Today most have been in therapy or 12 Step recovery programs and were ready to "clean up," to repent, and be among the first vets in history willing to tell non-vets how war really is. They were full of anger, grief, and remorse.

So was I. As I looked at my life twenty years ago, I saw my shattered family, my scattered children, myself in a psychiatric hospital because I "couldn't cope." I saw how we acted out against one another, that our values had vanished, that truth was a slippery approximation; love had gone; family had disappeared. We were all suffering; we couldn't find one another. We had lost everything.

Then I looked farther; I looked at the lives of friends, the lives of strangers, the lives of Americans in the '60s. Day after day there were new drug deaths, new divorces, new abused children, new children disappeared, and new and more deadly weapons . . .

Suddenly I saw it wasn't all my fault. I felt slip from me the guilt that had stung and burned me all those years. I saw that the war wasn't only in Vietnam. It was here, in us. It had pervaded our lives, our homes, our schools, and our churches. I saw, too, that it's worse now and we're no longer conscious that untimely death, brutality, and global disintegration stalk us all.

And there we were together in a room, weeping for our lost innocence and regaining it—yes, regaining it through the telling of our stories, and grieving over them. We were really in recovery, for we began to forgive ourselves. And Thich Nhat Hanh reminded us of the task ahead. All he said was: "Do not do it again and you will be healed." As I looked at us, I wondered: can we awaken Americans without another war catastrophe? And thought, perhaps these veterans are sounding the awakening bell. Then I realized that we, all of us, might be messages and messengers of a new way, the way of transformation.

That evening, another vet, Gary, told me his story and what he had learned. "Even if our planet dies," he said, "it will be reborn in a creative explosion. The generals in the war-room are as worthy of our love as anyone. I love them because I see truth in them—the truth of their spirit. What is love? Feeling my pain is love. Listening to our stories is love. When you've got no place to go but to God, you're safe."

It was then I realized I was in the underground peace movement, the movement of transformation. We were quietly transforming our lives and could practice war no more.

Part V:
Soviet-American
Citizen Diplomacy

During the 1980s, when President Ronald Reagan was talking about the "Evil Empire," and the Cold War mindset loomed like a mighty glacier dividing East and West, Gene Hoffman was busy distributing seeds—margiold seeds—to Russians and Americans who yearned for peace. This trust-building project was called "Planting Seeds of Hope" and is described in Gene's opening essay to this section.

Gene Hoffman's tireless work on behalf of Soviet-American reconciliation was well known and admired among "citizen diplomats" during this period. Besides working on two significant book projects, Directory of Initiatives *and* Loving the Stranger, *she traveled to the Soviet Union numerous times during her six years of involvement with FOR's US/USSR Reconciliation Project.[93]*

One of Gene's most successful projects was called "Forbidden Faces" (a title derived from a poem by Catholic priest/poet/activist Daniel Berrigan). These were slides of Russian people of all ages that Gene presented on speaking tours throughout the United States from 1983-85.

Little did anyone then dream that in less than a decade, the Cold War would end, thanks in large measure to the work of "ordinary" citizen diplomats like Gene.

In "How We Ended the Cold War," John Tierman counters the conventional wisdom among conservatives that the Cold War and Reagan's military buildup intimidated the Soviets or brought them

215

to "exhaustion." He says what decisively influenced American as well as Soviet politicians was the growing numbers of people who became involved in the nuclear freeze movement and citizen diplomacy:

> A veritable deluge of sister-city envoys, caravans of students, delegations of this union or that recreation club, ad infinitum…. had one salient virtue: They raised the temperature on politicians in Europe and the United States, a constant reminder that a popular will was escalating. When the local Rotary Club president visits Moscow, sees an apparent desire for better relations and returns to telephone the local newspaper editor and member of Congress, that is retail democracy at its most vigorous; repeated thousands of times—as it was—it sends an unmistakable message.[94]

When the Cold War ended, Gene's citizen diplomacy efforts turned from the Soviet Union to the Middle East, where she and others are spreading the message of hope through compassionate listening (see Part VII).

FOOTNOTES

---

[93] This is when the editor first came to know of Gene, and of Quaker peace activism. His first Quaker-inspired project was editing a collection of stories and poems by Soviet and American writers that was jointly published in the US and USSR in 1989. See p. 348.

[94] *The Nation*, Nov. 1, 1999.

Planting Seeds of Hope

Friends Journal, February 1, 1984

Last year, more than 60,000 US people visited the Soviet Union. Many saw for themselves that it is not a land of gray cement buildings and drab, dreary people, but that the Soviet people are very much like us.

They are proud of their nation and proud of its development. Their cities have many gray cement condominiums, but they are starred with parks, and the Kremlin is a handsome old red-stone fortress surrounded by gardens. The people are interested in fashion and wear brightly-colored clothes. One can talk openly of the longings of the human spirit for peace and well-being in the world. More powerful than any other impression was that they do not want another war.

In connection with my work for the Fellowship of Reconciliation, I traveled in a group to the Soviet Union twice last year, and several illuminating experiences led to many new perceptions. One such memorable experience was a visit to the Independent Group to Establish Trust between the United States and the Soviet Union. They are members of the unofficial (which means illegal) peace movement in Moscow. They were grateful for all peace-movement visitors. They said it protected them.

Friends who had arrived ahead of us prepared them for our visit and, fortified only with an address in Cyrillic, twelve of us rode in four taxis to the outskirts of Moscow, where we came to a clutch of high-rise apartments. We found the right door and were warmly received by six members. We met in a three-room apartment, furnished in vintage Swedish modern. Framed family photographs were all around, as well as lots of books. We sat on the floor and shared who we were, where we were from, and why we had come.

We learned that the group had formed and surfaced in May 1982. Most of its members were academics or professionals. A good number of them were Jewish and refuseniks—people who had asked for an exit visa and had been refused. As a result, many had lost or were in the process of losing their jobs. They received no mail, most of their telephones had been disconnected, and they were under constant surveillance.

The group is illegal because no peace action outside the Peace Committee-sanctioned rallies and demonstrations is permitted in the Soviet Union. The government's reasoning is that the Soviet government is for peace—so why is there need for private citizens to act?

The Group to Establish Trust felt differently. They saw that no steps toward disarmament had been taken by the United States or the Soviet Union. They felt that new initiatives were needed and that without grassroots activism humankind would have no future. They understood and wanted to promote nonviolence. So, they sent 21 peace proposals to the Soviet Peace Committee. Since these were not acknowledged, the group decided to act without government approval. They held an exhibit of the peace posters of Sergei Batrovin, the group's founder, in an apartment. The posters were confiscated, several members were imprisoned, and Batrovin was sent to a psychiatric ward.

They received a very harsh punishment for actions we in the United States take for granted. I believe a great amount of confusion has arisen because of this. Many of us have decried these punitive measures, and many others have condemned the Soviet government and the Soviet Peace Committee because they employ such measures for what seem to us such innocent acts.

We forget that the Group to Establish Trust is breaking a law of their land. Such laws seem repressive to us, if not foolish. But are they different from our laws that say that you must kill to be a patriotic citizen, or that holding a prayer vigil on military property is illegal and that you must be arrested or fined?

Breaking a law in most countries brings retaliation, so it seems strange that we (or the Group to Establish Trust) would expect to do so with impunity. I think we must celebrate their great courage and salute them for the risks they are willing to take, but we must not turn our backs on the established government simply because it behaves like established governments. As peacemakers I believe it is our task to seek to understand, to speak truth, and to act with compassion for the oppressor and the oppressed.

The Moscow Group to Establish Trust has been the only nonviolent group to surface in the Soviet Union, but I was told there are hundreds of like-minded people in other cities. After many cups of tea and lots of delicious little sandwiches, we all joined in singing "Shalom." Then we distributed Fellowship of Reconciliation marigold seeds with a poem in English and Russian on the packet: "Let us plant a garden together, flowers not fear; marigolds, not missiles. Together let us choose life so that we and our children may live."

One exciting aftermath of this visit was noted in our national newspapers this spring. The news release told how two members of the group, Maria and Vladimir Fleischgakker, planted a peace and friendship garden with our marigolds opposite the police station in Moscow. They surrounded it with peace posters. The police, the story said, did not interfere with the planting, but they did remove the signs. In the same period I received a letter from Vladimir and Maria inviting me to return to Moscow to see the garden.

When we left Moscow, the entire group saw us off at the station and gave us their buttons on which was written their legend: "Mutual trust can disarm the world."

I wonder if anything else can.

To Live Without Enemies

Fellowship Magazine, July/August 1985

On a warm, sunny September day in 1983, I walked into a building in Moscow that was surrounded with gardens and trees. I was led into a cool, dark room with big windows, where I sat alone and waited. Soon a woman with soft blonde hair and a gentle, yearning face came to greet me, carrying a gift: a recording of one of Tchaikovsky's Masses.

Nina Bobrova and I had met the previous spring at a Soviet Peace Committee meeting. She was the representative of the External Relations Department of Filaret, Metropolitan of Byelorussia and Minsk, who is known for his keen interest in peace. I was representing the Fellowship of Reconciliation's US-USSR Reconciliation Program. We talked of our longing for peace between our two nations, of our coming to really know one another's people. "Could you," Nina asked, "bring together Russian religious women with American religious women in the United States?"

"I don't know," I responded. "But I will try."

Four months later, arrangements in America were well under way. Don George, director of La Casa de Maria, an Immaculate Heart retreat center in Santa Barbara, California, offered their beautiful facilities for the retreat at no cost. The national office of the Fellowship of Reconciliation agreed to organize a national tour for the women. The Resource Center for Nonviolence in

Santa Cruz would organize a California tour. We began to select the fifteen American participants.

One year later, on January 28, 1984, flower-laden members of Santa Barbara's FOR Chapter met the four Soviet women at the Santa Barbara airport and took them in triumph to their retreat home for four days. The American participants, from across the US, had been selected for their lives of religious commitment and peace activity. Denominations represented included Presbyterian, Roman Catholic, Quaker, Jewish Reformed, United Church of Christ, Mennonite, Lutheran, Buddhist and Russian Orthodox. Ages ranged from 20 to somewhere in the 70's.

As the retreat leader, I used the discussion guide I'd created for our US-USSR program, "Learning to Love the Stranger," and a Quaker process called Creative Listening. Its purpose is to dialogue using an [open-ended] question [sometimes called a "query" in Quakerese] and to listen carefully to one another's responses without answering or challenging them.

In our first sessions we explored our childhoods and our significant spiritual experiences.

Nina Bobrova, who led the Soviet delegation, was born in Japan to a Russian family. Her first language was Japanese. Her family was very religious, but her school friends were Japanese Buddhists; thus she learned ecumenism early. She went to Soviet Union when she was twenty-two.

Tatiana Volgina, born in Moscow in 1943, lived in a huge house with other families and loved the open-door neighborliness of it. Her family was also very religious. She works in the editorial department of the Moscow Patriarchate.

Tatiana (Tanya) Novikova, the youngest member of the delegation, works in the ecumenical department of the Patriarchate. Her father is a priest of the Orthodox Church.

Mother Marfa Kovalevich, a nun from a village in Byelorussia, was born in an animal shed at the height of World

War II. The family home and barn had burned to the ground. Her parents were very religious and her happiest memory was the "Fairy Tree" at Christmas, decorated with toys made from paper.

The Americans, all of them peace activists, included a rabbi with a congregation in Albuquerque, a black peace and civil rights leader from Harlem, a minister in the Lutheran Church of Santa Barbara, teachers, community leaders, Catholic sisters and a university student.

Religious experiences among the Americans were varied. One had a period of deep wrestling to determine she had gifts equal to men and that God transcended male clergy! (She was not alone in this.) Another was startled into a life of spirituality by Dietrich Bonhoeffer's words: "Act and then belief will come." Another's transformation came when she took severe personal risks to help integrate a black school. One person found her spiritual life through living for eight years with a diagnosis of terminal cancer and a death experience. Another found it alone in a tiny room in New York where she was studying to become an actress. She described how the room became radiant as she feverishly wrote a poem about her life as a journey into God. One woman's turning came at a Mennonite college where she heard the Bible she had rejected transformed by new interpretations. Illness, injustice, the pain of discrimination or just early training were some of the promptings that turned these women toward a life of the spirit.

Among the Soviet women, three were raised in the Eastern Orthodox tradition from birth and did not have the struggles of the Americans. Only Nina Bobrova, who was born in Japan, was exposed to another religion: Buddhism. She came to her life work for peace and the Orthodox Church through a Japanese Orthodox priest.

In each session we addressed different questions:

Have you felt a spiritual power in your life that Gandhi declared has the energy equal to the force of an atom bomb? Can you describe a way you have invited goodness from a person who has harmed you? How might you express concern for an oppressor when you work for justice? Describe a way you might live to reduce the pain of others; a way your nation could do the same.

One afternoon we explored what brought us joy, pain, anxiety and hope. And finally, how we and the Soviets might save one another's lives. The most fruitful question was the one that exposed our differences, separated us in anger and tears and brought some healing.

Even though we recognized that the Soviet women had to speak from within the framework of the religious and political policies of their State, it was hard, if not impossible for us to accept that. There was some relief when we recognized similar attitudes among ourselves. One Catholic Sister remarked, "They're just like we were before Vatican II. We knew the shortcomings of our orders, the errors, even the corruptions, but we were so imbued with an idea of loyalty that we would only whisper about them among ourselves. To the outside world, we presented the face of unity, if not of love." Here are some actual conversations we transcribed.

"Can you describe ways you might break the chains of violence and injustice in the world?"

Kathy: I see the sanctuary movement as breaking a chain of violence in America, and actually saving lives. It is inspiring that some of us are willing to take great risks to save lives of people our government would send back to their countries to be killed. Another is bringing people here so we can actually understand what is going on in other parts of the world and thus change our misperceptions.

Tatiana: I think maybe there is no fear of Americans in the Soviet Union, only of weapons. To break the chain of these fears, I think we must learn more about each other. We must speak about common things first, things which do not divide us, but can join us together. Perhaps after we learn, we know, we understand, we can speak about things that separate us.

Gene: I feel I could break a chain by looking for things in my nation and my government I can affirm. I feel there is so much in my culture I fear and disapprove of that I've lost my love for things American. If I can keep seeking the good in my country and my people and share these discoveries with others, a chain of violence, fear and injustice in me would be broken.

Nina: There's not enough knowledge about each other. We want to give you more information about the reality of our life. Very little is known of our idea of peace and beauty and our work for it. So I think it is important to know what we are doing, and how we can unite ourselves to do what you call the peace strike. Another thing: we don't talk about the "enemy." We talk about the militaristic tendencies of your government; we do not consider your people as enemies. But in America, you put us all together as Soviets and you are against us. The word "communism" is a fearful word here. You forget that not all of us are communists and those who are are also human beings.

Fran: I've had a kind of secret here and I've been trying to cover it up. About a year ago I was on India Airlines and when they said, "Now you're traveling over Moscow," I felt afraid. I'm a peace activist and I'm supposed to have all the right feelings. I was shocked to find that I felt afraid.

I was raised in a conservative place in the '50s, when Communism and the punishment of Communism were very dominant. Even at that time, I thought it was kind of crazy.

But only once before have I ever met a Russian in my whole life. I can accept philosophically that we should be friends; I can even accept it practically. But when it comes down to speaking my truth to you, I'm afraid. I mean, we really have to be honest about our feelings with each other even if it doesn't make us look so glorious. There are a lot of differences I don't understand and I think we're afraid to question very deeply because there's so much at risk. And a friendship that has as much to risk as our friendship is very difficult even to begin—and that makes me afraid, too. And I'm crying about that....

Beverly: As long as Fran is willing to share her secrets, I want to share mine. And I say this with, hopefully, humility. I feel we're vulnerable. I think that Nina wants to speak only of the positive and begin our friendship there. I do, too (*in tears*). There is so much to repent of in my country. You've told me that, and I want to. But isn't there repentance in your country? It seems to me it's dishonest to come to each other speaking only of the wonderful things we have in common. There is terrible injustice in my country against your country, and I hate that. But there must be things, too, in your world—and we have to come with equal hands. It's not all my culture, my guilt; that's a heavy load for me to bear.

Gene: I think there's something we're not dealing with: that we are each dangerous to the other. Your weapons are as dangerous to us as our weapons to you. And if you can acknowledge that you are dangerous to us, I think it would be a truth our friendship could begin with.

Nina: The weapons, wherever they are, are dangerous. They are for killing. But actually, our country has been all the time trying to make initiatives for peace and we Russian people are afraid of war, much more than you. We know what war is. None of you has gone through being under siege by the Nazis; none of you has had to dig a hole in the ground and live there. That is why our country is afraid. Twenty million of us were killed, and more than that were homeless. In 1946 my country said immediately we must get rid of all armaments. So I just can't sit here with these big differences of understanding. Please don't call us enemies.

Margaret Rose: I think we have two things in common right here. We are all children of God and we're all women. I really believe that the major problems are the political systems in both our countries. I honestly think it's a sort of "old boys" system. It's a male, hierarchical one that has kept women silent. And that's what I'd like to see us begin to talk about. I'd like to see us explore ways the women of the world could set up a new model.

Anne: What I see is that from both sides there has been a negative influence on the Third World. But I believe we can both cooperate to have a positive influence. Some of the best inroads toward US-USSR reconciliation can be made on common ground: fighting disease and fighting hunger, which are enemies of the whole world. If we use the gifts of technology, the gifts of education that our countries have to help the rest of the world, then maybe something can be done between us.

Mary Evelyn: I thank Nina for helping me experience and understand the reality of the terrible suffering in World War II. The task for us is to realize that what you described and what you suffered can never be repeated because that kind of war cannot be fought.

Mariquita: There is a Buddhist practice: if you feel anger and aggression against someone, give that person a gift. You cannot continue to feel the anger and aggression while you're thinking about giving a gift. What gifts can we give each other?"

And so the retreat ended. I've only been able to give you a taste of what happened; there was much more. We discussed the question of whether Believers could be in high government positions in the Soviet Union. The answer was no. We discussed, with frustration, the status of Jews in the Soviet Union. We drafted a statement. We honored one another by worshipping in the different modes we represented. We recognized that to begin any friendship we'd better study one another's histories.

Some of us left the retreat satisfied that we had made some small beginnings. Many of us did not get our questions answered. But all of us tried to listen in love and keep open to one another and I think we did that.

Two ideas emerged for our US-USSR Reconciliation Program. One is that the FOR initiate a nationwide, week-long US-USSR teach-in and that we invite the Soviets to initiate a USSR-US teach-in at the same time. We would encourage every peace center and every school, every college, every university in the country to join in it. Each community would use whatever resources it has.

The second is to cooperate in areas where both our nations agree we have problems; for example, the Soviets admit they have problems of alcoholism and a high divorce rate. So do we. We could pool our knowledge and wisdom on those two subjects.

In this way we would be giving gifts to one another, relating as equals, and exploring both our differences and our common ground. In this way, too, we would begin to answer Abraham Lincoln's question: "Do I not destroy my enemies when I make them my friends?"

Creation Continues

Fellowship, March 1990

In 1983, I made my first visit to the Soviet Union with the Fellowship of Reconciliation. We came out by way of Poland and there met with the highly esteemed professor of mathematics and proponent of nonviolence, Andrzej Grzegorczyk. He described the Soviet Union and Communism as "triumphalism without change." He felt the Soviet Union was frozen and inflexible. Last year he met with another FOR group and acknowledged that vast changes were afoot.

The Soviet Union has changed—creation continues! This past December I attended a US/USSR Conference on the Universal Declaration of Human Rights hosted by the Soviet Peace Committee. The intention of the participants—citizen diplomats from the USA and leaders from the academic and peace community and government from the USSR—hoped that the conference would move beyond confrontation to cooperation. We wanted to emerge with concrete opportunities for cooperation.

On the opening evening, Generik Borovik, the handsome, urbane journalist and playwright who is chair of the Soviet Peace Committee, welcomed us. He reminded us that no one would have thought that Soviets and Americans would mark the 40th anniversary of the Universal Declaration of Human Rights by meeting together in Moscow. This brought into sharp relief that we were indeed present at a unique international event.

We were invited to choose one from five task forces that would discuss: education for human rights, community and human rights, threats to global ecology, terrorism, and an exploration of various freedoms from religious to ethnic self-expression. I decided to meet with the task force on terrorism because that seemed to me the one most closely related to the need for nonviolent alternatives. Our American chair, Dr. Mary Duncan, had studied terrorism in Northern Ireland for fourteen years and was writing a book on children and terrorism. Our Soviet chair was Dr. Gleb Starouchenko, member of the USSR Academy of Sciences and author of many papers on terrorism.

Mary Duncan is a knowledgeable woman who has strong opinions on the treatment of terrorists and she steered a fine course among the differing opinions of her US contingent. Gleb Starouchenko is a bright, twinkly man with a phenomenal memory, and a sympathy for "humanitarian solutions." He at once accepted the American position that we wanted to put a "human face" on terrorists and explore new responses to the problem. From there, it wasn't so easy.

We quickly agreed that "terrorism is the enemy of the world" but we couldn't succeed in dealing with state terrorism so we focused on non-governmental forms of terrorism. We and the Soviets were divided. We all recognized the danger and suffering caused by individual acts of terrorism; the Soviets pursued the idea of devising new punishments while the Americans sought more humanitarian means. For a while, except for Professor Starouchenko, it appeared the division was between those who wished to control and express terrorism and those who wished to listen to grievances and devise new methods, as the understanding increased. We came together initially by agreeing that we should identify individual terrorists and, so far as possible, study their history and culture so we could know the context from which they emerged. We discussed the possibility of training special groups who would seek to settle conflicts through mediators who were acceptable to all parties. We saw early intervention as a creative opportunity. We felt we had a charge to listen to everyone concerned, and we agreed to encourage citizen diplomats to visit nations where terrorism is practiced and express an interest in the people and their grievances.

At the end of seven sessions, we came to consensus that our task force would write and solicit brief manuscripts from Soviets and Americans on "humanitarian ways to preventing and overcoming terrorism." Professor Starouchenko said the Soviets would fund their work, and we agreed to publish any of our articles in *XXth Century and Peace*, the Soviet Peace Committee's journal. We Americans agreed to place Soviet articles in journals to which we have access and to raise funds for our work. We set deadlines for the articles and talked of meeting at the next forum in the US next October. We hoped our process would be a prelude to trust and a wider dialogue.

While we became convinced that there is a new freedom to speak without fear, we also learned that a careless move might bring *perestroika* tumbling. The Soviets want to make it irreversible. They want the right to elect representatives. They want to develop private property and are looking for new methods of ownership. They want to decentralize the economy and they are examining areas they have in common with capitalism. There is no Supreme Court in the USSR; the system of checks and balances was said to undermine popular opinion. The Soviets are reconsidering both of these positions.

On the last afternoon of the conference, a most unusual event occurred: members of Soviet independent (unofficial) groups were invited to speak. Six seats were assigned to them, each with a microphone, and the "dissidents" were each given five minutes to present their thoughts and grievances. They spoke on such things as wanting the right to choose their place of residence and their job, being allowed to subscribe to banned magazines, and the right to inherit land and to better one's economic position. Two anonymous women took microphones. One called herself a victim of lawlessness, describing how she was evicted from her house and put in a psychiatric hospital. She demanded to be taken to the procurator to have her case heard. The other spoke passionately about ecology, and described "genocide against the earth in the Soviet Union." The last speaker, from a Jewish group, was seeking a positive basis to oppose anti-Semitism, to stop the destruction of Jewish cemeteries, and to open public buildings for Jewish museums. This has since happened, with the opening of a Jewish Center in Moscow in February.

At the end, Gregory Lokshin, Soviet chair of the conference—a man who takes everything in stride and is able to move with the surprises—told us that the government is ready to take full responsibility for human rights. He said Soviet citizens "deserve concrete promises; they have been disappointed too often and we must listen to them." He concluded by saying, "We are working to show you what actually is going on here. We need your help. We need your advice." I found this a remarkable note on which to end. It was certainly a new model.

Between sessions, I managed to have lunch with Gregory Lokshin, a longtime friend of the FOR, and he made suggestions of new things we might do. He described a new institute he hoped would develop, with branches in both our countries. He called it the Institute of Consent (or Reconciliation), a place "where citizens' grievances could be addressed and people could study all types of meditation and reconciliation." He suggested a conference on nonviolence to be held in Moscow and sponsored by the Soviet Peace Committee. They are eager to learn more about nonviolence, he said, especially in light of conflicts like that between Azerbaijan and Armenia. The roots of many conflicts in the Soviet Union are religious, he said. We talked of training intermediaries who might move between adversaries.

Out of the Forum for Human Rights, out of many similar meetings all over the world, out of *glasnost*, out of *perestroika*, out of initiatives that blossom forth every day—out of these majestic human enterprises may come the new consciousness we need to create a society that is worthy of human beings, one that will include peace and goodwill to all.

This could be a new turning point. Creation does continue!

Part VI:
Reflections on the Spirit

"Activist mystics, turning up everywhere, always being inventive, impatient with institutional structures of every kind...."

—Elise Boulding, describing Western Friends whose stories appear in *A Western Quaker Reader, Writings by and about Independent Quakers in the Western United States, 1929-1999* (Friends Bulletin Publications: Whittier, CA, 2000).

The phrase "activist mystic" may seem an oxymoron, the joining together of apparent opposites (like "military intelligence"), yet when you study the lives of notable Quakers, such as Gene Hoffman, this term makes perfect sense. Inward transformation—the experience of connectedness with the Divine Presence—has led many Friends to seek social transformation. Many Friends regard activist mysticism as the heart of the Quaker experience.

As the lives of well-known Friends such as 18th century abolitionist John Woolman, 19th century social activist Lucretia Mott, and 20th century philosopher/mystic/activist Rufus Jones testify, the Quaker experience of mystical identification with God and/or humanity has not been a blissful retreat from the world, but rather a wake-up call to action. Howard Brinton sees the Quaker mystic as a prophet who "rises up in protest":

Whenever and wherever religion becomes too formal and institutional, too dependent on external expression, the mystic rises up in protest and points the way to a religion which is internal, independent of outward forms or organization and centered in the direct apprehension of God... (Friends for 300 Years, *p. xii*)

Gene's protest against dead outward forms differs from that of many Quakers in that she also celebrates the creative power and potential of each individual. (Until the 20th century, most Quakers felt that music and the arts were distractions.) An actress, poet, and "holy fool," Gene calls us to experience a God who not only cares about peace and justice, but also frees us to follow Inner Light-heartedness and fulfill our creative potential.

Over the years Gene has led creative writing as well as compassionate listening workshops. In 1991 she published a book of poems called All Possible Surprises. *In her introduction to this book, she says that ever since she was a young girl, phrases would flash into her mind, and she would write them down, and they would become the seeds of poems. "It was years later I learned I was writing instructions to myself on how to live my life," Gene notes. After becoming a Quaker, Gene realized that these phrases came from her "inner voice" and were directing her to areas where she needed growth. For Gene, the act of creation is also an act of listening, and responding, to one's inner voice.*

Jesus, the Christ, Quakers and I

Friends Bulletin, January1975

I was born into the Christian tradition and I loved it. I loved the idea of Jesus—ever-present, succoring, aware.

But, very early, questions came. Early I began wrestling with the idea of Jesus as uniquely divine, that only he lived a sublime life in history, that only he was the example of God in time, eternity on earth.

These ideas troubled me because I couldn't make sense of them. The questions persisted: "Why should the New Testament statement of the Golden Rule be 'higher' than the same statement by Buddha? Why is Jesus' injunction to love our enemies any more divine than that of Lao-tse, Socrates, or Gandhi? Why is a book from Palestine any more holy or authentic than a book from China, India, or America? What does it profit me to have set before me the example of a person who is *uniquely* sublime?" . . . so many troubling whys and wherefores. . . .

So I attended various churches, read the literature of mystics and religious thinkers, ancient and modern. Wondered and sought and wondered again.

Then came the time for me to join with others in the spiritual pilgrimage and I sought a group where I could be I, and yet could share. So I explored the thinking-feeling of people who belonged to various religious sects—and I went home and wept.

I wrote a poem about why I wept. I'd like to share part of it with you. It's called "How God Might Laugh":

> How God might laugh,
> If God could laugh—
> The laughter brimming tears—
> at having given us mind
> And thought and intellect
> And energy and imagination
> To conceive greater, farther horizons—
> And then discover that we fear
> Our own divine imaginations.
>
> Oh yes, we imagine,
> Each of us some truth of our own
> And yet, another says
> "No, that cannot be true.
> your mind has not conceived
> What my mind has conceived.
> Therefore,
> You do not know 'The truth'. . . ."
> That's why I wept.

Then I learned about Quakers. I learned they were a jubilant people because, through [Quakerism's founder] George Fox, they made the wondrous discovery that each of us can have a direct relationship with God, that all people are of the elect, that men and women are equal vessels of the Spirit, that the seed of Truth lies in everything, and that we're all bearers of new Revelations.

And I learned from [20th century Quaker philosopher/ mystic] Rufus Jones that the Light manifested itself differently in each different being. "This light must be *my* light. This truth must be *my* truth. This faith must be my very own faith." To one such as I, nourished from childhood on the writings of [Eighteenth Century free-thinker] Thomas Paine and [20th century atheist] Robert Ingersoll, it was a great illumination that I could belong to a group and still be free.

From [20th century Quaker theologian/mystic] Thomas Kelly I learned I had to try to "be the message," that the ". . . blazing discovery which Quakers made long ago is rediscovered again and again by individuals. The embers flare up. The light becomes glorious. There is no reason why it cannot beak out again today. . . ." and that the discovery is sometimes like being down "in the flaming center of God"; is sometimes "a living immediacy," sometimes a "sweet presence."

And—for me—sometimes God was literally a "pain in the neck."

Since I frequently had a pain in the neck (and other places), since I wanted the Sweet Presence, and since I also wanted to blaze up and flare out—I joined the Society of Friends at Orange Grove Meeting in Pasadena, California.

There I found a body of people who included and accepted many fascinating and diverse members. (We had Christians, Jews, one Buddhist and many Deists.) I found a gathering that encouraged each of us to be and become our various selves—a people who celebrated me being "me," and I celebrated them being "them."

And I loved the passion and the silence and the "waiting upon the Lord."

As I grew in my awareness through worship and study, Jesus, instead of being the one supreme revelation in history, became one of many prophets and mystics who comforted and inspired me by their examples. From Jesus' teachings (and many others), I learned that the core of my life must be worship—listening for and following my leading even if it be faint—tiny as the grain of mustard seed.

I rejoiced that I need not accept totally anyone else's Truth; to discover I sprang from different seed, in different time, that my destiny grew from *my* condition and *my* unique experience of life. I rejoiced that I could live the life of Holy Obedience as it was revealed to *me*.

Originally, of course, my leadings came to me in Christian terms, for that is my conditioning. And Jesus was like a good friend to me; perhaps another simile would be that he was like a parent who holds the child's hand until the child can walk by itself, then sets it free to do just that.

For a long while I needed to refer back to Jesus' teachings; then as my knowledge of the legacy left us by other God-inspired people grew I would include theirs. (Often, when I lose my own vision, I must still refer to others. Often others lead me on to new visions of my own.) But more and more, God, the Presence, speaks to me in my own words—uniquely fitted to my own condition.

The teachings of Jesus turned me toward the right direction, then set me free to discover my own Revelations—to stumble, to fall, to make my own mistakes which, when I learned from them, turned out not to be mistakes, but steps necessary to my own growth. Yes, the teachings of Jesus, the Christian teachings, pointed the way for me—the way to my own unique capacity to love, to be, to learn, and to live.

But, says my Spirit, I am not to seek to live his life. I am to live my life, informed by the same spirit which informed him. This leads me to Quakerism and its place in my evolution. Through becoming a Quaker I learned how to worship in silence—both with others and alone. I learned how to listen, and gained the courage to follow what came to me out of the worship in my life outside it.

Formerly, in my time-bound life, I thought I had no time for daily worship. There was so much I could and wanted to do—how could I take "time out"? Now I find I can't do what I want or need to do without the worship.

When I am in touch with my Spirit, I find I am suffused with energy. Being in tune means I am available for whatever happens—whatever needs arise; I am in touch with people, involved with more activities. But different kinds than formerly—important kinds, not urgent ones. And, I am not desperate (when I am in touch); I move serenely through whatever is required of me. By "waiting upon the Lord" I sometimes literally *do* renew my strength . . . run and not be weary.

This brings me to joy. As I follow the path of my Spirit, great Joy comes to me. Because I see everything is necessary—indeed, I am often permitted to see the meaning and the holiness in everything, even that which we call evil and depraved. When I am in tune, everything is a miracle to me; everything is a message bearer; there is meaning in each moment; every bush is a burning one; every leaf is aflame; every instant is from heaven—guiding, wooing, instructing me, leading me through my astonishing life.

As I see the promise in my own life, so I see the promise in our combined life. For I believe we Friends have the possibility of being among the most creative people on earth—for we know and we have proven that all things are possible through the Spirit. And we know that we have proven that the Spirit is within us. By attending to it faithfully and following its leadings, miracles can and have happened.

And I believe they will happen as we move more into worship together and apart. We will have available to us any talent we need. We will once again walk and talk with princes and with kings, or with wayfarers and with strangers. We will understand everything and speak in love to everything—to flowers and animals and plants and stones.

And who knows—maybe if we pour our love upon the machines of war and the disconnected people making the war—maybe if we pour the oil of our love upon all those troubled waters—the waters will clear and become calm.

And we will rejoice in our variousness: that each of us is a unique and irreplaceable message, none speaking to all conditions, each speaking to some conditions.

Maybe (for me) singing and dancing in the streets, maybe ministering prophetically, maybe turning out the seams of my life for you to see.

Maybe for thee, wandering over the country, a guitar slung over the shoulder, a handful of songs in the pocket. Maybe, for thee, laboring among the poor, typing in an office, speaking Truth to power, or silently tending a garden.

And through all this, our variousness, maybe coming alive again to the wonder of it all—to the wonder of the Spirit which is wider than the world we live in, greater than any particular idea any of us has of it—the Spirit which cannot be confined by any system of beliefs whether they be Hindu, Buddhist, Muslim, Christian, or atheist. The Spirit which breaks through all our efforts to limit it, reduce it to a size we can easily comprehend and yet, is still as close to us as "the great vein in our neck,"[95] holds us with "everlasting arms,"[96] and still "over the bent World broods with warm breath and with ah! bright wings."[97]

FOOTNOTES

---

[95] "We are closer to him than his jugular vein," Quran 50:60.
[96] A phrase used often by Rufus Jones and Thomas Kelley, taken from a Christian hymn.
[97] From Gerard Manley Hopkins' poem, "God's Grandeur."

God and Horror

Fellowship Magazine, January/February 1994

The way we respond to suffering determines the future of the world.

Unhealed trauma is, I believe, the cause of many of our psychological ills such as fear, greed, anger, and violence. Many of us must move beyond psychology, into a spiritual dimension, in order to heal ourselves.

I do not believe God creates horror or trauma. We human beings do because of our ignorance. We become infatuated with temptations—pleasure, security, riches, power, success—and we lose sight of our journey, which I believe is into compassion.

It is well recognized that there are horrors in everyone's life, among the affluent no less than the poor, in every culture, race, and denomination. Suffering, like rain, falls on the just and the unjust. The horrors in my life immersed me in pain and shame, and catapulted me into a psychiatric hospital.

Fortunately, in those years, there was a psychiatrist by my side who was known to be "radical." He made friends with his patients, as well as house calls. He was Dr. Benjamin Weininger of Santa Barbara. He not only practiced psychiatry and psychoanalysis, he was a powerful teacher and a spiritual friend. He embraced Christianity, Hasidism, and Zen Buddhism. He introduced me to new perceptions of each of these great traditions. The therapy I cherished most was his use of stories and precepts from them.

After the hospitalization, Ben gently led me back to reality, to a place where I could again say, "I love my life." Through his guidance I moved to a saner life where I could function on my own. New opportunities opened for me as I pursued these rich new spiritual resources. With Ben as my mentor I received an MA in Pastoral Counseling.

My interest in religion had blossomed early. At the age of nine I had my first "spiritual experience" and my life wish unfolded. I went with my family on a six-month tour of Europe. I was well prepared. I was an omnivorous reader and my mother provided books about every country we visited. I saw places where some of the world's horrors had taken place.

I visited the bloody Tower of London where Anne Boleyn and Lady Jane Grey had been beheaded. In those days they displayed the instruments of torture—the block, the lash, the rack. I absorbed these into my consciousness.

We visited the prison housing the first gas chamber for capital offenders, and I learned that we kill people who kill people, and in horrible ways.

I was taken to Flanders Field and saw the crosses "row on row," and to other famous battle sites. There I saw my first wounded veteran—a man without a nose. Instead, he had a gaping hole where his nose had once been. His shattered visage haunted my dreams, and he, I believe, was responsible for my conversion to pacifism.

Soon after these experiences, I was taken to St. Peter's Church in Rome and sat through my first Mass in Mary, Queen of Angels' Chapel. I was awed by the music, the incense, and the intoned Latin of the liturgy. Moved by I knew not what, I determined to dedicate my life to goodness and truth.

The three streams of Christianity, Hasidism, and Zen, along with psychology, have fed me on my journey.

Quakerism

I joined the Religious Society of Friends (Quakers) in 1951. I am a Quaker Universalist. Jesus is a great teacher and not God to me. My Meeting is a silent one. Our worship is akin to Catholic contemplation. I have no minister, no priest, no church, and no scriptures more sacred than the truths revealed to me in silence. At the heart of Quakerism is the faith that "there is that of God in every person." All life is sacred, and we think of our worship as experiential. We sometimes feel the presence of God in ourselves and in our Meeting. This presence is felt differently by each of us. It is from within that our ultimate truth comes. We are urged to follow this truth even if, after careful exploration with our Meeting, we learn that most of the others are against it. We believe revelation is ongoing.

We can meet anywhere: in seventeenth century England, when our Meeting houses were destroyed, we would meet sitting in the street. If, during the silence, a member feels moved by the Spirit, he or she stands and speaks (preferably briefly) from the heart and from experience, and then sits down. The words are absorbed in silence. There may be more than one speaker, and sometimes we are gathered into an epiphany where the spoken words coalesce into a truth none of us could have imagined. We seek to be "spoken through," and we are spoken through as much by silence as by speech.

Ours is a faith of social action—which sometimes derails our spiritual intentions! We seek to alleviate suffering. Many of us would rather be killed than kill, and many of us believe we must cherish the oppressor as well as the oppressed, for both suffer and each is a bearer of truth.

Perhaps we are best known for our peace testimony. Because we believe all life is sacred, most of us abjure killing. As we become sensitized, we are more aware of the violence within and around us. We seek to be a compassionate people. We fall short, but we are on a path which sometimes leads us into harmonious places.

It is by looking at life as a holy adventure, at Quakerism as a holy experiment, that I find strength to continue life and to go through the pain of it. I know there are hidden gifts of understanding and spiritual growth in pain, and these enable me to live and grow in compassion. To illustrate this, I give you the story of Emil Fuchs, a German Quaker who passed through great suffering. He speaks to me with authenticity. He wrote:

> I was dismissed from my professorship and imprisoned because I would not be a Nazi. My youngest son hid himself because the students at his university threatened to lynch him for being a leader of anti-Nazis. My eldest son and daughter were in great danger.
>
> One night I became nearly mad. I saw my children cruelly killed and lying before me. In this hour of utter despair I heard a voice saying, "What do you want? Shall they save their lives by losing their conscience?" I knew it was Christ in my cell, and peace came to me. From that moment I could bear the hardships my children had to go through.
>
> That I saw Christ, that I heard his voice—might have been imagination. What cannot be imagination is the new life, the strength and the insight which his presence gave. No imagination ….can give a father the strength to face danger to his children and remain certain and full of peace because they go the way of their conscience.[98]

Hasidism

Hasidism was the popular communal mysticism that transformed the face of East European Jewry in the eighteenth and nineteenth centuries. It arose in Poland and spread until it included almost half of the Jews there. [Jewish philosopher]

Martin Buber expressed and interpreted Hasidism eloquently for us today. As he portrays it, it is a mysticism which hallows community and everyday life rather than withdrawing from it. Buber's idea was to "draw God into the world—to make shine the hidden divine life in all persons, all things, all experience." 99

Here are some of my touchstones from Hasidism. They are Buber's interpretations of ancient Hasidic tales.

The Zaddik [teacher of righteousness] was asked: "Can you show me one general way to the service of God?"

The Zaddik replied: "It is impossible to tell people what way they should take. One way to serve God is through learning, another through fasting, another through prayer. Everyone should carefully observe what way his heart draws him and then choose his way with all his heart."

* * *

There is something that can only be found in one place. It. . . may be called fulfillment of existence. The place where this can be found is the place on which one stands. The environment which [is my] natural one, the situation which has been assigned to me. . . the things which claim me day after day; these contain my essential task. . . for it is where we stand that we should try to make shine the hidden divine life.

* * *

A person who frets himself with repentance, who tortures himself with the idea that his acts of penance are not sufficient, withholds his best energies from the work of the new beginning. . . Rake the muck this way; rake the muck that way; it will always be muck. In the time I am brooding, I could be stringing pearls for the delight of heaven.

* * *

Evil is the lowest rung of the good.

* * *

When a woman is pregnant and the child begins to come in the eighth month, the doctor does everything he can to prevent it. When the child begins to come after the ninth month, the doctor does everything to help the mother through any pain and suffering to enable the child to be born. My friends, the world is in the ninth month!

Victor Frankl was a survivor, not a victim, of Auschwitz. This is part of his story. One of the tenets of Hasidism is that life has meaning and that it is our task to discern it. Out of the historical horrors they experienced, the Hasidim devised a spiritual meaning for themselves. This enabled them not only to survive, but also to live.

I do not know whether Victor Frankl was a Hasid, but the story of his concentration camp experience surely has the flavor of Hasidism. In his book, *Man's Search for Meaning*, he describes horrors beyond our imagination and demonstrates that it is possible to remain human while suffering them.

He does not tell us how to do it; he suggests it can be chosen, and the choice comes from something I would call Grace. The following quotation is part of the postscript of his book. Frankl called it "The Case for Tragic Optimism."

> I speak of tragic optimism, that is, an optimism in the face of tragedy and a view of the human potential which ... always allows for turning suffering into a human accomplishment. . .

Frankl conceives of conscience as a prompter indicating the direction in which we have to move in a given situation.

> . . . There are three main avenues on which one arrives at meaning in life. The first is by creating a work or by doing a deed. The second is by experiencing something or ... someone with love. Most important

is the third avenue: ...Even a helpless victim of a hopeless situation, facing a fate he cannot change, may grow beyond himself and change himself. He may turn a personal tragedy into a triumph. We have the freedom to choose our attitude and that may be the ultimate freedom we have.

Out of his transcendence of the experience of horror, Frankl was able to write thirty years later:

> ...Everything is irrevocably stored and treasured.... Do not overlook the full granaries of the past, the deeds done, the loves loved, and last. . . the sufferings gone through with courage and dignity.

He was able to live out the commandment of Irving Halprin's book *Messages from the Dead* where those who experienced the Holocaust are admonished not to "look too long into the fire. To dwell too exclusively and obsessively on the pain and loss of the Holocaust is to invite the risk of deadening one's capacity to perceive what is life-giving in the present."[100]

I hold Viktor Frankl's example as an assurance that God is. For me it exemplifies the greatness of a spirit which can hold the dark and light in balance.

Buddhism

There is no deity in Buddhism. Instead, there is what is called "the Buddha Nature, our true nature." I interpret this as the Informing Presence, the Spirit of God in me. To contact this Spirit, or Nature, "[w]e need time and space, so that free from all interruptions and distractions, we can, at least once a day, collect all our psychic energy and concentratedly bring it into direct contact with our inner, most powerful resources. Then all our psychic energy, which has been scattered as a result of our pursuits and internal conflicts, is collected into a unity again." [101]

One of my teachers is Thich Nhat Hanh, Vietnamese poet, teacher, peacemaker and Zen Master. From him I learned the value and process of reconciliation. A paragraph from his book *Being Peace* has deep meaning for me; I have sought to let it permeate my life and work.

> In South Africa, the black people suffer enormously, but the white people also suffer. If we take one side, we cannot fulfill our task of reconciliation and bring about peace. Are there people who can be in touch with [both sides]? . . . understanding the suffering of each, and telling each side about the other? . . . Can you be people who understand deeply the suffering of both sides? Can you bring the message of reconciliation? [102]

Zen meditation practice and Buddhist teachings increase my awareness of differing realities by giving me glimpses of life as it really is, a process which is never completed. A practice I find essential is the "Breathing Through Meditation" as described by Joanna Macy:

> With Saint Shanti Deva say, "Let all sorrows ripen in me." We help them ripen by passing them through our hearts, making good rich compost of all that grief ... By breathing through the bad news we can let it strengthen our sense of belonging in the larger web of being ... It reminds us of the collective nature of both our problems and our power. When we take in the world's pain and our own, accepting it as the price of our caring, we can let it inform our act without needing to inflict it as punishment on others ...

Another meditation helpful to my sanity is "The Great Ball of Merit." Of it Macy writes:

> Compassion which is grief in the grief of others... is also joy in the joy of others. This is very important... because we face a time of great challenge, and need more commitment, endurance, and courage than we can ever dredge up out of our individual supply.
>
> In this meditation, we open ourselves to our fellow-beings.... In each of these innumerable beings' lives, some act of merit was performed. No matter how stunted and deprived the life, there was a gesture of generosity, a gift of love, an act of valor.... From each of these beings... arose actions of courage, kindness, of teaching and healing.... No act of goodness is ever lost. It remains forever a present resource for the transformation of life.[103]

* * *

Quakerism teaches there is that of God in each of us. Hasidism teaches gratitude to God for all things, both light and dark: each serves God's purpose. Buddhism teaches ways to achieve compassion and harmlessness toward all living things. Psychology teaches us how to examine our lives for the healing of our wounds.

I find these resources necessary to my efforts to live a sane life in our tragic world and I think they lead to a better one. I am confident creation continues.

FOOTNOTES

---

[98] Emil Fuchs, *Christ in Catastrophe* (Wallingford, PA: Pendle Hill, 1949), Pamphlet No. 49.

[99] Martin Buber, *Hasidism and Modern Man* (NY: Harper Torch Books, 1958).

[100] Irving Halprin, *Messages from the Dead* (Philadelphia: Westminster Press, n.d.).

[101] Ralph Hetherington, *Universalism and Spirituality* (Wallingford, PA: Pendle Hill, 1993), PamphletNo.309

[102] Thich Nhat Hanh, *Being Peace* (Berkeley, CA: Parallax Press, 1987).

[103] Joanna Rogers Macy, *Despair and Personal Power in the Nuclear Age* (Philadelphia: New Society Publishers, 1983).

Listening for Truth

"Listening for Truth" was presented as a talk at the June 1994 conference of Pax 2100 in San Jose, Costa Rica. This conference included a visit to the Quaker Settlement in Monte Verde. Pax 2100 is a project for peace initiated by the Goleta Presbyterian Church of California. Its intent is to introduce the peace religions of the world to people who wish to learn about them.

Gandhi once declared that if he had not been born a Hindu, he would have been a Christian because he so revered the teachings of Jesus. He felt that to teach Jesus' way in India, he had to reveal similar teachings in Hindu scriptures. In one of his booklets he transposed a familiar phrase and gave it new meaning. The title of this booklet is *Truth is God.* This made a radical change in my thinking. It means to me that anything my mind clings to as Truth is not God and is temporary and transitory; it exists for me until a fuller Truth is revealed.

As a Quaker I believe that revelation is ongoing: God is constantly revealing new Truths to human beings. I also believe that each person may perceive a portion of this Truth, and that listening for new revelations can be a daily discipline. I am not suggesting that we are to abandon our familiar Truths and religions—only that we open our hearts to those we discover in other people, religions, and parts of the world. I believe God provides everyone with Divine Truth, and peace in 2100 will not come about unless we listen for Truth in peoples, cultures, nations, religions, and interpretations of religions quite different from our own. Because listening will often be difficult, strange, even antithetical to our own perspective, we must listen with the open heart.

Ecclesiastes tells us this when he says, "To everything there is a season, a time to sow and a time to reap; a time to seek and a time to lose; a time to break down and a time to build up ...." Ecclesiastes says to me that nothing is without Truth. God has been revealed to people in a fashion suitable to their time and place. To the Jews was revealed the Torah; to the Christians, the Gospels; to the Hindus, the Bhagavad Gita; to the Buddhists, the Sutras; to the Moslems, the Koran.

We are on a journey to learn how the Truths of peace and nonviolence were revealed through different religions. We listen to Quakers to learn how they adopted and practiced Truths in their lives. We may find ourselves richer by listening and honoring their experiences. In the quest for peace, we need to open ourselves to new perceptions our culture often denies. And so, we listen.

I am not talking about listening with the human ear. I am talking about "discernment," which means to perceive something hidden and obscure. We must listen with our spiritual ear, the one inside, and this is very different from deciding in advance what is right and what is wrong and then seeking to promote our own agenda. We must literally suspend our disbelief and then listen to learn whether what we hear expands or diminishes our sense of Truth.

Our call, as I perceive it, is to see that within all life is the Mystery—God. It is within the African and the Afrikaner, the Iraqi, the Serb, and the American. It is within each religion on earth. Our task is to sift the wheat from the chaff, because in each religion there is both. Through nonjudgmental listening, we may awaken to it in both strange and familiar places and thus learn the God that resides in a religion or in an individual.

For peace to happen, I believe there must be peacemaking groups who can be trusted by all sides, that find the divine in the "enemy," and carry that message wherever they go.

I began with Gandhi and I shall close with him. I will give you a talisman which has always inspired me. Gandhi reminded us that there exists within each person a power, an energy, equal to the force of an atom bomb—a loving power, a caring power, a healing power for peace. I believe it is time for us to release this power in new ways.

Selected Poems from
All Possible Surprises

Transformation

Something was about to be—
    the silence sang of it
    the dark earth heaved
    the leaves whispered to
    one another—
    the birds waited—
    no wind stirred—
    all earth's people were silent
    looking inward at their hearts

Everyone—everywhere
    stopped striving
    stopped working
    stopped scolding
    stopped pursuing pleasure

Everyone sat in silence
    thinking caring thoughts
    about one other person

And all the world
was joyous
and at peace

American Gothic

"To grow a cemetery
I shall need seeds,"
cried the nursery man,
War,
Smoothing his soiled
Garden gloves.

And we believed him—
"He protects us—
just like we want
Our daddies to..."

And so
we sowed
Our sons.

Prayer

Mark me with a miracle
   oh my Lord
I cried—
   I need one so—

then panicked
to discover
I'd be living
in one all
the time—
my life

Holy Fools

Friends Bulletin, July 1997

I have been wondering about risks, wondering what risk I'm willing to take in this end-time of astonishing anger and fear; when abused people and the abused earth rages in earthquake, flood, and fire... When so many cry for mercy, and so few give. I've been wondering about risks that others are willing to take as well—wondering whether, in this time of shatterings and eruptions, we are called upon to imitate the great risk-takers— the Holy Fools...

So I began to explore the lives of Sacred Clowns—the Holy Fools. I learned that in Tarot readings the Holy Fool is one who often leaps into the unknown without considering the consequences. He or she is, in a deep sense, innocent, trusting, naive, enthusiastic, and embarked upon a journey whose end cannot be known. We often describe such behavior as irrational. Impulsive behavior is frequently considered irresponsible in our culture. It's sometimes destructive, sometimes creative, sometimes both. The Fool plunges into the experience that calls him or her. It might endanger his/her life. It might prove fruitless— but often it yields a totally unexpected treasure—a surprise—a new beginning.

Whether we recognize it or not, we, too, are standing at the threshold of such a journey. We can have inward promptings that call us to strange new endeavors. If we do not heed these calls, we may wonder why we feel despair, depressed, empty of enthusiasm for life.

We cannot know where the new beginnings will guide us; we cannot know whether we will reach the end and whether that end will be safe. Further knowledge is not given us. In some sense I believe we must be faithful to our inner voice—our intuition—or die to hope.

Dare we, trusting in heaven, take the risks required of us if we would live out our truth within? There's no such thing as a risk without fear, and acting on new insights is daring. Dare we let go of our precious security? Dare we abandon seeking the fruits of our efforts? Dare we relinquish our comfort zones—knowing the risks may bring us disaster?

Holy fools/Sacred Clowns have existed in every tradition since the Middle Ages, and perhaps before. Here are examples of some:

St. Xenia lived in the 18th century in Russia. She was a member of the Orthodox Church. She was also very wealthy. After her husband's death, she began giving her fortune to the poor, refusing a life of comfort and privilege. She felt compelled to live by Jesus' teaching to sell what we have, give it to the poor, and follow Him. To prevent Xenia from impoverishing herself, relatives sought to have her declared insane. However, the doctor who examined her concluded that she was the sanest person he had ever met.

Her clothes were threadbare; her home was in the Smolensk Cemetery. When she died at age 71, her grave became a place of healing pilgrimages. She was canonized during the Gorbachev years.

* * *

Another was a boy named Israel who was born in Poland at the beginning of the eighteenth century. He learned early in life that he was destined to be a great leader of the Jewish people, and that he must hide this knowledge from everyone until the time came for him to reveal himself. For many years he lived a wandering life as an ignorant fool who stammered. He dressed in rude clothes and was a poor shepherd. In this guise he met his wife-to-be and proposed marriage. She must have recognized the hidden spirit in Israel for they married.

Later he revealed himself as the Baal Shem Tov, Master of the Good Name, and the wise and great leader of a new sect of Jews called Hasidim, who praised God and sang and danced their times and sorrow and suffering.

The Baal Shem Tov shared his knowledge through terse, but loving wisdom stories. This is one of my favorites:

A young man came to him and said, "Oh Master, the world is in a state of great danger. It may be destroyed. What shall I do?"

The Baal Shem Tov replied: "When a woman is about to give birth, and labor begins in the eighth month, the doctors do everything to prevent the birth, but in the ninth month, they urge her to go through her pain and suffering so she may have a good birth.

"My son, the world is in the ninth month."

****

In the early days Quakers were no less odd. They thought the world was in the "ninth month," and many behaved like these Holy Fools. Today, alas, most of us are quite respectable. In the eighteenth century, we were persecuted for declaring that we can hear the voice of God within, that revelation is ongoing, and that we do not need a minister or church building, because God speaks directly to everyone and we can worship in the middle of a street, if need be. We called ourselves a peculiar and harmless people—and we were peculiar! We spent much time in prison for our peculiarities.

Some seventeenth century Quaker behavior would be shocking even by today's standards. Some decided to remind people that "nothing could be hidden from God" by walking naked through the streets proclaiming "this Truth." They were accompanied by fully dressed Friends to protect them.

But Friends were not simply eccentrics; they had much in common with court fools. Court fools were the ones who dared to speak truth to kings and rulers. They spoke with masking wit and humor and their truth could be easily dismissed. But often it struck deep, and they were protected by rulers who, it seemed, hungered to hear truth at no loss of face. Friends' "foolishness" often brought imprisonment and death.

We still have Sacred Fools and Holy Clowns today. Dorothy Day was one of them. It was she who created the famous Catholic Worker Houses of Hospitality. There anyone of any condition or color could come at any time, find shelter, food and clothing, and stay as long as they wanted or needed. She was an ardent pacifist and was often arrested for participating in demonstrations. The world found her work foolish. But when people called her a saint, she admonished them by saying, "Don't call me a saint; I don't want to be dismissed so easily."

Martin Luther King, Jr, practiced what he preached, and told his opponents: "We will match your capacity to inflict suffering with our capacity to endure suffering. We will meet your physical force with our soul force—and in winning our freedom, we will win your freedom as well."

Of course, Mohandas Gandhi, that master of spiritual *jiu jitsu*, also urged us to take suffering on ourselves instead of retaliating, and never to be concerned about the fruits of our efforts.

Mother Teresa—a Holy Fool who cares for the diseased and dying with a courage only matched by AIDS caregivers. She is able to see, I'm told, each as an individual, a sacred individual; indeed, she sees them as "Christ in distressing disguise."

These Holy Fools challenge us with our locks and keys and schemes to outwit destitution, suffering and death. And the challenges of today are no less than life and death for us and our lovely planet. I hope we will all explore what risks we're willing to take for healing ourselves and it.

Is it, in fact, such a wonderful thing to be regarded as sane? The chief administrator of the Holocaust, Adolph Eichman, was pronounced sane by psychiatrists. Surely these same psychiatrists would declare all those I have described as insane. Would you?

The story of Xenia was adapted from "Holy Fools" by Jim Forest, which was published in Forerunner, *a publication of the Russian Orthodox Fellowship of St. John the Baptist, Winter, 1996.*

Part VII:
Compassionate Listening in the Middle East

"Great ideas, it has been said, come into the world as gently as doves. Perhaps then, if we listen attentively, we shall hear, amid the uproar of empires and nations, a faint flutter of wings, the gentle stirring of life and hope."—Albert Camus.

The idea of "compassionate listening" did not originate with Gene Hoffman. It had been fluttering in the air, as it were, for several decades, nurtured by people of various religious persuasions. Vietnamese Buddhist activist Thich Nhat Hanh called it "deep listening." Zen Buddhist voice pathologist Rebecca Shafir called it "mindful listening." Psychologist Marshall Rosenberg called it "creative communication."

One of Gene's important contribution to compassionate listening was to take it to the Middle East and to recognize that all sides—including terrorists—need to be heard.

During the 1980s Libyan President Muammar Qaddafi was accused of masterminding the West Berlin discotheque bombing that killed two US soldiers and wounded over 200 civilians. He was called a "mad dog" by President Reagan, who authorized 100 US Airforce and Naval aircraft to strike five Libyan military targets in April 1986. During this attack, 30 people were killed and over 200 wounded. Qaddafi's 15-month-old adopted daughter was among those killed and two of his sons were seriously injured. The main target of the attack was clearly Qaddafi himself.

Gene's response was to write Qaddafi a letter telling him that she "grieved for the suffering that we caused him and his people, urged him to explore a nonviolent response, and said I hope one day to listen to his grievances." He wrote back, thanking her for her concern.

The cycle of violence did not end, of course. In 1988, Libyan terrorists allegedly blew up a Pan Am passenger airline over Lockerbie, Scotland, killing 270 people. In revenge, American planes downed two Libyan planes in January 1989.[104]

In response to this escalating violence, Gene Hoffman and Virginia Baron, then editor of Fellowship Magazine, *went together to Libya with a Fellowship of Reconciliation (FOR) delegation. Their story is told in "Listening to the Libyans." Because US citizens were forbidden to go to Libya, no US official would listen to what Gene and her delegation had to say about their experiences.*

What would have happened if the US had taken a different approach to terrorism and listened to the grievances of the Libyans instead of reacting with violence? It is hard to say.

What we do know is that people and situations change. Once considered a fiery revolutionary and a terrorist supporter, Qaddafi has publicly renounced terrorism and denounced the September 11th attacks on the New York World Trade Center and the Pentagon.[105] He has offered to pay 2.1 billion dollars in reparation for the Lockerbie incident (10 million dollars per victim) if the UN and US lift their sanctions (the US has refused, but the UN has agreed). Neither of these actions have altered the views of hard-liners in Washington, who believe that the world can and must be divided into the Bad Guys (who must be eradicated) vs. the Good Guys (who must triumph, no matter what the cost).

Compassionate listening does not try to force people to change, but it assumes that people are changeable and that listening to their concerns can facilitate transformation. Gene is convinced that the cycle of violence can be broken only when the victims (and perpetrators) of violence learn to listen to each other. The following story suggests how listening can produce astonishing personal transformation:

When Nachson Wachsman was captured by Palestinian terrorists, his family was thrown into a storyline all too familiar to both Israeli Jewish and Palestinian families. Within one week, a botched rescue attempt startled the terrorists, who responded by shooting and killing young Nachson.

His father, Yehuda, was still mourning the loss of his son when the father of the man who shot Nachson called him; his son's actions had convinced him that enough blood had been shed between Israeli Jews and Palestinians. Wachsman agreed. They arranged to meet in Jerusalem, and from that moment on the father of a son killed in conflict and the father of the killer joined together to work for peace and tolerance in Israel. [106]

These two fathers have taken part in the Compassionate Listening Project inspired by Gene Hoffman's work.

Another "terrorist" who has undergone many changes is Yasser Arafat. Even though he was once regarded by the United States as unredeemable, just like Qaddafi (some in the current administration still feel that way), Arafat took important steps towards a peaceful solution to the problem of Israel/Palestine. In 1994, his efforts in Oslo earned a Nobel Peace Prize for him as well as for Simon Perez and Yitzhak Rabin (who was assassinated a year later by an Israeli law student opposed to the peace process).

The peace movement was no doubt a factor in helping Arafat to consider nonviolent alternatives. In 1992, Gene was invited to join a delegation from the American Friends Service Committee to meet Arafat. Gene proved that she was not only a good listener, she was also willing to speak out. When Arafat was lecturing the delegation on the grievances of the Palestinians, Gene suddenly interrupted and said, "You ought to learn about nonviolence, and you ought to meet with Richard Deats."

Arafat was open to the idea and met with Deats to discuss it, but the dream of a peace center in Jerusalem never materialized due to lack of resources (why are there always funds for "smart bombs," but not for peacemaking?). One wonders what would have happened if some of the billions spent on arming Israel had been used for humanitarian aid and peace building efforts in the West Bank and the Gaza Strip.

Military and political solutions alone cannot resolve the profound psychological traumas that decades of bloodshed have wreaked upon the Middle East. The more time Gene spent in this region, the more she realized that both the Israelis and the Palestinians were deeply traumatized people. In order to heal, and to make peace, they needed to learn how to listen to each other, and be listened to, at a deep level.

Events in the Middle East demonstrate all too clearly that responding to violence with more violence is counterproductive. As Gene reminds us, amid the deadly uproar of empires and nations, we need to listen for, and nurture, the quiet stirrings of life and hope.

FOOTNOTES

---

[104] Libya did not initiate the cycle of violence involving the shooting down of aircraft. In 1973, four years after a bloodless coup in which Colonel Qaddafi ousted King Idris and became leader of Libya, Israelis shot down a Libyan plane over the Sinai, killing over 100 passengers. Libyan victims of this downed passenger jet have tried in vain to receive compensation from Israel, which claims that did nothing wrong in killing innocent civilians. In 1981, the US shot down two Libyan fighter jets off the Libyan coast.

[105] In an interview with Qaddafi that appeared in the conservative French newspaper *Le Figaro* (March 11, 2003), Charles Lambroschini wrote: "The young revolutionary Muammar al-Qaddafi has become a wise elder statesman. He has renounced terrorism—which, in his interviews with the American press, he consistently denies having ever countenanced: 'It was liberation movements that I supported,' he says. Al-Qaddafi stresses, too, that he became aware of the danger from Islamic fundamentalism long before Washington did. As early as 1986, he closed down about 50 Islamic institutions in Libya, accusing them of

being fronts for extremist subversion. And he was one of the first Arab leaders to publicly denounce the attacks on the World Trade Center and the Pentagon on Sept. 11, 2001. But in Washington, George W. Bush's most hard-line advisers are reluctant to forget al-Qaddafi's past. In their eyes, Libya remains a 'rogue state.'"

[106] "Compassionate Listening to the Israelis and Palestinians," by Kari Thorene. *YES! A Journal of Positive Futures*, Fall 1998.

Listening to the Libyans

Pax Christi USA, Fall, 1989

In 1986 American planes bombed Libyan civilians and Muammar Qaddafi's home and family in Tripoli. I was so shocked I wrote a letter to Qaddafi telling him that I grieved for the suffering we caused him and his people, urged him to explore a nonviolent response, and said I hoped one day to listen to his grievances. He sent a reply, an angry one, and thanked me for my concern.

In January of 1989, American planes downed two Libyan planes. This time a member of the Fellowship of Reconciliation (FOR) called the national headquarters in Nyack, NY, and said we should do something about it.

Virginia Baron, editor of *Fellowship Magazine*, agreed, and near midnight on June 27, 1989, ten FOR members from the US arrived in Tripoli. I was one of them.

We were met at the airport by a delegation of "The Libyan Arab Solidarity and Peace Committee" amid a flash of TV and newspaper cameras, led to our blue and white bus, and whisked to the Kabir Hotel, Tripoli's five-star finest.

At 9:30 the next morning, we met in the Kabir's huge meeting hall and began seven days of deep exploration of Libyan grievances, our differences, and what we might do about them. The Libyan committee consisted of fifteen members—all men— until our redoubtable delegation leader, Virginia Baron, asked where the women were. They quickly produced two remarkable ones: young Salma Abdul Jabbar, a teacher of philosophy at Tripoli University, and stunning Rawhia Kara, perhaps Libya's greatest feminist, an associate professor of English at the same university.

We introduced ourselves as "The Libyan Listening Project" and they quickly dubbed us "The Committee of Good Intentions." We hoped we would be both.

Most of our host committee were "westernized," which means they had lived in the United States and had either studied or taught at American universities. The majority were doctoral professors; there was one journalist and several were members of the "Solidarity and Peace" or other governmental committees. One was the former ambassador to the United States. All welcomed us warmly. Most thought very highly of the US and longed to return. An exception was the former ambassador who had been summarily deported in 1980; he did not share the others' enthusiasm. All told us how dismayed they had been with President Reagan's policies. When criticized for inviting us, the committee had responded by saying: "These Americans want to sift out solutions. They want to hear from us and tell their people what we say."

We learned that not everyone agreed with Qaddafi, but all held him in high esteem. We also learned that Libya is a secular Muslim state. It is called a state, not a nation, because Qaddafi's goal is to unite all Arabs into one mighty nation. Libya would be a state in that nation.

Today, Libya is wealthy because of oil discovered in 1959. Until then, the people were impoverished, uneducated, and under Italian occupation. After World War II, the Soviets and Americans divided up much of the world. Among other areas, the Americans were given bases in Libya. The United Nations appointed a king, who was deposed in the 1969 revolution at the time Qaddafi rose as a leader.

Moammar Qaddafi was born a Bedouin boy with unusual intelligence. He advanced in the military service and was a colonel at the time he became the country's leader. Qaddafi felt deeply about social issues and the sufferings of the impoverished Libyans, and he wrote a book of policies called *The Green Book*, which is presently banned in the US.[107]

Qaddafi rejects both capitalism and communism for a form of peoples' democracy through Basic Peoples' Congresses and Peoples' Committees. He believes the people should have direct control over their lives, and his form of government promotes that goal. I don't know whether it works, and people we interviewed were divided about it, but all agree their situation has improved beyond belief. Qaddafi has remained the unofficial head of Libya and its final arbiter in decision-making.

Since we had come to listen to grievances, we heard them—from Solidarity and Peace Committee members, from the International Green Book Studies Centre, from the permanent secretariat of the Arab Congress, and from private citizens.

Libyan Grievances

The Libyans' main concern was our attempted assassination of Qaddafi and the killing and wounding of his family, as well as many other civilians, in 1986. Next on the list were the economic sanctions against Libya, the embargo on all trade, the freezing of Libyan assets in the US, the banning of all Libyans from the United States, the ban on the travel of US citizens to Libya, our efforts to dismantle Qaddafi's regime, and the campaign of disinformation about Libya in the US. "Since the Libyan peoples' bureau was closed in the US in 1980, no Libyan voice is left to tell the Libyan point of view . . . the history of Libya is ignored in the US," we were told.

"We have been occupied for centuries—by the Turks, the British, the French, the Italians, and by Americans who fought their battle with the Germans on our soil during World War II. General Patton and General Rommel left our country in shambles. Villages were destroyed, our people were killed, and thousands of mines were sown in Libyan soil.[108]

"After World War II, we asked for aid from the Marshall Plan. We were denied it. We asked the Americans and Germans to remove the mines. They refused. Each year many people die from these abandoned mines. And now you bombed two of our planes last January in our own waters [*i.e. within the limit considered territorial rather than international waters*].

"The sad relationship with your government is due to a misunderstanding about our government and about the Libyan way of life. We want to live free as an independent state. We will never submit to any power, Soviet or US. We are rich and must control our resources and must evacuate all foreign people from our shores.

"Human rights means aiding people in solving these problems. You do not do this.

"As to your treatment of us: our rights are violated every day in the Gulf of Sert. Many areas of the high seas are in our own back yard. What the US fleet does in our high seas is a matter of life and death for us. Your maneuvers are one of the basic problems between us. We are bitter about what has happened. Your military aggression, embargo, and refusal to sell civilian planes to us are indefensible. The UN has adopted a resolution that we should be compensated for our suffering—but when? We want to be friends with your government and with the US people—but how?"

A member of our delegation posed this challenge: "We see a contradiction in your government. Libya wants dialogue and coexistence; in this we stand in solidarity with you. But American people perceive that you stand for the liberation of any governments and groups, no matter how violent. American people fear this will bring a reign of terror to the world."

271

Ibrahim Aboudhzam, vice-president of the People's General Assembly, answered: "As a basic principle we support independent movements which fight for justice; we support them but do not intervene in the process they choose. We support peaceful means to achieve independence, but sometimes they don't work. If we had used Gandhian means, I do not believe we would have achieved independence. Did the US gain independence by dialogue?"

Not all our experiences were so austere. The meetings were punctuated with delightful and delicious meals, as well as morning and afternoon breaks for coffee, tea, and ubiquitous pastries. We were banqueted and entertained. There was a memorable evening of Libyan tribal dances which had a power and vitality I'd rarely experienced. There were early morning walks along the Mediterranean, an afternoon at the exquisite ancient Roman ruins of Sabratha, and a "free day" at the Janzour sea resort.

And there were the people!

The Human Faces

There was Dr. Ali F. Kushaim, a member of our host committee. He is a gentle-spirited man, full of delight at our presence. He was an author, a mystic, a professor of Islamic philosophy. He invited me and two others from our delegation to his home.

There was Salma, a tall, dark-eyed, dark-haired young woman who stood queenly in her slim elegance. Salma was part of the Libyan delegation and came into my orbit by asking if I were a poet, "because," she said, "when I first heard you speak, I felt poetry in your speech." Salma taught philosophy at the University of Tripoli and hungered to know our poets and our philosophies.

Salma took me to the "*souq*," the old city market, where she carefully described the customs and the wares for sale in the tiny stalls. In one of the wedding stalls were three Bedouin women holding a lively conversation. She told them I was "one of the Americans" and they chattered excitedly like morning birds.

Then the spokeswoman for the three turned to me and spoke in flowing Arabic which Salma translated. She looked at me keenly with flashing black eyes. As she spoke, I observed her delicately blue-tattooed chin and forehead, her desert headdress, full skirt, loose bodice and flowered scarf tied across her breasts. "You are American," she said. "Please do not bomb us again. We want to love you; please do not bomb us. Let us have love between us. Salaam." The other two Bedouin women nodded in agreement and reached out to touch me with their work-worn hands.

There was Rawhia, a woman of statuesque proportions who had studied at Berkeley University and now taught in the English department of Tripoli's university. Full, rich mouth, penetrating eyes, hair drawn back from her finely carved face, a high bridged aquiline nose; this describes Rawhia— in part. She was the feminist; her passion to take her women out of slavery was intense. She referred angrily to women who wore the Myt Hejba (headdress) and the Juba (long gown), saying these were symbols of their willingness to be inferior to men.

There was Nada, Rawhia's vivacious daughter, who had lived in Berkeley, California, the first ten years of her life. She returned there when she was eighteen to attend the university. Breathlessly, she asked me if I had seen "Rain Man." When I said yes, she replied, "I have too. I loved it . . . We have video clubs and we get the newest films from the US." I was astonished. I had been told there were no American imports in Libya.

Nada described the day we bombed Tripoli and Qaddafi's home. She was in Berkeley, on the bus, when a man sitting beside her turned to her and said angrily, "If I saw a Libyan, I'd smash his face in." Nada knew it was time to leave. She got off the bus at the next stop, frightened and quaking. Soon the US government deported her, and she hasn't been back since.

There was the little girl who sat next to me at lunch. She turned to Mary, one of the American delegates who spoke Arabic, and said, "You must love war." When Mary protested that she was peace-loving and that was why she had come to Libya, the child gazed at her from candid gray-blue eyes and remarked, "You *must* love war. You bombed us. I saw the bombs falling."

There are many more faces etched in my memory. Even with these few I can clearly see that Qaddafi is not Libya, nor is our American view of it the real Libya.

Our last dialogue was with the attorney general of Tripoli. He was Sassi Salem el Haj, who is on the Executive Committee for Human Rights. He came from a Berber tribe. His eyes were warm and blue; he was open and very responsive.

"Two months ago we formed a committee on Libyan human rights. We have not yet organized our work, but we want to do something for human rights not connected with the government. We sent our committee's constitution to Amnesty International; we have had no response from them yet.

"As to the prisoners on the Amnesty International list you gave me, that list is old (*and it was*)[109], and I know many of them. Almost all of them are released; just a few are still in prison. I am in touch with all of them; I can take you to meet some of them, if you wish. (We could not—we had no time.)

"After 1988 most political prisoners in Libya were released. There were more than 500 and now there are only about 20. Qaddafi himself destroyed the first jail for political prisoners, and we plan to have no more."

Toward the Future

Finally, our delegation and the Libyan committee met to determine what we could do to continue the dialogue and to educate Americans about Libyans. The FOR agreed to pursue the possibility both of a return delegation of the Libyan committee to the United States, and of a conference of Christians, Muslims, and Jews which would include Libyans. We also agreed to see if foreign student departments would petition our government to permit Libyan students to return. Another goal is a campaign to "put a human face" on Libyans for Americans by creating slide shows, posters, and postcards of Libyan people, and by exhibiting Libyan children's art. The Libyans also agreed to invite more Americans to visit Libya.

Thus, our "days of dialogue" came to an end. We all felt we were wiser than when we came. I have little direct knowledge of Libyan hearts and minds, but I do not believe that Libyans as a people can be called terrorists. Probably though—as in every country—some of them are, for everywhere there are those who are hopeless, angry, those who feel their grievances will never be addressed, and so they turn to violence.

What I do know is that Libyans are people just like us, who laugh and weep and sing and die. I hope to help Americans see Libyans as human beings hungry for life and love and friendship, in precisely the same ways we are.[110]

---

[107] Copies are currently available online through amazon.com and elsewhere.
[108] Estimates of the number of landmines in Libya vary. The US State Department says that there are approximately 100,000 mines on Libya's territory, the majority of which are World War II-era German, British, US, and Italian mines. Libyan officials have stated that there are "millions of landmines buried in Libya." It

has been estimated that as much as one third of arable land in Libya cannot be used because of landmines.

[109] Gene Hoffman's aside.

[110] When Gene and her delegation returned to the US, they were forbidden to speak to US officials about their experiences in Libya because of US law.

Palestinians and Israelis: Two Traumatized People

(HopeDance June 2002)

I have long loved Israel. When I was there in the sixties, I found that little country a rare and refreshing spiritual, political, and social experiment.[111] It had taken, I felt, the best from a variety of governing systems and had blended them in a remarkable way. I had hoped each of my sons and daughters would spend time on a kibbutz.

When I returned in 1980, I found a very different ambiance. Israel was heavily armed, frightened, defensive, and persecuting the Palestinians. What had happened to this promising nation and its people to become so bellicose?

A whole new chapter of my life opened. I wondered why people tortured other people, and I thought that if I could know that answer, there might be new possibilities for peacemaking and reconciliation. And, as a Quaker pacifist, I believed I should have no enemy and should care for the wounded on all sides of every battle.

That year I worked on both sides of the Green Line [*the geopolitical border separating the West Bank from Israel proper*], moving back and forth, interviewing peace people, both Israelis and Palestinians. The suffering of the Palestinians under Israeli rule was horrifying. It seemed madness, and I wondered whether the behavior of the Israeli government and the military had anything to do with the suffering from the Holocaust. I began reading everything I could find on the Holocaust syndrome. In the ensuing years I learned about post-traumatic-stress disorder (PTSD), a tragic condition which frequently affects soldiers when they emerge from battle, or years later—battle fatigue, as it was formerly called. Any catastrophic event "outside the range of normal human experience" can cause similar symptoms, which can include depression, isolation, withdrawal, rage, numbing, alienation, intrusive thoughts, horrifying flashbacks, a force of hyper-vigilance akin to paranoia, and more.

I looked at the histories of these two adversaries, the Israelis and the Palestinians. I saw them as two traumatized people who have suffered from and committed acts of terrorism and violence against one another. Today the Israeli government is in a position of power and is oppressor to the Palestinians. There is, of course, retaliation. While there is a strong and active peace movement against the Israeli government's policies (at least 50% of Israeli citizens are said to disagree with their government), the people have not been able to change its policy to one of just and peaceable coexistence.

Today it's easy to see the Palestinians' suffering and the injustices they experience. It is not so easy to see the suffering of the Israelis. I feel that many of us have taken sides against the Israelis and consider them brutal, relentless, and unapproachable.

I have a different opinion: I have come to believe that violence springs from unhealed wounds. I don't believe we've made an effort to listen to them compassionately, to explore their history and their fears. While we stand steadfast against cruel actions, our attitude toward violent people requires this compassion toward them.

I began to study the Holocaust Syndrome and returned to the area many times to learn about the syndrome of both peoples. I felt it might be the unseen and unhealed wound of both parties to this tragic conflict.

There is a new consciousness of the long-term effects of the concentration-camp experience on the survivors and the children,

278

even grandchildren, of survivors. There is a new awareness that no healing processes were available at the time people were released from concentration camps, and a disturbing lack of care since then. Some people are beginning to refer to the violent actions of their government, and the refusal to grant the Palestinians a home of their own, as PTSD. The survivors experience a deep fear, both from surfacing memories and that it will happen again. Many Israelis appear to be affected by a siege mentality, and there is no way of their not believing they are in a dangerous "war zone."

I met with Rabbi Jeremy Milgrom, who was born in the US and is now an Israeli citizen, the head of Israel's Clergy for Peace. This tall, slender young man, intense, and compassionate, said, "The Holocaust left many Jews so scarred that they believe powerlessness is a sin. They feel the whole world is hostile to us. This is a sick behavior. Our politics are the opposite of forgiveness, namely rebellion against mistreatment suffered in the Holocaust and violent treatment from Palestinians who demand their freedom." Rabbi Milgrom, in the second generation from the Holocaust, finds his government's politics irrational because the Jewish State has been implemented at the expense of the Palestinians (partly) and because spiritual Zionism has changed into statehood after the Nazi persecution. "There was a war with the Palestinians which we won and our agenda is corrupt because we're not permitting Palestinians to re-unify. We Jews feel guilt toward the Palestinians and we're unwilling to have a dialogue with them because it will be so unpleasant."

Rabbi Milgrom was also struggling with the issue of forgiving the Germans, for he said, "As long as we withhold forgiveness of the Germans, we're corrupted. It's very hard to trust after the Holocaust, but if we can have this redemptive dialogue with the Germans, then we can break down the resistance to having it with the Palestinians. Forgiveness is a release from the past. You don't have to forget."

Rabbi Yonasson Gershom, in his article, "Breaking the Cycle of Abuse," writes: "On a conscious level, the Israelis are not purposely punishing the Palestinians for the Holocaust. The very suggestion is horrifying to most Jews; didn't we collectively vow never again? True. But it is also true that people who have been abused will, when they come to power, abuse others because they do not have healthy models for exercising power. Abuse is passed down from generation to generation...unless there is some kind of therapy to teach new ways of coping with frustration and anger."

Rabbi Gershom also addresses the question of abuse in its application to nations: "What is true of individuals can also be true of nations. It is relatively easy to overthrow a government, but far more difficult to oust the internalized oppression which causes us to demonize others. The abuse cycle is not logical. It is a set of totally irrational behaviors based on pain, fear, shame, guilt, and anger.... Rather than forgive and forget, we need to forgive and move forward. Nonviolence does not mean passive resistance; it means holding to the truth, using truth, faith, and love as our 'weapons' for waging peace."

I agree with Rabbi Gershom. There is a Buddhist tale of the snake who learned to practice nonviolence. Like the snake, I reserve the right to "hiss" and warn others of danger.

Last, I met with the editor-in chief of *New Outlook* Magazine, Chaim Shur. He is a generous, gentle man who told me, "The Holocaust is the worst trauma in Jewish history. The whole world was killing us. No one did anything to prevent it. The Holocaust Syndrome invades a large part of our lives. Five hundred thousand people in Israel are Holocaust survivors or descendants."

When I asked him if he thought survivors suffer from PTSD, he answered, "PTSD is not a scientific diagnosis. I don't accept it. I have a daughter-in-law whose parents are Holocaust survivors."

After that journey, I returned to the Middle East to listen to Palestinians. By this time I had learned new things: that people become "terrorists" when they feel their grievances are not heard, their concerns not addressed; I believe that our work as peacemakers is not to take sides but to seek truth, that there will never be peace unless both sides are listened to. We must care about those who hurt others, and listen with respect to those who disagree with or oppose us. I believe that through such listening we can open new avenues for communication where people are in conflict. We hope that one day they will be able to listen to each other.

Now to Palestine, or the Occupied Territories

How can I make Gaza real to you? Gaza is a Muslim strip of land on the Israeli-Egyptian border, the most densely populated area in the world. Perhaps telling you how people looked, what they said, and what I saw and heard might help.

In the outskirts of Gaza, fruit trees blossom, wild grasses cover the fields, and people suffer.

The main street had chuckholes full of dirty water, broken buildings, blind stores, their locked doors covered with anti-occupation graffiti. A woman walked down the broken sidewalk, a baby on her hip, talking and gesticulating excitedly, a barefoot old man carried a knotted staff, limping.

Gaza: prostheses, crutches, braces, scabies, 15,000 demolished homes, miscarriages from gas attacks, rubber fragmentation bullets, plastic bullets covering an explosive metal core, prison sentences of 150 years, 700,000 people in 360 square kilometers, 45% of the land confiscated by 2,500 Israeli settlers, xeroxed pictures on lamp posts of sons of Gaza who were martyrs: young men and children shot for throwing stones, refugee camps, rag walls on houses, sewage flowing in the central gutter, down narrow streets with not even enough room to carry the dead through, malnutrition, worms infesting the people.

And still, there is life in Gaza.

Out of the general and into the particular. We drove into a parking lot across a shallow lake of dirty water left by the rains. The buildings are a faded blue and white. A sign reads "American Friends Service Committee: Early Childhood Education Center." We are taken to a pale green room with a desk and chairs. We wait for Mary Khass, a Palestinian Quaker and pacifist who is the director of this little center. She has suffered the fate of most Palestinians: a son was killed, her family disrupted, desolation and despair. Yet Mary is said to have a sturdy faith in life. She lives in this childcare center.

Mary Khass enters. She is full-figured, Western-dressed. Her face is carved into lines of pain and compassion. She stands before us telling her story. I trust Mary Khass.

"My deepest concern is the children. We and the Israelis are raising a generation of haters. It is important for the Palestinians and Israelis to come to an understanding before the Palestinians lose all the land. There is no survival without sharing. We and the Israelis will have to live here, the sooner, the better.

"What can you do to help us? Work hard for the two states. Respect and support Israeli progressive groups, but remember, they haven't done enough unless they refuse military service in the occupied territories. If they are against the occupation, they must not serve."

And then, her cry of anguish: "How can they sleep? There is a hospital next to this place. I have seen Israeli soldiers raid the hospital. They shot and beat patients, nurses, doctors. I saw an Israeli soldier crying and beating his head against the wall. A Palestinian mother comforted this soldier. 'Malesh. It's all right, my son.' That young man could have said, 'No.' Why didn't he say No? Can Israelis not see it's more courageous to work for peace than war?

"We have unwanted refugees all over the world. We didn't cause the Holocaust. We advocate a peaceful and just solution for both. But my people have learned that depending on justice and the politicians is fruitless. We must pay the price and bring about change ourselves. Our children are suffering emotional horror, hypocrisy, violence, and fear. The little ones learn how to solve problems with violence. They are out of control. They are controlling us. The hand that throws the stone needs understanding and love. Educators need education to deal with opening the minds of these little ones.

"Recently a bullet was shot in a camp. Nobody was hurt. All the camp was placed under curfew for 12 days. One hundred and eighty young men were arrested. All the citrus groves were demolished. Three houses were destroyed. Many men between the ages of 16 to 60 were beaten.

"The Israelis must learn to live with guilt. To do this, they must stay in camps with us. As long as they don't stay in our camps, they haven't crossed the line emotionally. As long as they don't discourage their military from serving in the territories, they wipe my tears with one hand, and slap me with the other."

That night we heard shooting in the streets; fires blazed in the sky. The next day, fighting continued with rock throwing and sporadic shots. Soldiers and rock-throwers faced off on a street in which we were riding; our driver turned hastily and left. We later learned a nine-year-old boy was killed.

We were taken from refugee camp to refugee camp: more stories.

"I was in prison and so was my husband; he [was sentenced] for 440 years. I was pregnant, near term. The guards insisted the baby should be born now, dead. They said I have five living children. This one must die. They drove me for two hours over rough roads. I was forced to lie on my stomach. The baby did not come. They took me to a room in the prison and manacled me to the bed while they threatened and probed and pushed.

Still the baby did not come. They called my baby a terrorist. At last, my baby came. He lived; I called him Yasser. God wanted Yasser to live."

More voices in the camps: "I have two martyrs in my family, two of my sons were shot. See their pictures on the wall." "My son was seventeen when he was killed by open fire on demonstrators." "Mine was shot in the head." "My son is in Anssar III, the prison of suffering." "My youngest son is serving his ninth prison sentence."

"Do not feel sorry for us. We are parents of martyrs. We are proud. For 38 years we were silent and compliant. Then we began the Intifada, our uprising. We do not use weapons. We use our skills. We now have hope and a purpose. We will not stop until we get our independent state and our own identity."

This was before the latest war. Palestinians are now returning to use of violence, and so are the Israelis. The situation seems hopeless.

I feel there are always "possibilities" if we look for them. The therapist Alice Miller is confident that we can find ways to free ourselves of hatred and rage by doing the painful and rewarding work of feeling and experiencing it "in its original context." She is confident that we can save life on our planet by "questioning the present dangerous and ubiquitous blindness (denial), above all as it exists in ourselves."

I agree with Alice Miller and I feel if we can see the sorrow and suffering of those who commit heinous violence, I think whole new dimensions will open for our lives and for peacemaking. I see peacemaking as a healing process and know that if we include this dimension in our efforts, they will have new power and persuasion.

FOOTNOTES

---

[111] Gene went to Israel as part of a delegation from Center for the Study of Democratic Institutions. See p. 19 and footnote.

Crevices in the Rock

Fellowship Magazine, 1981

I was about twenty-two when my grandmother told me my grandfather was a Bohemian Jew. That knowledge had been hidden from me by my parents. Perhaps she thought it was time. I was thrilled and returned home in great excitement to tell my parents how glad I was to be a Jew.

They denied it.

But I continued to cherish this awareness of the Hebrew seed in me, the seed of prophets and of seers.

The other half of my heritage is Danish. I have always been proud that my relatives in Denmark were in the Underground against the Nazi occupation, and, though no Jewish blood (if there be such a thing as Jewish blood) coursed through their veins, they joined their king and countrymen and wore the yellow star when the Nazis ordered it for all the Jews in Denmark.

When I first visited Israel in 1961, I found it a Promised Land, and thought of it as one also promised me. I was a guest of the Israeli government and saw Israel from its most flourishing kibbutz to dinner at the home of Golda Meier.[112]

I am dismayed at how ignorant I was at that time. I hadn't done my homework. I knew nothing of the plight of the Palestinians. I did know that the Jews, who had suffered so much and who had been rejected in their homelands, came there seeking sanctuary and acceptance and met still another painful rejection by the Palestinians. Only later did I understand that Palestinians felt the Holocaust was a Western problem that should be solved by Western countries, by re-absorption of the Jews into the Western world.

I knew the suffering of the Jews by heart—but I was beginning to have some doubts about the progress of Israel. For even then I saw the foreshadowing of cruelty caused by so much absorption in one's own suffering. My training in psychotherapy taught me the difference between being centered-in-the-self and being self-centered. When we are self-centered, we know only our own grief, our own sufferings, and we lose our capacity to feel into the suffering of others. I saw some Israelis subtly becoming like those they feared.

Last summer I returned to Israel. It was part of a world pilgrimage to visit peace centers and learn what new creative acts were being taken for peace that I might bring home. I was also searching to understand why some people emerged from great suffering with compassion while others were twisted by it into bitterness and the desire for revenge.

I found much to celebrate in new efforts for peace. I gained some understanding about the different effects of suffering. In Israel (as in our own and other countries) I saw the brutalizing effect of militarism. I saw the truth in the poignant cry of Joseph Abileah, Israel's leading pacifist, about his beloved land: "These people don't defend me. They cannot, because they defend only an institution which is called the State."

On the day I rode to Haifa it was Sunday. The bus was crowded, the aisles full of standing passengers. Most were Israeli soldiers. Young dark-eyed, dark-haired boys with scarcely the first fuzz on their chins—submachine guns slung over their shoulders. Long, slender fingers, short, practical fingers, hands of half-grown children easing around the triggers.

Children of terror, children of the trauma of fear. How many generations must this fear be visited upon? Children who should be playing violins, planting wheat, surfing in the sun—children growing into adulthood who should be exploring the delicate wonders of sex and love, the miracles of creation.

For days I'd been in the dust-dry land of despair—had been with Palestinians choking on grief, on anger, on unshed tears, on fear. For days I walked their deserts with them and saw their lives under Israeli occupation. Saw demolished houses where Palestinian children had once thrown stones at Israeli military vehicles; their families were now consigned to tents and prevented from rebuilding their homes for two years. Saw villages with all but one exit sealed by cement, saw houses sealed by cement, their owners forced to find residence elsewhere because they were suspected of being unsympathetic to Israel.

I met women under house arrest because they had dared to seek civil liberties meeting with others; saw new ground being broken for new settlements even though the United Nations had declared their construction a violation of international law; met shopkeepers who were forced to reopen their shops at gunpoint when they had closed them in nonviolent resistance. Learned from the Mennonite director of refugee children's education about the beating of a young Arab boy by an Israeli soldier outside the Quaker meeting house. Learning some of the causes for Palestinian acts of violence, I learned, too, that the Palestinians are an unarmed people under Israeli military occupation.

And I wondered: How could it happen that those who suffered so grievously from oppression had turned oppressor? How could it happen that this land, so longed for, knows no peace?

An answer that came to me was "fear and memory of fear." This was substantiated by Joseph Abileah, who said that the Israeli militarists were "suffering from the trauma of fear."

Later, in Holland, J. Bastiaans, psychiatrist and professor in the department of psychiatry of the State University of Leiden, expanded on this theme.

In 1945, Dr. Bastiaans began his study of the effects of the concentration camp experience on people who survived. He discovered a series of stages each goes through, not unlike those discovered by Kuebler-Ross in her studies of the effects of death upon family and friends. For those who survived, there was first a period of shock, withdrawal, and repression. For those who received help when they came out—a warm, caring environment where they could do their grief work, remember and talk about the horrifying experiences, purge themselves of memories and guilt—life held new promise and they were able to fulfill themselves as human beings.

For those who did not receive this caring treatment, for those who had to return to the competitive world, to find a place in it without friends, without family, without sharing their memories, without doing the work of grieving, another direction opened.

According to Dr. Bastiaans, it is one of closure and repression, with the repressed (sic) returning in terrible ways—as hostility, as anger, as aggression. Today, thirty-five years after the end of World War II, the aggressive stage is flowering.

If this is true—or even partly true—there is at least some explanation for the behavior of the Israelis who have caused such suffering among the Palestinians.

It explains, too, the behavior of their children—those in khaki and berets, black submachine guns slung over their shoulders. We used to say, "The sins of the fathers are visited upon the children." Dr. Bastiaans would say, the children are infected by the fears of their elders and respond to them in similar fashion.

When I reached Haifa, I was immediately taken to Ibillin, an Arab village in Galilee, where Father Elias Chacour, an Arab Christian priest (who was born there), was creating educational centers for young and old, while seeking to teach them Christian nonviolence toward the "enemy."

Three settlements had been built around Ibillin. Settlements are Israeli "housing developments," usually built on confiscated Arab lands. Sometimes they are cement-block houses surrounded by high fences and barbed wire. Sometimes they are huge prison-like structures which have a sweeping view of the countryside. Sometimes they house the expanding Israeli population; sometimes they are homes for the Gush Emunim, fanatical Zionists who believe any violence is God's will if it preserves Israel. They usually keep caches of arms in case of a Palestinian uprising. Whenever there are settlements, there is increased fear, anger, and hostility.

Father Chacour greeted me warmly, and I sat in the spacious welcoming room of his church compound. The interview began. Father Chacour sat across—no smile, no welcoming now. It had vanished. He grieved. Anguish, pain darkened his face. "They are building the fourth settlement in our village. Now we are surrounded. Surrounded by fortresses of hate. What can I *do*? What can I say? How can I tell them any more to love their enemies? Do good to them that hate you? No, I cannot. What *can* I do?"

That was all. I sipped the coffee. He went into his office to prepare for a wedding that evening.

We have to have a deep, patient compassion for the fears of men, for the fears and the irrational mania of those who hate....

So wrote Thomas Merton.

Fear, the return of the repressed and the cruelties that spring from it are one side of the coin in Israel, one face of suffering in this beleaguered land.

But there is another face—fresh grown, cracking the cold stone of pain.

One Palestinian woman, whose son—the president of Birzeit University—had been deported several years ago, remarked: "The most sorrowful thing about all this is that our younger generation doesn't know what it is to love a Jew. Does not know they are people and can be loyal friends. I grew up with Jews—they were my schoolmates. With some, our families were as one family. One of them, my best friend, gave me a blood transfusion. I do not forget that, ever."

There are Israelis who have not forgotten—and their children have been "infected" by different memories...

There was the day Naftali Raz came to lunch. A five-star day! Naftali is a short, compact man, intense, young, surprisingly gentle. His face tells of harsh experiences as a paratrooper. Yet smile lines crinkle around his eyes. In them I saw his depth of concern for his people, the Israelis, and for the Palestinians.

Naftali is a Zionist. He believes the Jews had to find a homeland after the Holocaust, and it is right that it is on this soil. But Naftali had an experience that changed his life. As a boy he lived in a "settlement." It was built over three destroyed Arab villages. As he grew older, he questioned this. Why should Israelis build a Jewish city where Arab cities had been flourishing? There was plenty of land. Why were the Palestinians forced to flee, and to where?

This concern lived with him through all his days of service in the Israeli army. When he was discharged, he knew he had to work for peace.

Two years ago, "Peace Now" was born. It began with a letter signed by 358 reserve military officers and soldiers. The letter was sent to Prime Minister Menahem Begin on March 7, 1978. It called upon him to choose the path of peace by developing neighborly relations with the Palestinians, halting the building of settlements on Palestinian territory, and relinquishing rule over one million Palestinians.

They felt that ". . . true security will be achieved only with the advent of peace" and that the course the government was on "would damage the Jewish democratic character of the state" and make it difficult for them to support the goals of the State of Israel.

A leadership committee of fifteen was formed. Naftali was one of the original signers and is on the Leadership Committee today. They began to formulate policy they thought appropriate to true Zionism as defined by Theodore Herzl in 1904: "Zionism . . . contains not only the aspiration for a secure piece of land for our unfortunate people, but also the aspiration for ethical and spiritual perfection." They saw that Israel was not moving toward any ethical or spiritual perfection.

So they set to work. Today they have over 250,000 names on their mailing list and are vibrating all over Israel with demonstrations, papers, statements, letters, meetings, and "happenings."

In brief, "Peace Now" seeks negotiation and believes the Israeli government must be willing to meet any kind of Palestinian representative on one condition: negotiation is the only appropriate method.

They want no advance decisions or preconditions brought to the negotiating table. They demand a freeze on building new settlements, on the Jerusalem law, and on Begin's plan to move his offices to Jerusalem.

To educate their countrymen and to persuade their government to move in this direction, they have held many demonstrations and performed many acts of protest and of reconciliation. The largest demonstration they held amassed some 100,000 people. They had two demonstrations of 80,000 protesting the obstacles Begin created to peace with Egypt.

At one time they demonstrated against the building of a new settlement by surrounding it with ripples of larger and larger circles of people holding posters of protest. At another time the Gush Emunin cut down the vineyards in the West Bank. The "Peace Now" people brought Jewish and Palestinian children together to plant new ones.

A year ago they demonstrated against more settlements next to Nablus; 6,000 people occupied the area for two nights and two days, blocking the tractors. The army surrounded them and set up roadblocks so they could not escape. They asked to speak to the Minister of Defense. Minister Weizman came in a helicopter. They negotiated with him and agreed to leave if he would make the "Peace Now" position clear to the government and if the army would remove the roadblocks. Their requests were met.

"All our demonstrations have been nonviolent," said Naftali proudly. I then asked him about extending nonviolence beyond the borders of demonstrations, into the direction of disarming Israel. He replied without pause: "Being an Israeli, I can't even think of Israel without a defense force." I appreciated his forthrightness.

Just before I left Israel I learned about the most recent peace rally. It sounded like a "happening" to me. A group of young people called The Young Guardians created a "sing-in." The event was called "The Song of the Dove."

The "Peace Now" people joined it, as did the Abie Nathan Peace Ship people. Between 50,000 and 70,000 people gathered at Yar Kon Park in the outskirts of Tel Aviv the last weekend in August. They had a few professional entertainers, but most of the singing was by the participants, who sang for twenty-four hours, with time out from 11:00 p.m. to 7:00 a.m., "to give the neighbors a rest." From the description by two exalted, enthusiastic young women who told me about the event, I decided the neighbors probably had a great time!

Morning in Haifa, bright sun slanting through the dining room window. Breakfast on fresh cucumbers, tomatoes, cottage cheese, bread, marmalade, and steaming tea. Out the window, fresh green of trees, and in the distance, the silver-shimmering sea.

The phone rang. It was Ibrahim Si'man, Israeli-Arab, a Christian, a Baptist, a man of tender tireless passion for the redemption of all peoples. A man of gusto, humor, and suffering. A man of peace.

"Would you like to go to a burial today?"

"A burial? Of whom? What burial?"

His answer was quick and surprising. "This is to be a very unusual burial—this evening we shall bury hatred on Neve Shalom."

Neve Shalom! That mystic mountain. Neve Shalom, "Oasis of Peace," where Jews and Moslems and Christians have begun their experiment of living together on the harsh, unyielding land. Of course, I wanted to go to Neve Shalom, where the vision of Father Bruno Hussar, a Dominican priest, had come into being.

On the way, Ibrahim described a little of what I might expect: Under the aegis of a rather new organization called Partnership, a camp of young Israelis and Arabs (one of Partnership's many projects) had conceived the idea of the burial of hatred. More than that he would not tell me.

My introduction to it was at the community hall, where about thirty people were sitting in face-to-face pairs. The wooden room quaked with their laughter and chatter. I later learned the Israelis were speaking Arabic and the Arabs Hebrew. It was a first for most of them.

Partnership is another vision, a vision of a remarkable woman, Rachel (Rosenschweig) Bat Adam, who believes that Israel can exist only if Israelis and Arabs come to live in full partnership, recognizing the importance of the contributions each makes, as well as their dependence on one another. Others have caught fire from Rachel's energy and enthusiasm. One is Ibrahim Si'man, who is now its chairman.

The evening was the culmination of days of deep sharing and working together. The participants came from Arab villages in Galilee. The Jews came from various places in Israel, and some (including the leader) were from America.

At the end of the conversation time, the campers formed a circle, and each was asked to describe why s/he had come and what it had meant. Here are some of the responses:

Yusuf: I came to test and strengthen my view that Arabs and Jews can live together.

Judi: For my conscience's sake. I see things need to be improved; I'm trying to learn now.

Khaled: I believe the Neve Shalom way of life suits this country—there can be peace between Arab and Jew.

Fatima: To let them know me, to know them, so we can live together.

Claudia: To see how it works, this cooperation, to see what's possible in the future.

Amal: I came to hear and to listen to what they know about us, and to give them of myself, and to talk about politics.

Oren: I am for common life and for this we need to strive together. There are problems: we need to bring them out, discuss them.

It was dinnertime. We walked to the dining hall, thoughtfully, after the open exchange. Dinner was delicious. I sat with Father Hussar, who told of his delight in the three new "citizens" of Neve Shalom—three babies in the past two months.

After dinner, we filed out. And there, before us, was another vision. The top of the mountain was wreathed in light, in glowing candles. We stood silently for a moment, then formed a procession to the top, each of us holding in our hands a piece of paper on which we had written what we wanted to bury.

At the top we stood in a silent circle as various members of the group read passages of peace in Hebrew and Arabic from the Old and New Testaments and from the Koran. Then we walked, one by one, to the grave, and threw into it what we wished to bury.

Some read aloud what they were burying: Disrespect, misunderstanding, bad people, dark spirits, hostility between Arabs and Jews, feelings of superiority, suspicion. I buried fear.

After all were cast into the grave, someone came with a torch and began to light a banner that stretched across the grave. It spelled peace in both Hebrew and Arabic. One by one the letters began to blaze, catching fire from the torch.

Suddenly the banner fell to the ground in a flaming heap.

There were cries of "Oh, it is a bad omen! How awful. Our ceremony is spoiled." Words leapt to my lips and I cried, "No, it isn't a bad omen— this means peace has come to earth in Israel." My words were taken up by others. There was laughter, still some doubt, but some release. Then silence.

Out of the silence came a song—a song for peace. Other voices took it up. And there, in the soft night, a golden moon rose. It shone upon the mountains and the valleys, and the six or seven houses of Neve Shalom. And it shone upon us as we sang in Arabic, in Hebrew, and finally, almost unobtrusively, in English.

For someone began, "We Shall Overcome." Slowly, we put arms around each other and began the customary rhythmic swaying, singing verse after verse, believing in that moment the truth of what we were singing, making it true by the singing; somehow, opening some crevice in that stony desert of hatred and despair to let some love flow through—feeling, in that moment, that our Shaloms and Salaams and hopes for peace could flower in all the worlds we came from.

FOOTNOTES

---

[112] She went with a delegation from the Center for the Study of Democratic Institutions. See p. 19.

After the Peace Accords—
What?

Harmony: Voices for a Just Future, 1994.

I met Yasser Arafat twice in 1992, in April and in October. The first time, with a delegation from the American Friends Service Committee, I learned that President Arafat and the PLO were hungry for new nonviolent initiatives in the conflict with the Israelis.

The second time, I had written him a letter—some of us from the Fellowship of Reconciliation wanted to present some alternatives to violence. Sami Musallam, Director of the President's Office, responded, inviting us to come.

Four of us went: Richard Deats, Director of FOR's Interfaith Program and an intrepid nonviolence trainer; Scott Kennedy; Karim Alkadhi, Chair of FOR's National Council; and I, long-time worker in the Middle East vineyards for peace, and a member of FOR's Advisory Council.

On the October visit, we arrived in Tunis on October 20. We were met by Zudhi Terzi, former PLO representative to the United Nations, now a Senior Aide to President Arafat. On our first meeting he told us: "The more nonviolence is unfruitfully pursued, the more room there is for fanatics who will oppose the peace process out of desperation. There is the danger of the rise of Islamic fundamentalism. Fundamentalists reject any political settlement and consider the peace negotiations treason. The hope Hamas (the Islamic fundamentalists) offers

296

are arms, money and the belief that the Palestinian-Israeli deadlock will be broken with the 'help of God.'"

After meeting with Terzi, we were taken to President Arafat, who greeted us warmly, and told us of his and the Palestinians' new suffering. We all suggested courses the PLO might take to avert violence. Richard was particularly impressive when he described some of his experiences teaching nonviolence in the former Soviet Union, particularly Lithuania. I told him I was eager to bring Israeli and Palestinian mothers together, to share about how the conflict was affecting their children. President Arafat wanted us to form a new nonviolent center in Jerusalem, made up of five Americans, because, he said, "You cannot be arrested, tortured or shot—you can only be deported."

Leaving, I reflected on what I had said at the previous visit: that I didn't believe that he could count on President Bush and the Americans to help him in his struggle for a State, and that I suggested that he do something dramatically nonviolent to capture the world's imagination. I wondered if we had suggested any such thing this time?

Since then, both he and Israel's Prime Minister Yitzak Rabin made nonviolent initiatives to each other that were beyond my wildest dreams! President Arafat became a strong leader again. He struck out the words in the PLO covenant about destroying Israel by "pushing it into the sea." He began small (as some Israelis hoped he would) by accepting only the territories of Jericho and Gaza, and he made other enormous concessions.

The Israelis made the unprecedented offer to talk with the PLO and to relinquish some West Bank territory. They and the Palestinians have reached mutual agreements and signed papers confirming them. They were televised for all the world to see, shaking hands on the White House lawn.

To me, some of the great results from the peace accords are that Israelis and Palestinians may visit one another and the PLO without being imprisoned. They may hold public discussions about mutual peace without fear of imprisonment, being called traitors, or worse. They may resume trade relations, if both agree. These are great new freedoms for both.

Thomas Jefferson said that we have nothing to fear so long as Truth is in the marketplace—if true, great fears have been lifted from both sides, and they may hammer out more peaceful solutions.

But they're not out of the woods yet. The woods may have grown thicker. Since the fighting in Kuwait, funds sent to the PLO to support the Palestinians have dropped to nearly nothing. It is now the Hamas fundamentalists who pay the bills for West Bank Palestinians, education, medical care, food, and much more. It is they who have armed the Palestinians and inflamed them with a sense of injustice and an impatience for retaliation.

Another critical problem is the settlers in the West Bank, who are armed and feel mortally threatened. I hope they can be dealt with equably and not compelled to leave the West Bank, for this would cause further terror and bloodshed, perhaps war. One Palestinian suggested to me that the settlers should be permitted to stay so long as they became full Palestinian citizens and obeyed Palestinian laws. This will work, if at all, if the Palestinians make no punitive laws against them, and the settlers accept these conditions.

I see this step as needed for real and enduring peace: First, both the Palestinians and the Israelis are wounded people. Each has caused great suffering to the other.

Thomas Merton wrote, "We have to have a deep, patient compassion for the fears. . . and the irrational mania of those who hate or condemn." We must seek a truth to match this. One truth which might serve was described by the Buddhist peacemaker Thich Nhat Hanh who said, "For peace and reconciliation, one thing is necessary. We must listen to the suffering of both sides with deep compassion."

Listeners must be trained to be non-adversarial and sensitive, to listen without judgments or rancor, and, above all, to not talk too much! After listening to one side, they must go to the other and tell of the suffering of the first. Then they repeat this with the second side. Eventually, it is hoped that through this delicate process each side will be able to listen to the other. It helps to heart-memorize Longfellow's wisdom: "If we could read the secret history of our enemies, we should find in each person sorrow and suffering enough to disarm all hostility."

Listeners must be trusted by both sides, able to see the human face of the "enemy," so that message can be carried across battle lines. Listeners must also be convinced that *there are always new possibilities!*

After such an exchange may come the epiphany: forgiveness. Forgiveness, in my book, is not about establishing a warm relationship—it means giving up the option to punish or revenge, freeing oneself from resentment.

How do we come to this? By seeing that both Palestinians and Israelis have been traumatized by the horrors they have experienced. Both need healing from what has occurred during their conflict, and long before. Unhealed wounds leave us with a legacy of violence, and telling our stories of suffering helps heal these terrible wounds.

There are many ways to heal traumatic stress. Some Vietnam veterans whom I know said the greatest healing for themselves was to be forgiven by some Vietnamese. Some of them attended a retreat given by Thich Nhat Hanh in Santa Barbara, California, in 1988. They told their horrifying stories of the war. Some Vietnamese who had fought in the war also attended. The vets asked forgiveness from the Vietnamese and were forgiven.

They discovered that they wanted something more, perhaps reconciliation. They decided to go to Vietnam, to acknowledge the harm they had done to Vietnamese people, in places where they had fought. They wanted to restore, with their own hands, places they had destroyed. Finally, they wanted to ask for forgiveness. Reconciliation can come after forgiveness, if it's right. It means to me mutual forgiveness, mutual responsibility for harm caused, and then mutual commitment to make a new relationship work. This happened between some Vietnam vets and some Vietnamese.

This experience was the beginning of the Vietnam Vets Restoration Project, which is still working. Forgiveness and reconciliation are still taking place for both sides, because hatred and fear have ceased.

I see similar healing needed by both sides in the Israeli-Palestinian conflict. Both people suffer from post-traumatic stress disorder. Both would benefit from people who would listen with compassion to their stories of suffering. We hope they may learn to listen to each other and perhaps to forgive one another and ultimately reconcile.

There are voices on both sides saying the conflict will never end until forgiveness takes place. Yehezkel Landau, former head of the religious peace organization "Oz ve Shalom," is one. He urges both Palestinians and Israelis to acknowledge the harm they have done one another, to forswear any such future behavior, and to ask one another for forgiveness. He maintains that only from mutual forgiveness can come reconciliation and true peace and security everyone longs for. He's not alone.

Nafez Assailey, the creative and vital Director of the Palestinian Center for the Study of Nonviolence, echoes Yehezkel's words. He, too, is not alone.

How do we encourage such behavior? I think, by modeling it.

I've just returned from a week in our Revolutionary and Civil War country. I've learned that those rifts haven't healed yet. Our nation had bloody beginnings, wars with Native Americans, the British, abuse of Africans by slavery, and many wars. Rarely, if at all, have I read of any American party to these atrocities asking for forgiveness of the other sides. Those wars ended with victors feeling justified and the vanquished being oppressed.

The modeling: I think we could begin modeling peace by following the lead of the Vietnam vets. We could look into history, and begin pilgrimages, in little groups, to the places where we have harmed people through war. What if we made pilgrimages to Germany for the harm we caused by firebombing Dresden, to Japan for the horrors of Hiroshima and Nagasaki? What if we moved through Grenada, Cuba, Nicaragua, Panama, Vietnam, Korea, Iraq, describing our sorrow for the harm we had done? What if we offered to make amends and asked for forgiveness?

Might we not plant seeds for an evolution of human beings into a world where we *would* "turn our swords into plowshares and our spears into pruning hooks"? Might not such actions lead to the transformation of humanity some of us feel is necessary if life is to continue on earth?

I think they might. It would prove that, as in the forming of our nation, a small group of dedicated people can make mighty changes. [The Oslo Accords, the first peace agreement between Israel and the Palestinian Liberation Organization] happened in Norway because a small group of Norwegians with vision were willing to take risks. How much more might happen if small groups of Americans took such risks for peace on earth? Admitting we have done wrong, over and over, would be a huge first step.

If the Vietnam vets are any example, true reconciliation, mutual healing, mutual understanding and mutual love might spring up between strangers who were once thought of as enemies. It might mean the continuation of a healthier planet and a nobler human race.

An Enemy Is One Whose Story We Have Not Heard

Fellowship Magazine, May/June 1997

In the spring of 1996 I received a phone call from Leah Green, Director of the Middle East Program for Earthstewards Network. She wanted to talk with me about my writing on compassionate listening, a process in which people open up to new thoughts and ideas when they are carefully listened to. Sometimes they even change their opinions as they learn to listen to themselves. Over the years I have doggedly kept visiting the Middle East, pursuing this process. Leah invited me to come to Israel and Palestine in November of 1996 with a group dedicated to compassionate listening.

On November 10, a party of eighteen left the United States—all committed to listen to both sides non-judgmentally, non-adversarially, compassionately. This article is about some of the people we encountered during that remarkable experiment.

The first night we were there, we met with Mikado Waraschawski, Director of the Alternative Information Center in Jerusalem. I'd known him for some time as the founder of Yesh Gvul. *Yesh Gvul* means "There is a Limit." To Mikado and many Israelis of military age, it meant they would not serve in the Israeli Army of Occupation on the West Bank.

Mikado was the same vivid, clear-thinking and clear-speaking young man, with hints of Asian ancestry, that I'd met before. He spoke to us about the hundred-year struggle between

Israelis and Palestinians, "two different realities in a very small land." The Oslo Declaration of Principles was based on important joint assumptions that recognized the mutual legitimate rights of both realities. But this is now being undermined by the Netanyahu government that "is replacing this mutuality with domination." Mikado also spoke of the fear in both societies of war between Jewish and Muslim fundamentalists, as well as deep concern over "the collapse of Israel's internal cohesion" if the militantly orthodox and extreme nationalists continue to grow in political power.

Sara Kaminker describes herself as a "devoted Zionist and a Jew." She is a former Jerusalem city planner and City Council member. She wants Palestinians on the City Council so that they can air their differences. Sara is a handsome, bold woman—larger than life, with an arresting voice. Her apartment is tastefully decorated, full of color, with rare Impressionist paintings, Persian rugs, furniture of rich woods, and large windows opening onto patios and views of Jerusalem. She is beloved by Palestinians, for she is a public voice on their behalf.

Sara described to us how land is distributed in East Jerusalem—a burning issue for Palestinians. In the past three and a half years, Jerusalem municipality policy has destroyed 291 Palestinian homes. In the worst cases, the municipality gives families five minutes to two hours to take what they can and leave the area. Then bulldozers demolish their houses. Sometimes demolitions are held up for months in the courts. "Jerusalem," she told us, "was expanded after the 1967 war. In 1967 there were 164,000 Palestinians in East Jerusalem and no Israelis. Seventy thousand *dunhams* [*sic*] were then expropriated and annexed to West Jerusalem." Today there are 170,000 Israelis in East Jerusalem.

To use Palestinian land, Israelis confiscate it for public use. This includes parks, schools, public buildings, the apartment complex in which Sara lives, and settlements. The Palestinian villages in East Jerusalem have been designated as "yellow areas." "Green" land is owned by Palestinians, but they are not allowed to live there or to build. Palestinians are always offered some compensation for their lands, but no Palestinian who values his life or reputation would accept it, since seeking this compensation denotes a traitor. The Israeli government offered twenty-five million dollars for certain Palestinian lands. No one took it, and the government confiscated the land anyway.

"Once they have lost their homes, Palestinians have the choice to live under poor housing conditions in 'yellow' areas, leave Jerusalem, or build new houses on 'green land.' No permits are issued to Palestinians to build on 'green land,' nor are there any subsidies. Homes on 'green land' are regularly demolished, often as soon as they are built. The Israelis have subsidized 60,000 apartments in East Jerusalem for Israelis, and only 5,000 for Palestinians. It is obvious," continued Sara, "that they want to populate Jerusalem with Israelis."

Sara Kaminker is an amazing woman. I feel Israel is blessed with her presence.

From Sara's we went to Beit Horon, a settlement in the West Bank. There we were met by Yehudit Tayer, Associate Director of the West Bank Yesha Settlement Council. Yehudit is a slim woman with long blond hair. She was born in the United States and has a fragile look. But she is far from fragile; her delicate chin is set; her brown eyes flash; she is a militant Zionist who believes unwaveringly that God gave this land to the Jews as an irrevocable gift. She lives with her husband and two small children in Beit Horon. We met with her in the settlement's synagogue, a handsome building with stunning and unusual stained glass windows. "We moved here," she began, "because we are Jews and want one homeland. Here is where it is: these Judean mountains were biblically given to us. The first settlers here had the beginnings of a friendly community. There were lots of empty mountaintops, plenty of room to live here for both us and the Palestinians. I oversee the 141 settlements of 150,000 Jews here in the heartland of Israel. We have a bypass road for the safety for our children; our drivers speak Arabic.

"I deal with the media. We residents are always depicted as fanatics. It would have been easier if in 1967 we had just thrown the Palestinians out. When we establish settlements we live on our ancient land. Hebron was established by Jews, and then we were 'ethnically cleansed' from there. We want to return; we have the right to return. We want to live in peace with the Arabs. Despite all the problems, we have grown. We have a high-tech economy, security doors, educational opportunities, even education for disabled girls. Terror attacks are blamed on us. The Government de-legitimized us by not allowing us to expand. Hebron should not be given to the Palestinians. All Jewish children in Beit Horon are targeted by the Palestinians— they are calling for the blood of the Jews. This message is coming from mosques: 'First we kill the Jews, and then the Christians.' A few weeks ago our houses were under fire. Palestinians are afraid to come here as friends...."

We left feeling downcast—we could sense her pain. Next we went to Gaza and, at long last, met with a leader of Hamas, the Islamic Resistance Movement best known in the West for acts of terrorism, such as suicide bombings. We were to meet Ghazi Ahmed Hamad, 31, head of the Center for Research on Palestinian Issues and spokesperson for the political wing of Hamas.

The office we entered was small and full of plastic chairs for us. Soon Ghazi Ahmed entered and sat at the worn desk. He was a slim, handsome young man with a surprisingly gentle face. There was something about his presence that caught my attention. He explained to us that during the Intifada, Hamas was militarily oriented, but that now it is more politically and socially oriented, helping poor families, families of prisoners, and women's activities. "We don't want to throw Israel into the sea; we want independence like any other people," he said.

"The Israeli government," Ghazi Ahmed told us, "exacts severe punishment from Palestinians in its effort to keep them under control. We may not export to anyone but Israel. There has been a four month curfew, and Palestinians may not go anywhere outside their own cities."

Then Ghazi Ahmed spoke about his personal life. He told us how his father and uncle were assassinated before his eyes when he was seven years old. How his mother had been shot, wounded in the lungs, had undergone surgery, but never healed. How on the night before the birth of his first child, while he and his wife were talking about possible names, Israeli soldiers dropped into their house from everywhere and arrested him. They told him to come with them for five minutes—and then told him he had committed acts against Israel, and was sentenced to five years in prison. He suffered thirty days of torture during interrogation. This was in 1989, during the height of the Intifada [Palestinian uprising]. He said he was never accused of anything specific; he did not know of what he was guilty.

"We live in isolation from the world," Ghazi Ahmed continued. "Here in Gaza we are in a big jail. We have lost the right to travel. The world should not blame a nation under siege. When we react to the settlers' violence, we are called killers. But I'm re-thinking violence for us—it doesn't do any good."

We asked him if his religion helped him. He responded, "My Muslim religion says 'Be patient.' If you do good and don't harass, you will survive. If you kill or harass, you and your state will be destroyed."

Our time with Ghazi Ahmed Hamad ended. We were all awed by the experience. I went up and spoke to him before I left. I told him, "You have great gifts—you can be a leader to your people. I hope you will explore nonviolence—it may be helpful to you." "You sound just like my mother," he replied. I told him I'd be glad to have him as a son. We laughed. He reached out to me; we embraced.

[Shortly after we left, Ghazi Ahmad Hamad joined in two nonviolent demonstrations in Gaza, as was widely reported in the US press. GKH]

After returning to the West Bank, our group joined a busload of Israelis going to visit a Palestinian woman whose husband had been killed by an Israeli soldier while participating in a nonviolent protest over the confiscation of his land. We passed through the main room of the murdered man's house and shook hands with his despairing family. The widow was pregnant with her eighth child. On our way out, I noticed a lovely woman with wavy gray hair. She must have noticed me too, because we walked out together toward the bus. We sat down and our conversation began. Her name is Chava Keller.

Chava lived in Poland in 1940. She had to flee from the Nazis, first to Russia and then to Lithuania. She spoke forcefully when she said, "Israelis are not committing Holocaust atrocities on the Palestinians. But if I don't do anything about the atrocities we *are* committing, I am like the Germans were."

I learned that Chava was the mother of Adam Keller, a famous Israeli pacifist who spent years in jail for refusing to enter the Israeli army. He is now editor of the magazine *The Other Israel*, which is committed to ending the Israeli occupation and undertaking many reforms. Chava is a long-time worker for peace and justice for Israeli prisoners, many of whom are Palestinian.

The following evening, we visited Chava in Tel Aviv. We were invited into a small apartment which, between chairs and the floor, was still big enough to contain our large group. It was warm and cozy, full of foreign souvenirs. There we met her husband Ya'akov and two of their friends and contemporaries,

Sara and Itzak. All four were veterans of the '48 war and were in their seventies.

In 1948 they, like Menachem Begin, had been members of the terrorist organization Irgun. They had all fought against the Palestinians. They were now against war and for the two-state solution.

They shared memories with us. Chava's feisty husband presented a picture of Jerusalem in 1948. "Few Jews walked with Arabs," he said. "Most were afraid to go to Arabs' homes." He had lived in Jerusalem. Parts of the city were destroyed by bombardments. His father lost his job. "We children were told to take Palestinian homes after the Palestinians left. My father said, 'Are you crazy? These people will return!"

Sara's husband Itzak was a writer; he reminded me of an elderly aristocrat. At that time, he had felt it was all right to kill. "The idea of killing Arabs gave me pleasure. 'Kill the tiger and become a man' was my motto." Later he became sympathetic to the Palestinians and began to think it was not right to kill them. "In wars everyone is right. Settlers feel they have a right to kill and die for the land." Itzak feels peace is impossible. "We can have Jews and Muslims in a secular state but if we're seeking to be a religious state, we cannot live together as equal citizens."

Sara, Itzak's wife, was a fine-looking dark-haired, dark-eyed woman—and a humanist. She had been in the army. She had watched the exodus of the Palestinians from their villages in 1948. She had brought Arab prisoners of war to work for Israelis. She had listened to Arab histories and had seen their villages flattened. She told the Palestinians to leave, to run away—but they would not. They knew they could not return.

Chava sees Zionism as built on religion. "I am an atheist," she told us. "I would like a humanist, secular state. I want partition for both Arabs and Jews. It's my state; I'm not giving it to the religious, to the Palestinians, or to the nationalists. I want it to be democratic and I want it to be free.

"My main work is with political prisoners today. Jews get a lot of legal understanding. No one takes anything into account with an Arab. I send lawyers to the prisoners and try to get good legal care for them. In 1948 we had an army; the Palestinians had no army. Israeli officers were mobile. It was a time of no choice about our survival. One of the sides would win. It was one or the other. If we lost, we would be exterminated. The 1948 war was more horrible than any other."

Again, we left in awe. If people who had believed so strongly in violence could give up their violence and feel compassion for their former enemies, even while they were fighting, there may be hope for humankind.

Beit Sahour is a Palestinian town (largely Christian) outside of Bethlehem, and has long been known for its nonviolent struggle. For many years its people have refused to pay taxes for the occupation, and have been severely punished, losing homes, businesses, and money. Yet they have gone courageously on. The people of Beit Sahour developed "Palestinian Time." They set their clocks and watches to hours different from the Israeli standard, causing many difficulties for the occupying soldiers. Their schools were closed for several years, and students were arrested if they were found carrying textbooks on the street. Yet they developed a curriculum for home teaching, and sent weekly lessons to parents. They held secret dialogue sessions with Israelis every fortnight, and called their meeting room the most democratic in the world.

On other occasions when I had met with the Beit Sahour group, they had been composed mostly of older people. This year, at the Center for Rapprochement, the majority were bright, eager young people, busy formulating policy and preparing new actions. Elders, who are their teachers, also attend. Planning involves activists from around the world. Recently a group of young people from Denmark visited and worked with them, and ended by inviting them to spend a ten-day holiday in

Denmark. The group's newest project, teaching conflict resolution in Palestinian schools, is supported by Austria. In 1996 the Center was the recipient of the US FOR's [Fellowship of Reconciliation] Pfeffer Peace Prize.

"The Israelis are frightened of us," they say. "They think we are killers, terrorists. After they stay in our homes, they are less frightened—but they take the risk of losing their jobs if they visit us. Some still do it, but settlers don't come here.

"We know we'll survive better if we use nonviolence. We need many leaders and teachers; the quality of the leader should be open-minded and aware of peoples' feelings on both sides."

The people of Beit Sahour told us they are happy with their commitment—not confident of peace, but still eager to practice nonviolence. They are daring, bright visionaries, open and aware. It began to feel to me that young people are once again becoming the hope of the world.

We returned home, deeply aware of the gulf separating Palestinians and Israelis, but also encouraged by openness where we hadn't expected it, and changes that adversaries can make. Both Israelis and Palestinians—like us all—may yet discover there really are divine possibilities in every situation.

Compassionate Listening— First Step to Reconciliation?

A talk given November 25, 1997,
at University of California at Santa Barbara

Reconciliation is the most difficult of peace processes because it requires the resumption of relationship between those in conflict. It means the coming together in harmony of those who have been sundered.

My sense is that if we would reconcile, we must make radically new responses to the radically new situation in a world where violence is mindless, hopeless, meaningless and almost every nation has nuclear weapons—if they don't now, they soon will. We must move beyond initiatives we formerly used, into realms we have not yet considered, not yet discovered, trusting that there are always open to us new divine possibilities.

We peace people have always listened to the oppressed and disenfranchised. That's very important. One of the new steps I think we should take is to listen to those we consider "the enemy" with the same openness, non-judgment, and compassion we bring to those with whom our sympathies lie.

Everyone has a partial truth, and we must listen, discern, acknowledge this partial truth in everyone—particularly those with whom we disagree. That remarkable saint, Thomas Aquinas, would support this, for he wrote: "We must love them both, those with whom we agree and those with whom we disagree. For both have labored in the search of truth, and both have helped in the finding of it."

311

To reconcile, we must realize that both sides to any violence are wounded, and their wounds are unhealed. From my study of post-traumatic stress disorder in Holocaust victims and Vietnam Veterans, I am persuaded that a great source of violence is our unhealed wounds.

In 1980 I had a life-changing experience. I was on a world tour of peace centers to learn what I could bring back to the USA. Outside the London Quaker Meeting I saw a huge sign that said: "Meeting for Worship for the torturers and the tortured." I'd long known I should listen to the tortured—but listen to the torturers? I'd never thought of that.

I began wrestling with the idea that I should listen to both sides of any conflict and when I arrived in Israel I began listening to Israelis and Palestinians. I found it changed my perspectives on each. I began to practice it everywhere I went.

In 1989 my work-focus became the Middle East, and in that year a small group of us from the Fellowship of Reconciliation went to Libya to listen to the Libyans after we'd bombed Libya twice, first to kill Qaddafi, and second, after we'd downed two Libyan planes over Libya. We knew our government's side and we wanted to hear the other. We did.

After ten days in Tripoli, as guests of the Libyan government, we learned a lot. We met with Libyan leaders, professors, government members, religious representatives. We had new messages to present to our government such as "Please remove the mines you've deposited in the Sahara Desert [during World War II]; we can't do it alone.[113] Please resume conversations with our government over our differences—and please let Libyan students return to American Universities."

Our government wouldn't listen to us, since we'd gone there illegally. So we wrote our articles, spoke publicly where we could and were considered "dangerous."

My next efforts were on my own. Between 1989 and 1996, I went to Israel and Palestine some seven times to listen to both sides. I listened to Israeli psychiatrists, settlers, government members, peace people, writers, publishers and plain people. In the West Bank, since I stayed in Palestinian homes, I had more opportunity to listen to the people: refugees, families, parents whose sons had been killed, some of their sons who hadn't, academics and peace leaders, and twice I met with Yasser Arafat. Out of those experiences came Pax Christi's Just World book of 1991 called *Pieces of the Mideast Puzzle.*

The breakthrough for beginning to practice compassionate listening in the Middle East on a broader scale came in 1996 when Leah Green, Director of Earthstewards' Mid-East Citizen Diplomacy project contacted me. She said she had read everything I'd written on compassionate listening and she would like to have her delegations to Israel and Palestine begin to practice it. We took a group of 18 people to Israel and Palestine in November1996 for a trial run. Now we are preparing for our first formal Compassionate Listening delegation, which will bring rabbis and Jewish community leaders to listen deeply to Israelis and Palestinians representing all sides of the conflict.

Compassionate listening is adaptable to any conflict. The listening requires a particular attitude. It is non-judgmental, non-adversarial, and seeks the truth of the person questioned. It also seeks to see through any masks of hostility and fear to the sacredness of the individual and to discern the wounds suffered by all parties. Listeners do not defend themselves, but accept what others say as their perceptions. By listening they validate the others' right to those perceptions.

I'm not talking about listening with the "human ear." I am talking about discerning. To discern means to perceive some thing hidden or obscure. We must listen with our "spiritual ear." This is very different from deciding in advance who is right and who is wrong, and then seeking to rectify it. And, it's very hard to listen to people whom I feel are misleading, if not lying. Hard to listen to such different memories of the same event—hard!

Here are two definitions of reconciliation we use. Thich Nhat Hanh, the Vietnamese teacher, peace-maker, and poet, describes it as "understanding both sides." Adam Curie, senior Quaker mediator from England, says, "We must work for harmony wherever we are, to bring together what is sundered by fear, hatred, resentment, injustice, or any other conditions which divide us. ...I begin with a concept of human nature based on the belief in a divine element within each of us, which is ever available, awaiting our call to help us restore harmony. We must remember this good exists in those we oppose."

I have since learned there are similar traditions and teachings in Judaism and Islam. In his book, *Jewish Renewal*, Michael Lerner reminds us that the story of Jonah, read in synagogues on Yom Kippur, reminds us that compassion must be extended to the enemies of the Jewish people—which means keeping in mind at all times that they too are created in the image of God, and that distortions of them that lead them to wish us ill are the product of a world of pain and cruelty that shaped them in this particular way.

From Islam comes this teaching by Abderrazak Guessoum, vice rector of the great Mosque of Paris. "...Islam is tolerance, service, and mercy...though it may surprise many non-Muslims to learn it. The Koran rejects all violence. Even the notion of Jihad—so often translated as 'holy war'—actually refers to the struggle of every Muslim not to stray from the path of Obedience to the will of God revealed in the Koran."

I believe that the call is for us to see that within all people is the mystery, the Spirit/God. It is within the Afrikaaner, the Contra, the Americans, Palestinians and Israelis—everyone. By compassionate listening we may awaken it and thus learn the partial truth the other is carrying.

Here is a partial process: Thich Nhat Hanh asks this of us: "In South Africa the black people suffer enormously, but the white people also suffer. If we take one side, we cannot fulfill our task of reconciliation. Can you be in touch with both sides, understanding the suffering and fears of each, telling each side about the other? Can you understand deeply the suffering of both sides?"

Finally, I treasure this quotation from the poet Longfellow: "If we could read the secret history of our enemies, we should find in each person's life sorrow and suffering enough to disarm all hostility."

FOOTNOTES

[113] See footnote p. 127.

Part VIII:
Listening for the Future....

If we can change ourselves, we can change the world. We're not the victims of the world we see, we're the victims of the way we see the world. This is the essence of compassionate listening: seeing the person next to you as a part of yourself.

We need to discern the internal conditions which create war: the belief that we have nothing in common with the next person, the next group, or nation. As the Compassionate Listening Project has pointed out, when you approach a moment without judgment and can connect with the sacredness of the agency of each soul, we can transform the moment—we can transform war into peace.

It is not too late to create a new world. Through compassionate listening we can create moments where we can evolve.

These words were spoken in Seattle, Washington, on May 25, 2003, by Dennis Kucinich, a progressive Congressman from Ohio's 10th district who has become an advocate for compassionate listening. The seeds of compassionate listening that Gene Hoffman planted are beginning to bear some remarkable fruit.

During the 1990s, Gene's expertise as a teacher of compassionate listening was increasingly in demand. Leah Green, then director of the Mid East Citizen Diplomacy project (now The Compassionate

Listening Project) describes how compassionate listening tranformed her program.

Gene was also asked to lead compassionate listening trainings in Alaska and in the state of Washington, where conflicts have arisen between indigenous people and professional and recreational hunters and fishers. She even became an "Internet Presence" (although she doesn't herself own a computer, preferring instead the telephone and typewriter).[114]

Gene's capacity to listen deeply has enabled her to become an extraordinary teacher whose students have themselves become teachers of compassionate listening. Included here is a very heartening report from Carol Hwoschinsky of The Compassionate Listening Project in which she describes training 70 Palestinians and Israelis in Compassionate Listening. In the aftermath of war and two years of violent intifada and repressions, it wasn't easy. But the participants felt that such work was essential. A Palestinian wrote:

> "I have never shared this with anyone, but because of how I have been heard here this weekend, I feel I can share it with you all. I have been afraid of what people would think of me, but I feel that the only way is to work with the Israelis. I participated in a march with the Israeli Co-existence Association a few months ago. And I know what some people would say about me because of this, but this weekend I realized that I did the right thing, and I will keep doing these things in order to make the peace."

An Israeli Jewish participant summed up his experience with these observations:

> "With each suicide bombing I realize it is only a matter of time until one of them touches my life, my family and friends. We must make the peace and with the help of this training we will."

As more and more people learn to listen and to trust, one can envision in the future a peace movement in the Middle East like the one that helped to end the Cold War during the 1980s.

If this happens, Gene Hoffman and Leah Green will be seen as important catalysts for this transformation. Leah Green observed, "I consider Gene one of my most treasured mentors. In fact, I consider her one of our national treasures."

Gene's approach has inspired others not only to practice, but also tto write about compassionate listening. Some of their essays are included in this section.

Although age and health has slowed Gene's pace, she continues to write a column for alternative publications, such as HopeDance, and is active in the peace movement. Her home in Santa Barbara is still a place where meetings are held and where peace activists and spiritual seekers find a friendly welcome.

FOOTNOTES

---

[114] Thanks to Dennis Rivers, two of her booklets—a collection of essays entitled *An Enemy is One e Whose Story We Haven't Yet Heard* and *A Compassionate Listening Handbook: An Evolutionary Sourcebook*—are available for free in PDF format at www.coopcomm.org. Leah Green has produced a compelling 34-minute video based on Compassionate Listening called *Children of Abraham* which is available at www.compassionatelistening.org. Another video called *Alaskans Listening to Alaskans* is in the works.

Listening: Key to Healing Wounds in Mideast

by Leah Green

Published in *HopeDance Magazine*, January 2001 issue (www.hopedance.org) and *Santa Barbara News Press*, Sunday, January 21, 2001.

I've been passionately involved with the Israeli-Palestinian conflict for the past 22 years. I started leading citizen delegations to Israel, the West Bank, and Gaza in 1990 in order to bring Jews and Palestinians and others together, to break stereotypes, and to work together for peace and justice.

At some point, I made a clear decision to work for reconciliation, and the delegations evolved into the Compassionate Listening Project. We also hold compassionate listening workshops now for Israelis and Palestinians.

Our project is based on Gene Knudsen Hoffman's pioneering work. She's been working to bring compassionate listening into the peace movement for the last 20 years. One of the first things I read of Gene's was:

> "Sometime ago I recognized that terrorists were people who had grievances, who thought their grievances would never be heard and certainly never addressed. Later, I saw that all parties to every conflict were wounded, and that at the heart of every act of violence is an unhealed wound."

Many Palestinians have asked me over the years, "How could the Jewish people, who have suffered so greatly, do such harm to another people?" The answer, of course, lies buried in the question—like the abused child who grows up to become an abusive parent. It's hard to miss the wounding of the Jewish people. Collectively, Jews are still locked into the victim role. And when you're a victim it's hard to see how you could be oppressing another. It's identical to the abusive parent who still identifies as the victim. We have to remember that all parties to a conflict are wounded.

Now, unfortunately, the Palestinians are undergoing the same cycle of victimization. Dr. Eyad Sarraj, a prominent psychologist in Gaza, told us a story last year. He was put in Palestinian prison for his open criticism of Arafat and the Palestinian Authority's human rights record. The large, central prison used to be an Israeli prison, and his Palestinian interrogators had all once been prisoners there, themselves, in the Israeli prison. While sitting in his cell one day, Dr. Sarraj overheard another Palestinian being interrogated. The prisoner wasn't answering and the interrogator became increasingly loud and angry, until he suddenly erupted, screaming and shouting in Hebrew, which of course was the language of his torturers. So again, at the heart of every act of violence is an unhealed wound.

The first premise for compassionate listeners is that we must acknowledge that every party to a conflict is suffering. And that our job as peacemakers is to hear their grievances and find ways to tell each side about the humanity and the suffering of the other. We have to find ways to bring conflicting parties to listen to one another—not to dialogue at first, not to argue or debate. Just to listen. We must drop any arrogance of thinking that we know how it is for another.

You might think listening is an easy thing to do. It's not! One of the most difficult listening sessions I've ever had was when 20 of us compassionate listeners presented our work to a large audience of Israelis at Jerusalem's prestigious Van Leer Institute. The audience was completely mixed—from far right to far left. Audience members attacked each other viciously—us too—if they didn't like what was being said. We were modeling compassionate listening really well—we had been practicing for two weeks at that point and we were getting pretty good at it. A woman stood up half way through and said, "You know, we Israelis have to admit that listening is a very radical concept in Israel, but I think these people are onto something." And there was actually a great deal of transformation that evening.

Compassionate listening is the first step of a peace-building process. I believe in it deeply. I know it works because it's worked for me and those who've participated in the project. I have found compassion for some Israeli and Palestinian extremists. It doesn't mean I condone their actions, but the point is: How can we sit in judgment of someone whose life we have not lived?

There are critical ways in which Israelis and Palestinians don't see one another. While Israelis find it difficult to see Palestinians as victims, Palestinians find it hard to see Israelis' sense of vulnerability and fear. They see Israeli tanks, helicopters, and missiles. They know Israel is the fourth largest military power. But if they had the opportunity to listen to Israelis as we have they'd experience their incredible sense of powerlessness and fear.

Israelis have failed to grasp how patient Palestinians have been with the Oslo peace process. Palestinians bought into Oslo with the goal of a Palestinian state in the West Bank and Gaza by the end of a five-year interim period. Here it is seven years later, and they've watched each year as more and more of their lands have been confiscated to expand Israelis settlements. The new Palestinian Intifadah (uprising) is a revolt against Israeli occupation, against settlements. We were all predicting it three years ago. You could see it coming. They are enraged and feel they have nothing more to lose.

Peace building is one person, one heart at a time. It's a slow process. And it's the only way. A paper peace—an agreement between governments for example—can happen literally overnight. But peace between people comes slowly, from relationship building.

It's no coincidence that the Israelis and Palestinians whose relationships have remained strong through this crisis are the ones who have worked to build relationships. I've read articles in the press these past months quoting both Israelis and Palestinians who are bitter that business associates they thought were friends haven't called to check in and make sure they are safe. They feel disappointed and betrayed.

But groups like Yitzhak Frankenthal's, whose remarkable Family Forum brings together bereaved Israeli and Palestinian parents who have lost their children to this conflict, are stronger than ever—even today. What's the difference? Groups like Frankenthal's have sat in each other's homes. They've met each other's children, and they've shared and acknowledged each other's pain. They've reversed the process of dehumanization.

I would like to see us create places here in the US where Jews and Palestinians could come together to learn from one another while making a public statement for peace like the peace tents that sprung up around Israel. We need to hear each others' stories. There are successful dialogue groups across the country that are changing the human relationship, and we need these in every city.

I have a vision: that one day, Palestinians will come by the thousands to the checkpoints, not with rocks but with candles or even flowers. And the international media will broadcast the mass nonviolent movement of the Palestinians and it will capture the imagination of the entire world. And Israelis will see that they don't have to be afraid.

Jews and Palestinians are cousins—we're Children of Abraham, and I believe we'll find our way back to one another.

Some of us already have. We have to be willing to listen—to know that *our* truth is not The Truth. We have to be willing to say, "I'm sorry." And if we want to work for peace and justice, we need to work with compassion.

Leah Green is the founder of MidEast Citizen Diplomacy which leads citizen delegations to the Middle East. Ms. Green can be reached at office@mideastdiplomacy.org.

Compassionate Listening Training for Israelis and Palestinians

by Carol Hwoschinsky, Training Director,
The Compassionate Listening Project

"I have never shared this with anyone, but because of how I have been heard here this weekend, I feel I can share it with you all. I have been afraid of what people would think of me, but I feel that the only way is to work with the Israelis. I participated in a march with the Israeli Co-existence Association a few months ago. And I know what some people would say about me because of this, but this weekend I realized that I did the right thing, and I will keep doing these things in order to make the peace."

Palestinian Workshop Participant,
Bethlehem, Israel, May 2003.

In May of 2003, a team of three trainers (one Jewish, one Arab American Muslim and one Christian) and two volunteers from The Compassionate Listening Project (TCLP) successfully completed a series of Compassionate Listening trainings in Israel and the West Bank.

Due to the conditions on the ground, we had to postpone this phase of the project until late spring. Yet our ground coordinators had no trouble recruiting over 70 participants for the four trainings we conducted. And though participants came in very skeptical and disheartened, the hope that they left with, and the outcomes and continued connections that they have sustained since, have been beyond even our vision at this difficult time.

In a period of two weeks, we offered three Introductory Compassionate Listening workshops and concluded with an Advanced training. The Advanced training was open to previously trained Israelis and Palestinians as well as those who had just completed the Introductory program. In total we trained over 70 Jewish and Arab Israelis and Palestinians from the West Bank in the skills and practice of compassionate listening. Most of them were leaders in their communities and included the head of the Women's Interfaith Encounter, The Council of Druize women, business leaders, therapists and educators, program directors, a rabbi and an author of a book for Palestinian girls.

Our first introductory training was in Bethlehem. Given the conditions, we were not sure if we would be able to enter the West Bank to work with Palestinians. However, we were able to conduct a full two and one half day workshop with twenty-five Palestinians there.

The training was received enthusiastically. Five women and twenty men participated—including four teachers and two staff members of The Hope Flowers School. (The Hope Flowers School has a very strong peace education program and teaches Hebrew to its Arab students). Our Bethlehem workshop was given at no cost to any of the participants, as many of them, though highly educated, had been unemployed for a long time. In addition to a generous grant from the Threshold Foundation, the trainers raised $2,500 for scholarships for this purpose.

Our Arab American trainer, and a Board Member of TCLP, Munteha Shukralla, wrote an article on that Bethlehem training which appeared in the summer issue of *Peacemaker* magazine. Here is a quote that describes the effectiveness of the program, as everyone in the room moved through the chaos of language and cultural barriers to deep connection with each other through the practice of compassionate listening:

> There were 25 Palestinians in the training and it was the most amazing thing I have participated in...There were countless things we did not anticipate, and we ended up re-vamping our entire training on the spot, in accordance with where people were, and their needs. There was simultaneous translation going on at all times, and at one point my co-leader and I just decided to stop the training and do what was actually needed, which was to sit and listen to them. There were lawyers, psychologists, Palestinian peace-workers, conflict resolution people, and teachers at the training, twenty men and five women, Christians, Muslims, old and young. We had to turn people away who wanted to participate at the last minute. Even with all our concerns about "are they getting it???" I just trusted that "I work, and the format works." At the ending circle the last night, we finally got it...they got it. One woman came up to me afterwards, crying, and told me that these were the best three days of her life, and asked when would we be back.....

One benefit of this training to all of us, including the leaders, was to have the opportunity to listen in depth to the many experiences of the people present. The advanced group committed at the start of the weekend to be truthful: to speak the truth and to listen to the truth even when difficult. Our facilitators were able to create a safe container for this to occur when things inevitably became heated. As a result, for most of the people, it was the first opportunity they had had to hear truth coming directly from people with such differing background and experiences. There were tough moments and they always ended with hugs and often tears.

This training went very deep and was challenged severely on the second day when a bus bombing occurred near Jerusalem. The training team was awakened at 6:00 AM by sirens. From the rooftop of Tantur, the Bethlehem checkpoint was in full view. Every single participant still came to the training, though one young man from Bethlehem was worried about getting stuck and decided to go back. The despair that morning was palpable and the leaders led the group in processing their grief and hopelessness with everyone listening deeply, expressing despair, rage and fear. At the end of the morning people were laughing and hugging again. They agreed that if the people in that training could continue to influence their communities, there would be a viable and lasting peace in the region.

Another "secondary outcome" is that one of the Jewish women from the Introductory and Advanced Trainings at Tantur, a Reiki Master, is now doing a barter exchange with the grandmother of one of the Palestinian men—teaching her Reiki in exchange for Arabic lessons so she can train more Arabic students in this healing art.

We want to close this with another quote from Munteha's article in *Peacemaker* magazine as she described her work in Bethlehem with Palestinian trainees:

I have felt as though I have been walking a tightrope. On one hand, I am a peacemaker; on another, I am an Arab in their eyes. I must gain trust, and stand for something. It has been very painful and hard for me. But I have been true to myself. I feel that they know this, and this is why they are able to listen to what I stand for; and really, the truth is, it is what they stand for as well. As one man put it, "you are not telling us anything new, but you are like the aim of the arrow, you will show us the way with what we already know, which is that we must love all people."

"Why There Is Hope for Humanity"

by Gene Knudsen Hoffman

[This article was written for a collection of essays called Hope in a Dark Time *(Santa Barbara, CA: Capra Press, 2003), edited by David Krieger, founder and president of the Nuclear Age Peace Foundation, and with an introduction by Desmond Tutu.]*

When I was asked, "Do you have hope for humanity?" my mind said, "No!" My heart said, "Wait a minute. Listen to me." I did. This is what I heard.

I think war and violence are human problems. That's why I'm hopeful. I've seen that humanity can change, and it has—not by force, not by threat, not even by cajoling, but by creating a safe place to be heard, to hear, to accept the other's right to his/her point of view, and to look for truth in it with which we can agree. I believe we all have fragments of truth in our points of view, and it's important we look for those fragments when we're deeply troubled by differences.

We all have secrets, and, it seems to me, secrets are part of our undoing. We hid how cruel the first settlers were to the Indians. These earliest immigrants came here following what I believe were skewed truths about freedom. They believed they had "discovered this land and had a right to it." They believed they had eminent domain over it, the people, the animals, and the vegetation they found here. And they had a right to use them as they chose. Many of us don't believe that any more and are seeking ways to heal this breach.

Many of us once felt it was right to own slaves, to keep people in bondage for our use and pleasure, because (we believed) these weren't "real people"—they didn't have souls. Today, many of us believe that was a tragic lie and are seeking ways to heal this breach, too.

We have believed the mountains and seas, animals and trees were "ours" because we found or bought them. Now many of us feel they are the heritage of all of us—and are our caregivers, our friends, and we must cherish them.

We have believed that we had the right to manipulate the earth and its gifts into weapons, to genetically change fruits and vegetables, to clone sheep, clone people, create deadly pesticides, spray them on food, and then, without warning, sell the food for us to eat.

We've long believed that it was our right to declare war against people and topple governments, if not civilizations, when they disagreed with us. We thought we had a God-given right to fight for our "self-interest." We thought it was right to atom-bomb Hiroshima and Nagasaki. Many of us now feel this was wrong, if not disastrous, thinking. Many of us now believe we should continuously be in dialogue, negotiation, mediation, or just plain conversation with those with whom we have ruptured relationships.

The Path of War

And the path of war is the path we still follow today. We are killing people, destroying lands and cities in Afghanistan. We are leaving war's remainders in that land—dead bodies, used weapons, and some weapons which are unfortunately still "alive." We have peopled that country with thousands of military personnel who, no doubt, believe we are ridding the earth of evil with our guns, and our tanks and our bombs. And we are keeping the deadly results secret from ourselves, the public. Instead, we see commercials, which tell us of delightful places we can vacation, basking on beaches in the warm sun, exotic new automobiles to buy, and the right cosmetics to make all women beautiful.

Meanwhile, we are told by our president that we are providing "security for our homeland," with a war that will go on and on while we beat a bloody path to "victory over evil."

And now we are readying our weapons of terror to continue this war. We are threatening to take it to countries other than Afghanistan—anywhere people do not agree with our American ideas of freedom and democracy. These wars are spontaneous, unapproved by our Congress. We are terrifying people with our ever-present threat of revenge on those who take revenge on us for past injuries and harm. Through our determination to "destroy evil"—which is an abstraction-we are committing assassinations and making them look respectable. We are on a dangerous path.

"How then," might you ask, "do I have any hope for humanity?"

Revenge Does Not Bring Peace

My reply: Many of us believe the path we are following leads to disaster. Acting out of revenge does not bring peace—it invariably provokes retaliation in some form. I don't believe we want to live under this threat.

Some of us have learned there are limits to what is allowed us. We have been given freedom, not license. We are being offered lessons we cannot practice until we have a heart that yearns for peace for you. I do not believe we will have ongoing peace until we realize that all life is sacred, and we need to listen to the suffering and grievances of all sides to any conflict.

There are laws we may not disobey without jeopardy to ourselves and all we love, for if we do not honor our limits we enter "chaos and old night." When we fight wars, we are in that chaos. When we harm the earth, we enter chaos. When we do not do our work to heal our wounds—which are a cause of hate, anger, wars, and violence—that chaos is in us.

I believe there is hope for humanity because many of us are relinquishing our secrets and ignorance. Some are moving from denial to acknowledgement of mistakes in our past or present. Some are even asking for forgiveness.

We are learning we cannot make peace if we do not listen to our "enemies" with the same compassion, non-judgment, and caring we ask for ourselves. Indeed, as [19th century American poet Henry Wadsworth] Longfellow wrote, "If we could read the secret history of our enemies, we would find sorrow and suffering enough to dispel all hostility."

The Power of Forgiveness

Last, we might reach a depth of understanding that would enable us to ask for forgiveness and forgive—for I do not believe there can ever be real peace without forgiveness. This is hard, because we're not accustomed to admitting that we are wrong.

There are places in the world where people are discovering the need for acknowledging the harm they have done, asking for forgiveness and forgiving. For example, Desmond Tutu, Episcopal Archbishop in South Africa, maintains, "There is no future without forgiveness." Yehezkel Landau, one of the great peacemakers in Israel, writes:

> "Diplomats are contriving formulas that might bring Israelis and Palestinians together. The focus, I feel, is missing …is a readiness to admit the harm done to the other side, and to demonstrate repentance for that behavior. This is a challenge diplomacy tends to ignore—this may be why all [peacework] in the Middle East comes to naught."

The hardest and most essential sacrifice required for genuine peace is that of one's self-image as the innocent victim at the hands of a cruel enemy. Imagine how cathartic it might be if [Israeli] public figures said words like these:

> "In defending ourselves, we projected on you demonic stereotypes.... The violence you waged against unarmed Jews caused us great pain and anger.... Yet we hope you can forgive our violence against you and ... for so many of you in exile from the land. Now, let us together transform this legacy into a hopeful future by agreeing to partition land into two states for two peoples who claim it."

Israelis need to hear similar words from Palestinians such as:

> "We Palestinians were the majority in Palestine when European Jews began settling the land—this meant the loss of our land and our political rights to people who weren't born here. Looking back with greater compassion, we can forgive you... for the same nationalist excesses that we, too, have been guilty of. Let us transcend the antagonism of the past, affirm our recognition of one another, and accept the rights and needs of both sides."

Desmond Tutu, one of the founders of the Truth and Reconciliation Commission in South Africa, maintains, "...on the foundation of forgiveness can be built the transformation of conflicts. Forgiveness-based negotiations start with the premise that conflict leads to death. Not merely physical death, but the death of trust, the termination of relationships, the sowing of deadly hatred."

Forgiveness in Action

What might happen if some of us followed the lead of remarkable men such as Desmond Tutu? What if we began making pilgrimages in little groups to places where we have harmed people through war? What if we went to Japan to acknowledge the horrors that our atom bombs unleashed upon the Japanese, and asked for forgiveness? What if we went to Korea, Vietnam, Granada, Cuba, Nicaragua, El Salvador, Iraq, and Afghanistan to speak our sorrow for the destruction we caused them? What if we offered to make personal restitution and asked for forgiveness?

Might such actions lead to the transformation of humanity that some of us feel is necessary if life is to continue on earth. I think they would, and it could be a proof that a small group of dedicated people can make mighty changes. I think true reconciliation, mutual healing, mutual understanding, mutual love might spring up between strangers who were once enemies. And it might mean the continuation of a healthier planet, and a noble human race.

Aging: A Time of New Possibilities?

by Gene Hoffman, *Fellowship Magazine*, October 2001

At last I've discovered that I am *aging*—and I never really believed it would happen. I didn't mind the business of growing older because something new and fascinating was always entering my life. My early life was absorbed in the theater. My mother told me she had made up her mind that if she had a girl, she would be educated to become an actress. That was one of my mother's passions. True to her vision, I was born a girl, and educated for that profession, and I loved it. Later there were two marriages, seven children, and other things beckoning. I discovered that I didn't want to speak another's words and opinions: instead I wanted to write my own. So I developed a companion career. I became devoted to peace and other "radical" ways of thought, and began to write about what I saw and heard in an advertising column that was syndicated in the Los Angeles newspapers for eleven years. That ended when I began writing about nonviolence and other controversial subjects. I was fired.

By that time I knew about peace and psychology magazines, so I wrote for them. As a result, I was hired as the first white columnist on Harlem's outstanding newspaper, *The Amsterdam News*. These experiences led me into fifty years of writing of my adventures—and I'm still doing it!

When my children had grown I began to travel all over the world to learn new peace initiatives for the US. In the middle of my travels, I took time out to become a therapist because I felt it was essential to understand psychology if I wanted to work for peace. In the 1980s I worked for six years with the Soviet Union, seeking to help Americans recognize that the Soviets are human beings, and creating the US/USSR Reconciliation Program for the Fellowship of Reconciliation. When that was finished, my work moved to the Middle East: I traveled there through the 1990s. During that time I developed the Compassionate Listening Program, which is beginning to flourish in the continental US, Canada, the Middle East, and Alaska.

Then, a year or so ago, I discovered I couldn't live that exciting, adventurous life anymore. I no longer had the energy to make semi-annual journeys all over the map. I began discovering I was an elder, and had better stay home.

I began to wonder what an elder was supposed to do. Visit friends and family? Read novels? Write my memoirs? A little of each is great—but that didn't feel quite right to me. I began to explore being an elder when I was asked to write this article.

I suddenly flashed on a question Jack Kornfield, Buddhist sage, had asked on one of his tapes. He said, more or less, "At the end of your life the only question worth asking is, 'Did I love enough?'" My internal answer was, "Of course I haven't, and perhaps never will. But I can begin trying. Whatever happens, it will keep me well occupied for the rest of my life."

I have six grandchildren. I began looking at the ways I loved them. I felt I could love them better, and discovered my first step is learning to "let them be," to accept them as they are, and with gratitude.

Another thing I've learned recently is that if someone offends or hurts me, I don't need to make a scene. I've long thought violence springs from our unhealed wounds. If I'm really trying to be a loving presence in others' lives, and I can remember

Laura Huxley's phrase "You are not the target," I'll be healing myself, and something may spill over.

Life is full of not-knowing-how-to-love and finding new ways to act, to be, to respond, to live. Since I think this may take several lifetimes, I can't waste any more time. The assignment is before me: I'm here to focus on being a warm, loving human being, just like my sons and daughters are already. Maybe I'll be able to listen more compassionately to them and my grandchildren—and I'm sure never to be bored.

Bibliography

Books and Pamphlets:

All Possible Surprises: Poems. Berkeley, CA: Parallax Press, c. 1991.

Compassionate Listening: A Reader. Santa Barbara, CA: Project Crossroads, Univ. of Calif. at Santa Barbara, UCSB Bookstore Custom Publishing (1997).

Dialogue on Women by Esther Milner. Indiana: Bobbs-Merrill, 1987.

Dimensions of the Future: Alternatives for Tomorrow. Compiled by Maxwell H. Norman. N.Y.: Holt, Rinehart and Winston, 1974. "Sexual Equality is Not the Issue" by Gene Hoffman.

Forming Spiritual Base Communities in the U.S.A. Madison, WI: Interhelp, 1988.

Hope in a Dark Time, edited by David Krieger. Santa Barbara, CA: Capra Press, 2003. "Why There is Hope for Humanity" by Gene Hoffman.

Loving the Stranger. New York: Fellowship of Reconciliation, 1983.

My Sister Tatiana, My Brother Ivan: Learning to Know the Soviets. Helen Bailey, ed. Elgin, Ill.: Brethren Press, 1988. "To Live Without Enemies" by Gene Hoffman.

From Inside the Glass Doors, Brooklyn, NY: The Turning Press, 1977.

No Royal Road to Reconciliation. Wallingford, PA: Pendle Hill Pamphlet #321, 1995.

Pieces of the Mideast Puzzle: Israelis and Palestinians. Erie, PA: Pax Christi USA, 1991

Spirit and Trauma: a Universalist World View as an Instrument of Healing. Landenberg, PA: Quaker Universalist Fellowship, 1994.

"Toward Turning," unpublished masters thesis in pastoral counseling and psychology, Goddard College, 1976.

Waging Peace in the Nuclear Age: Ideas for Action. Edited by David Krieger and Frank K. Kelley. Santa Barbara, CA: Capra Press, 1988. "Councils for non-violent solutions" by Gene Hoffman.

Ways Out: The Book of Changes for Peace. Edited by Gene Knudsen-Hoffman. Santa Barbara, CA: J. Daniel, 1988.

Articles from periodicals

"After the Peace Accords—What?" *Harmony,* 1994.

"Aging: A Time of New Possibilities," *Fellowship Magazine,* Oct. 2001

"An Enemy Is One Whose Story We Have Not Heard,", *Fellowship Magazine,* May, 1996.

"A Peace Pilgrim's Progress to Inner Healing," *Awakening,* Feb. 1990.

"Crevices in the Rock," *Fellowship Magazine,* 1981.

"Compassionate Listening in Alaska" and "Compassionate Listening about Makah Whaling," *Friends Bulletin,* September 2001.

"Creation Continues," *Fellowship Magazine,* March 1989.

"Jesus the Christ, Quakers and I," *Friends Bulletin,* January 1975.

"Let the Rage Uncoil," *Liberation* March 1967.

"Listening to the Libyans," *Pax Christi*, Fall, 1989.

"Redeeming Some Sparks Through Divorce," unpublished paper, 1974.

"Reflections on Meeting with Richard Nixon," *Friends Journal*, November 1, 1986.

"Quakerism and Creativity," *Friends Journal*, March 15, 1979

"Sowing," *Fellowship Magazine*, 1984..

"The Oath and I,"*Fellowship Magazine*, February 1, 1955

"Trapped by Thomas Jefferson," *Liberation*, February, 1959.

"Trauma: Tragedy or New Creation?" *Harmony: Voices for a Just Future*.

Our thanks to *HopeDance, Hope in a Dark Time, Harmony: Voices for a Just Future, Fellowship Magazine* (publication of Fellowship of Reconciliation) and to *Friends Journal* (an independent magazine serving the Religious Society of Friends) for permission to use their material in this book. All the articles from *Friends Journal* have their copywright and those seeking permssion to reprint excerpts longer than 200 words should direct inquiries to: *Friends Journal*, 1216 Arch Street St 2A, Philadelphia, PA 19197-2835. Telephone: 215-563-8629. info@friendsjournal.org. Website: friendsjournal.org. *Harmony* can be reached at PO Box 210056, San Francisco, CA 94121-005.

Index